Dr Lee Gatiss is the Director of Church So~~
Church History at Union School ~~
Fellow of the Jonathan Edwards Ce
of the Free State, South Africa. He
theology from New College (Oxford
Oak Hill Theological College (Lo
Theological Seminary (Philadelphia). F.   ~~ editor of
more than twenty books including *For* ~~ *and For Our Salvation*
and the editor of the *NIV Proclamation Bible*.

What people are saying:

Lee Gatiss' *Cornerstones of Salvation* is a model for historical theology done in service of the church. The scholarship is penetrating in its depth, yet written in an engaging manner able to speak to the general reader. Indeed, the historical questions have been aptly chosen for their clear relevance to the needs of the Reformed community today. What are the fundamentals of saving doctrine essential for contemporary audiences to hear? In the light of the New Perspective, can we still preach justification by faith? In fact, in an age of sound bites and video clips, should local congregational preaching still be the top priority? How should Christian parents present the faith to their children, assuming they are outside of the faith being beckoned in, or are they inside the faith being nurtured to grow? With contemporary culture demanding inclusion, is there room for some degree of doctrinal diversity amongst today's adherents of the Westminster Confession? With calls for unity in the face of Christianity's minority status in contemporary Western society, are there limits to making common cause with Protestants from other traditions? In short, *Cornerstones of Salvation* shrewdly mines the Christian past for helpful insights on essential issues facing the Reformed tradition today. Readers will be well rewarded by reading it cover to cover.

Ashley Null, DFG-Cranmer-Projekt, Theologische Fakultät,
Humboldt-Universität zu Berlin.

In these discussions of important issues from the sixteenth century to the present day, Dr Gatiss writes with clarity and impressive scholarship. These essays are both learned and accessible, deserving a wide readership. Their subject matter is not merely for antiquarians but has a significant bearing on the way the Reformed faith is to be articulated in our own times.

Robert Letham, Senior Lecturer in Systematic and Historical Theology, Union School of Theology.

Scripture commands us to contend for the faith and also to avoid foolish controversies; Lee Gatiss walks that fine line from which obedience in both directions remains possible, and shows us how often holy wisdom takes the form of a strategist choosing the right battles. In a collection that starts with Luther's decision to pick a fight with Erasmus and ends with Wesley's decision to pick a fight with Whitefield, Gatiss revisits some key contested places of Protestant history. Concise and crisply written, these are fine companion pieces to the history of soteriology in the Reformed tradition. Disagreeing heartily at several key points, I nonetheless recommend it highly as a lively, informative, and clarifying examination of things that matter.

Fred Sanders, Professor of Theology, Torrey Honors Institute, Biola University.

It is a truism too frequently unrecognised that all of our doctrinal convictions have emerged within set parameters of history and culture. This does not make them any less true, but it is a reminder that the Christian faith is above all a religion that must take history seriously. This collection of articles does just that: whether it is Luther battling Erasmus in the 1520s or debates about the extent of the atonement at Westminster 120 years later, Lee Gatiss superbly opens up to us the many-layered historical context in which a number of our central doctrines were shaped and moulded. A deeply rewarding read and reminder!

Michael A. G. Haykin, Professor of Church History & Biblical Spirituality, The Southern Baptist Theological Seminary.

Lee Gatiss' *Cornerstones of Salvation* is a historically informed and contemporary relevant introduction to the development, delineation, and definition of Protestant Reformation doctrines. Careful and nuanced scholarship. Edifying and engaging reading. Serving the church and academy. Warmly recommended.

Adriaan C. Neele, Yale University.

In *Cornerstones of Salvation*, Dr Gatiss unpacks historical debates on theological issues that are foundational to the Reformed tradition. In typical Gatiss style, these subjects are explored with an accessibility that opens them up for the novice reader who is unfamiliar with the area, while at the same time offering fresh insights which will prove to be stimulating for the specialist reader. I thoroughly enjoyed reading this book, and commend it wholeheartedly.

Ed Loane, Lecturer in Theology and Church History, Moore Theological College, Sydney.

In this super new selection, Lee Gatiss addresses themes of classical Reformed theology with characteristic clarity and verve. If the material on atonement, justification, and union with Christ is of capital importance, the account of Grindal's approach to preaching is groundbreaking and compelling. And there is much more besides. Here is an author with that rare and marvellous ability to analyse and articulate essential contours of confessional truth, through detailed yet lively conversation with great thought-leaders of the past, in ways that are at once profound and readable, incisive, penetrating, and weighty, without ever being heavy.

Benjamin Dean, Lecturer in Systematic Theology and Dean of Postgraduate Studies, George Whitefield College, Cape Town, South Africa.

Three of the common sources of confusion, error and disaster in the church today are disobedience to Scripture, neglect of theology, and ignorance or misunderstanding of the past. Lee Gatiss provides a remedy for these ills, and *Cornerstones of Salvation* gives us biblical, theological, and historical insights into issues of importance, such as the nature of free will, our union with Christ, the nature of justification, the importance of preaching and the training of preachers, the nature of salvation, and infant baptism. Here is a model of creative and productive interaction with Bible, theology, and history.

Peter Adam, Vicar Emeritus of St Jude's Carlton, and former Principal of Ridley College Melbourne.

In an era when the question: 'What is Anglicanism?' is hotly debated in North America, Dr Gatiss' *Cornerstones of Salvation* brings a welcome point of clarity and focus concerning eight critical doctrines of the church. Each of the chapters presents a balanced and careful examination of the doctrine in question. Gatiss also writes with an accessibility that will benefit both the informed layperson and pastor. His mastery of primary sources and his careful use of notes gives the reader a sound start to further reading and research. They are excellent studies. Every Anglican in North America should read them.

Henry P. Jansma, Canon Theologian for the Missionary Diocese of CANA (Convocation of Anglicans in North America) East.

God created history. Christian salvation is rooted in the historical deeds of Christ. Because of this Christians need to care about how God has worked through real people in the context of real human events. Lee Gatiss' latest work helps us to think biblically about key truths of the Christian faith; he also helps us to think historically about how these truths have been expressed over the centuries. This book is a true delight because it brings us into conversation with giants of the Christian tradition as if over tea.

Daniel R. Hyde, Pastor of the Oceanside United Reformed Church in Carlsbad, California.

Our day is one too often characterized by theological naiveté and historical ignorance. As a result, we are doomed to repeat theological missteps that could otherwise be avoided. Lee Gatiss, however, corrects this all too common problem by taking us back in time to the rich heritage of the Reformed tradition. Whether it is John Calvin, the Westminster Assembly, or George Whitefield, Gatiss reminds us why such voices must be heard afresh today. With careful analysis and erudite historical reflection, Gatiss is a superb guide to the controversies that define us to this day.

> Matthew Barrett, Executive Editor of *Credo Magazine* and Tutor of Systematic Theology and Church History at Oak Hill Theological College, London.

Christians don't have to reinvent the wheel. Too often when we do, the wheel is not that round. In *Cornerstones of Salvation*, Lee Gatiss has shown that the Christian tradition, particularly the Reformation vein, is inhabited with giants like Luther, Grindal, and Owen. He helps us climb on their shoulders so we can see further than before. Gatiss writes with energy and sparkle that gave me an excitement about the riches in our Reformed past. Please take up and read.

> Martin Foord, Senior Lecturer in Systematic Theology and Church History, Trinity Theological College, Perth.

One of my favourite scholars of Reformed theology has applied his skill to many important historical-theological doctrines. You can read this whole book through or pick and choose a chapter as you like. But whatever you end up reading will likely teach you a great deal.

> Mark Jones, Pastor at Faith Vancouver PCA

Cornerstones of Salvation

Foundations and Debates in the Reformed Tradition

Lee Gatiss

EP BOOKS

1st Floor Venture House, 6 Silver Court, Watchmead, Welwyn Garden City, UK, AL7 1TS

http://www.epbooks.org

admin@epbooks.org

EP Books are distributed in the USA by:

JPL Distribution

3741 Linden Avenue Southeast

Grand Rapids, MI 49548

orders@jplbooks.com

British Library Cataloguing in Publication Data available

ISBN 978-1-78397-195-4

Contents

Preface

The Reformed tradition in theology is both broad and deep. It is broader than a single figure, such as John Calvin. And it is deeper than any superficial summary, such as the infamous acronym TULIP, could ever encapsulate. In the chapters which follow I explore some of the foundational teachings and debates in the Reformed tradition, particularly around the subject of salvation. I have found over the years that there is an astonishing ignorance about what people such as Luther, Calvin, Owen, and Wesley actually taught, even amongst those who claim to be Reformation Christians. The following chapters were originally researched and written to fill in the gaps in my own knowledge, and I hope they will be useful to others too.

Here, people such as Luther are seen, 'warts and all', establishing the basic contours of Reformed thought on free will and predestination. Calvin's brilliance not just as a theologian but as an exegete and preacher of the Bible are made clear as he opens up the riches of 'union with Christ' in the book of Ephesians. Recent challenges to the foundational doctrine of justification by faith alone, which are often ultra-critical of the Reformation, are seen as unjustified and ill-thought through. The Reformation emphasis on preaching as 'the ordinary means and instrument of the salvation of mankind', as Edmund Grindal memorably put it, is brought into sharp relief during a furious conflict with the Tudor monarchy.

The variety in Reformed thought on the atonement, and the subtlety of its confessional formulas, especially on the controversial topic of 'limited atonement', is brought out. An often neglected sacramental angle is discovered afresh in an exposition of John Owen's doctrine of infant baptism and infant salvation. And eighteenth-century arguments between the great celebrity Revival preachers over predestination and justification are seen to be more foundational than the standard accounts give them credit for.

I have tried throughout to keep one eye on applications to the contemporary church scene in each of these areas, so as not to get lost in (albeit fascinating) historical and theological detail. I owe a great deal to many other scholars for their insights and sharpening interaction on the subjects discussed here. In addition to those I have thanked in the notes on each chapter, I would also like to express my gratitude to David Meager of Church Society and Stephen Boon of the Proclamation Trust for their invaluable help in proofreading and indexing this book.

I have found the Reformed tradition of biblical teaching exhilarating, edifying, and engaging at so many levels. I hope that readers will enjoy these explorations — all significantly modified, expanded, and updated from lectures and published research in peer-reviewed theology journals. I trust they will find them to be both stimulating to the mind and satisfying for the soul. My hope and prayer above all is that they will draw people to the glory of the Lord Jesus Christ, who has become for us *wisdom from God, righteousness and sanctification and redemption, so that as it is written, 'Let the one who boasts, boast in the Lord'* (1 Corinthians 1:30-31).

Lee Gatiss
Cambridge

The Manifesto of the Reformation: Luther vs. Erasmus on Free Will

This chapter is a modified version of an article first published in Churchman 123.3 (2009). I am grateful to Carl Trueman for commenting on an early draft of this. References to the English edition of Luther's Works (55 volumes; Philadelphia: Fortress Press, 1960-1975) are abbreviated throughout to LW.

The clash between Martin Luther and Desiderius Erasmus over the issue of free will is 'one of the most famous exchanges in Western intellectual history.'[1] In this chapter, we will examine the background to the quarrel between these two men, and two of the central themes of Luther's response to Erasmus – the clarity of Scripture, and the bondage of the will. In doing so it is critical to be aware that studying these things 'operates as a kind of litmus test for what one is going to become theologically.'[2] Ignoring the contemporary relevance and implications of these crucially important topics will not be possible. Whether thinking about our approach to the modern reformation of the church, our evangelism, pastoral care, or interpretation of the Bible there is so much of value and vital importance here that it would be a travesty to discuss them without at least a nod in the direction of the twenty-first century church. From Luther's perspective, as

---

1 Attributed to John W. O'Malley in R. Kolb, *Bound Choice, Election, and Wittenberg Theological Method: From Martin Luther to the Formula of Concord* (Cambridge: Eerdmans, 2005), 7.

2 Steven Paulson in G. O. Forde, *The Captivation of the Will: Luther vs. Erasmus on Freedom and Bondage* (Cambridge: Eerdmans, 2005), xi.

Gerhard Forde rightly says, this was not just one more theological debate but 'a desperate call to get the gospel preached.'[3]

Furthermore, this is a fundamentally significant dispute historically since it involved key players in the two major movements of the sixteenth century: Erasmus the great Renaissance Humanist and Luther the Reformation Hercules.[4] The debate between these two titans reveals not only the reasons behind 'humanism's programmatic repudiation of the Reformation',[5] but also gives us a clear view of the heartbeat of the Reformation itself. As B. B. Warfield wrote, *The Bondage of the Will* is 'the embodiment of Luther's reformation conceptions, the nearest to a systematic statement of them he ever made. It is the first exposition of the fundamental ideas of the Reformation in a comprehensive presentation, and it is therefore in a true sense the manifesto of the Reformation.'[6] If, therefore, modern evangelicals have lost Luther's clarity and faithfulness to Scripture on this issue of free will we will have lost something very precious and foundational indeed.

The Fly vs. the Elephant

Neither party in this grand debate was particularly keen on getting involved in a match against the other. Luther's position was precarious enough in 1524-25, so it is not surprising that, as Brecht puts it, he 'really wanted to maintain an attitude of charitableness and good-naturedness in dealing with his

---

[3] *The Captivation of the Will*, xvii.

[4] The title 'Hercules Germanicus' is given to Luther in a cartoon of 1522 which is most uncomplimentary to the Pope, the Inquisition, and the scholastic theologians. See R. H. Bainton, *Here I Stand: A Life of Martin Luther* (Nashville: Abingdon Press, 1978 [1950]), 93-94.

[5] H. A. Oberman, *Luther: Man between God and the Devil* (London: Yale University Press, 1989), 216.

[6] B. B. Warfield, 'The Theology of the Reformation' in *Studies in Theology: The Works of Benjamin B. Warfield volume 9* (Grand Rapids: Baker, 2003 [1932]), 471.

enemies.[7] He was aware, however, that despite their common stance against such things as relics, pilgrimages, indulgences, fasting, monastic vows, and the invocation of saints, there remained deep theological differences between them.[8] It was commonly said that with his early calls for reform and his groundbreaking linguistic work on the Greek New Testament, Erasmus laid the egg which Luther hatched.[9] Erasmus himself complained against this saying, 'I laid a hen's egg: Luther hatched a bird of quite different breed.'[10] Luther first became cognisant of Erasmus's theological animosity towards him in May 1522 after reading some of the humanist's published letters.[11] They held an uneasy truce for some time until a combination of factors drove Erasmus to declare hostilities officially open. Luther wrote to him privately in April 1524 thanking him for all he had done in the fields of literature and textual research but counselled him to leave theology to the experts: 'we have chosen to put up with your weakness and thank God for the gifts he has given you... [But] You have neither the aptitude nor the courage to be a Reformer, so please stand aside.'[12]

Such a rebuke stuck in the throat of the older man as the more eminent and respected of the two. With a prickly sense of pride, Erasmus was somewhat conceited, addicted to his own reputation,

---

[7] M. Brecht, Martin Luther: *Shaping and Defining the Reformation 1521-1532* (Minneapolis: Fortress Press, 1990), 219.

[8] As Bard Thompson says, Erasmus's impatience with the externals and formalities of religion made him even more radical than Luther in some respects. B. Thompson, *Humanists and Reformers: A History of the Renaissance and Reformation* (Cambridge: Eerdmans, 1996), 345.

[9] See e.g. J. A. Nestingen in *Captivation of the Will*, 2 and J. I. Packer, 'Luther Against Erasmus' in *Collected Shorter Writings of J. I. Packer volume 4: Honouring the People of God* (Carlisle: Paternoster, 1999), 103. See also the 1521 woodcut depicting Erasmus milling the flour of God's word from which Luther then makes bread in Brecht, *Martin Luther*, 214.

[10] B. A Gerrish, *Grace and Reason: A Study in the Theology of Luther* (Oxford: Clarendon Press, 1962), 162.

[11] Brecht, *Martin Luther*, 215.

[12] B. Thompson, *Humanists and Reformers*, 343.

and over-sensitive to criticism and challenge.[13] His friends and patrons, including Henry VIII of England, were urging him to write against Luther anyway,[14] so on 1st September 1524 not only did he not stand aside, he entered the lists against Luther by publishing *On the Freedom of the Will*.[15] With a tone of mock humility and possibly a side-swipe at the German's well-known verbose prolixity he asked, 'dare Erasmus attack Luther, like the fly the elephant?'[16]

The trick for Erasmus was to be faithful to his own principles while simultaneously putting some distance between himself and Luther without jeopardising his own calls for reform of the church. Although he disliked his rather unruly manner, Erasmus approved of much that Luther had said and done, and did not wish to split the rather fragile coalition driving reforms. Indeed, as Kolb says, 'he feared that both Luther's radical ideas and his boisterous advocacy of those ideas would alienate the powers and frustrate true reform, as he understood it.'[17] The ground on which he chose to fight was the issue of free will, because it enabled him to address some of his own core concerns about the improvement of manners (that is, morality), but also precisely because it was the

---

[13] See Oberman, *Luther: Man between God and the Devil*, 216 and Kolb, *Bound Choice*, 13.

[14] He told Cardinal Campeggio in February 1524 that he was thinking of publishing something on free will against Luther, at the urging of Henry VIII. See Brecht, *Martin Luther*, 218, 223. It is for these reasons that Packer (following Rupp) refers to Erasmus's book as his 'greatest act of appeasement' in 'Luther Against Erasmus', 103.

[15] In 1533 he perhaps had something of a change of heart when he wrote in a book on Church unity that 'The freedom of the will is a thorny question which it profits little to debate; let us leave it to professed theologians.' See J. I. Packer & O. R. Johnston, *Martin Luther on the Bondage of the Will: A new translation of De Servo Arbitrio (1525) Martin Luther's Reply to Erasmus of Rotterdam* (London: James Clarke & Co, 1957), 39-40.

[16] E. G. Rupp & P. S. Watson, *Luther and Erasmus: Free Will and Salvation* LCC 17 (Philadelphia: Westminster Press, 1969), 36. All citations of *On the Freedom of the Will* and Luther's *On the Bondage of the Will* in this chapter are taken from this edition.

[17] Kolb, *Bound Choice*, 13. Cf. R. Marius, *Martin Luther: The Christian between God and Death* (London: Belknap Press, 2000), 447 who says, 'If only Luther had not turned so vehement and so radical, Erasmus could have seen in him a comrade.' See also Bainton, *Here I Stand*, 195 for Erasmus's positive evaluation of Luther at this point.

subject on which he was closest to Luther's opponents. He was perhaps not entirely conscious at first of how very close it was to Luther's heart.[18]

Erasmus took exception to statements Luther had made about free will in several key documents. For example, in *The Heidelberg Disputation* Luther asserted that 'Free will after the fall exists in name only.'[19] In his response to the Papal Bull excommunicating him, the sarcastic *Assertions of All the Articles Wrongly Condemned in the Roman Bull*, Luther declares:

> Free choice after [the fall of Adam into] sin is merely a term, and when [such choosing] does what it is able to do [*facit, quod in se est*], it commits moral sin... So it is necessary to retract this article. For I was wrong in saying that free choice before grace is a reality only in name. I should have said simply: free choice is in reality a fiction, or a term without reality. For no one has it in his power to think a good or bad thought, but everything (as Wyclif's article condemned at Constance rightly teaches) happens by absolute necessity.[20]

Erasmus's response was elegantly written in a measured tone which in typical Erasmian fashion 'smoothed out the paradoxes, argued for peace over tumult, and pointed toward an ethics-

---

[18] See B. Lohse, *Martin Luther's Theology: Its Historical and Systematic Development* trans. R. A. Harrisville (Minneapolis: Fortress Press, 1999), 161 and Brecht, *Martin Luther*, 235.

[19] See Theses 13-15 in T. F. Lull (ed.), *Martin Luther's Basic Theological Writings* (Minneapolis: Fortress Press, 1989), 39-40.

[20] Article 36 of the *Assertion* as quoted in Kolb, *Bound Choice*, 11. In Lull, *Martin Luther's Basic Theological Writings*, 39 thesis 13 at Heidelberg mentions 'mortal sin' whereas Kolb here has 'moral sin', and on page 294 his footnote (number 1) incorrectly identifies the Heidelberg thesis being paraphrased in the *Assertion* as number 14 (it is surely number 13). The second part of this article from the *Assertion* is also quoted by Erasmus, *On the Freedom of the Will*, 64. For Wyclif's teaching, see e.g. John Wyclif, *Trialogus* (trans. Stephen E. Lahey; Cambridge: Cambridge University Press, 2013), 132 (*Trialogus* III.8).

centered religion.'[21] The thrust of his argument is that Scripture is not entirely clear on this issue of free will, but very few theologians have ever 'totally taken away the power of freedom of choice,' and so he would prefer to stick with the consensus view rather than follow Luther's new and divisive opinions. Besides, if Luther was correct (and there was much in the Bible against him it seemed) then 'what evildoer will take pains to correct his life'?[22]

Examining his argument in more detail, Erasmus begins by defining free will as 'a power of the human will by which a man can apply himself to the things which lead to eternal salvation, or turn away from them.'[23] This power of free choice was certainly damaged but not destroyed by the Fall.[24] In the body of the book, as he works his way through biblical texts, he asks time and time again, 'What is the point of so many admonitions, so many precepts, so many threats, so many exhortations, so many expostulations, if of ourselves we do nothing, but God in accordance with his immutable will does everything in us, both to will and to perform the same?'[25] The will cannot be powerless, though it is of course 'puny' and requires the assistance of divine grace.[26]

Erasmus expresses his approval for a patristic view which distinguishes three stages in human action – thought, will, and accomplishment – and which assigns no place for free choice in the first or third stages where 'our soul is impelled by grace alone.' In the second stage, however, 'grace and the human will act together, but in such a way that grace is the principal cause, and

---

[21] B. Thompson, *Humanists and Reformers*, 344.

[22] Erasmus, *On the Freedom of the Will*, 41-43.

[23] Ibid., 47. Brecht, *Martin Luther*, 221 accuses Erasmus's definition itself of being obscure since 'it did not differentiate between natural freedom and freedom granted by the grace of God. To be sure, Erasmus later constantly emphasized the support of grace, but this showed the inconsistency of his position.'

[24] Erasmus, *On the Freedom of the Will*, 51.

[25] Ibid., 87, but see also the similar point on pages 57, 58, 59, 60, 63.

[26] Ibid., 79.

the secondary cause our will' and 'even the fact that he can consent and cooperate with divine grace is itself the work of God.'[27] The contribution of free choice is, therefore, 'extremely small'[28] or 'exceedingly trivial'[29] but nevertheless real. Luther is right on many things and has good motives, godly sentiments worthy of favour, and writes 'in pious and Christian vein,'[30] says Erasmus, yet in propagating 'grace alone' he immeasurably exaggerates original sin and ends up saying that even a man who is justified by faith cannot of himself do anything but sin.[31] Thus it is better to follow his (Erasmus's) 'more accommodating view'[32] which takes a mediating position, guarding against things Luther was rightly concerned about but without throwing the baby out with the bathwater, so to speak.

In one sense, the Prince of the Humanists speaks for all learned intellectuals here with his emphasis on balance, mediating positions, and the rejection of extremes. But as Forde rightly complains, 'Erasmus' position reflects at bottom the same dreary moralism touted by everyone from the lowliest neophyte to the most learned professor.'[33] However, by re-asserting free will even in this apparently small way, Erasmus had attacked what Luther called 'the highest and most important issue of our cause.'[34] Nothing less than the Reformation doctrine of salvation by grace alone was at stake.

---

[27] Ibid., 80.

[28] Ibid., 89.

[29] Ibid., 90.

[30] Ibid., 86, 97.

[31] Ibid., 91-94.

[32] Ibid., 90.

[33] Forde, *Captivation*, 31.

[34] 'Assertio omnium articulorum M. Lutheri per bullam Leonis X' in WA 7.148.16 as quoted in Forde, *On Being a Theologian of the Cross: Reflections on Luther's Heidelberg Disputation, 1518* (Cambridge: Eerdmans, 1997), 53.

The Elephant Wades In

Luther's response to Erasmus had to wait for many months. He had more than enough on his plate already as the simmering discontent within Germany boiled over into the Peasant's War in the spring of 1525. His own bitter attack on the peasants, an inflammatory book called *Against the Murdering, Robbing Hoard of Peasants* came out around the same time as he broke his monk's vow and got married to Katherine von Bora, something of a PR disaster at the height of social unrest. He also remained busy on the intellectual front, continuing to preach, to publish a translation of Ecclesiastes, and to prepare a commentary on Deuteronomy while also falling out with Karlstadt, being occupied with Müntzer's revolutionary form of Christianity, and engaging in the newly initiated eucharistic controversy.[35] His sermons and writings from the first half of 1525 show that he had begun to wrestle with the issues presented by Erasmus,[36] and he had at least read *On the Freedom of the Will* (rather than using it as toilet paper as he often did with his opponent's attacks!).[37] His political support and protection was undermined and threatened but he lacked motivation and time to engage with Erasmus more fully. It was his wife who finally persuaded him to put pen to paper with *On the Bondage of the Will*, which finally appeared on New Year's Eve 1525 some sixteen months after Erasmus's opening salvo.

The Prince of the Humanists may have presented him as an elephant, but Luther would have been conscious of the fact that in reality, despite his recent fame, next to Erasmus he was merely 'a minor academic from a fairly new faculty in a small town in an obscure part of eastern Germany.'[38] Yet what he lacked in

---

[35] See Lohse, *Martin Luther's Theology*, 162-163.

[36] Brecht, *Martin Luther*, 224-225.

[37] Ibid., 224 which cites WA, TR 2, number 2086 for this entirely believable tale. See also LW 40:362.

[38] Nestingen in Forde, *Captivation*, 2.

elegance of style and firmness of reputation he made up for in sparkling theological insight and witty repartee. He confessed to being 'an uncultivated fellow who has always moved in uncultivated circles' and yet Erasmus's book struck him as 'so cheap and paltry that I felt profoundly sorry for you, defiling as you were your very elegant and ingenious style with such trash, and quite disgusted at the utterly unworthy matter that was being conveyed in such rich ornaments of eloquence, like refuse or ordure being carried in gold and silver vases.'[39]

This tone was not calculated to win friends and influence people in Erasmus's circle. It has not, however, prevented praise being heaped on the book in the last 150 years.[40] Referring to the extravagantly positive reception it has received, one recent biographer, Richard Marius (whose own religious position seems far removed from Luther's) chooses to dissent saying, 'It is not a judgment I share. The work is insulting, vehement, monstrously unfair, and utterly uncompromising' and it 'burns with rage.'[41] Erasmus himself was bitterly hurt by it: 'You have never written against anyone anything more rabid, and even, what is more detestable, nothing more malicious… What torments me and all honest people is that with your character that is so arrogant,

---

[39] *On the Freedom of the Will*, 102. A not unusual scatological reference after Luther developed severe constipation while confined at the Wartburg for his own safety in 1521-1522; Brecht, *Martin Luther*, 2 and Bainton, *Here I Stand*, 151-152.

[40] Kolb, *Bound Choice*, 9 makes a striking case that though it was a popular book at first, very quickly it 'utterly disappeared from the market… [and] remained in comparative obscurity for a quarter-millennium.' It was not until the nineteenth century that interest in *The Bondage of the Will* recovered.

[41] Marius, *Martin Luther*, 456, 465. Marius certainly does not share Luther's view when he expresses his own opinion that the New Testament is 'inconsistent and contradictory' and complains of the 'Hebrew Bible's propensity to make of God a somewhat petulant and changeable personality' (page 451). See also Bard Thompson, *Humanists and Reformers*, 410 who is more positive but still describes Luther's book as 'hard-hitting, sometimes offensive,' and blunt.

impudent, and rebellious, you plunge the whole world into fatal discord.'[42]

Luther would defend his passionate tone and rather bruising style by contrasting it with Erasmus who '[w]hen it comes to theology... does nothing in earnest.' It is manifest that 'deep-seated emotional differences underlay the conflict between the two reformers.'[43] Kolb sums up Luther's apocalyptic perspective well: 'Erasmus might be able to delude himself into thinking that a dispassionate, purely academic and reasonable discussion of the bondage or freedom of human choice in relation to God was possible. Luther was certain that their exchange was part of the final combat between God and the devil.'[44] It was the last times and God's truth must be vindicated against the devil's lies by wielding the sword of the Spirit!

Luther may be right that Erasmus's tone of 'bored detachment' towards the subject at hand was 'fundamentally irreligious and in a theologian irresponsible.'[45] Yet too many commentators sympathetic to Luther have failed to censure him for his sometimes excessively contemptuous and colourful language here. It does not appear to me that Luther's personal attacks on Erasmus were entirely free of 'vainglory or contempt' or that they were motivated by 'undisguised pastoral concern' for Erasmus, as Packer suggests.[46] At the time, Melanchthon urged moderation, fearing that Luther had only made things worse, and would have preferred a brief, simple explanation of the differences Luther had

---

[42] Marius, *Martin Luther*, 467. On the next page, Marius emotively adds that to many in the twenty-first century who have seen the effects of war and the results of zealots taking up guns, 'Luther's uncompromising rhetoric reeks of sadness and futility and of bloodshed to come in rivers of anguish throughout Europe and the Americas.'

[43] Gerrish, *Grace and Reason*, 164.

[44] Kolb, *Bound Choice*, 18.

[45] Packer, '*Martin Luther on the Bondage of the Will*', 45.

[46] Packer, 'Luther Against Erasmus', 107.

with Erasmus, shorn of the ugly insults and polemical rhetoric.[47] Luther himself had written that, 'in teaching, simplicity and appropriateness of speech is required, not bombast and persuasive rhetorical images.'[48] Yet he failed to follow his own rule.

Perhaps Luther was right; it could be that the Dutchman was 'the first Christian atheist',[49] an unconverted stranger to grace as Luther rather bluntly suggests. It is true, as Luther says, that 'no man perceives one iota of what is in the Scriptures unless he has the Spirit of God.'[50] Erudition and biblical learning alone make neither a theologian nor a Christian. Steinmetz pointedly draws our attention to the fact that, 'When Luther observes that a theologian is made by *meditatio*, *tentatio*, and *oratio* (meditation, temptation, and prayer), he wants to emphasize that theology is not a neutral discipline like geometry, which can be studied dispassionately in abstraction from the self and its concerns.'[51] This, of course, has led some to suggest that Luther allowed his experience to dictate his interpretation of the Bible,[52] and it is true that he is open about how it has affected him.[53] The ability to cite texts, marshal arguments, and muster the troops of tradition is good (Luther himself is very effective in using classical quotations, Patristics, Hebrew, and Greek) but it is far from sufficient. Hägglund also mentions Luther's idea of 'the school of the Holy Spirit' and how important tribulation is 'for a genuine insight into

---

[47] See Brecht, *Martin Luther*, 237-238 and Kolb, *Bound Choice*, 14 (on Melanchthon's continued moderation in 1526-1527).

[48] Luther, *The Bondage of the Will*, 170.

[49] Oberman, *Luther*, 213.

[50] Luther, *The Bondage of the Will*, 112.

[51] D. C. Steinmetz, *Luther in Context* (Bloomington: Indiana University Press, 1986), 26.

[52] See Oberman, *Luther*, 212 who suggests, 'the suspicion that personal experiences dictate scriptural interpretation may be a modern prejudice' and Kolb, *Bound Choice*, 21 who affirms that Luther found the bound will in both the Bible and his experience.

[53] E.g. Luther, *The Bondage of the Will*, 329. See also Brecht, *Martin Luther*, 233.

the Word.'[54] A fatal lack of insight into the gospel and personal experience of saving grace can render the most elegantly written, well-researched and well-received tomes utterly useless.

Yet Luther's deliberately cultivated bullish tone and his references to Erasmus's work as 'Madam Diatribe' and use of the feminine pronoun when quoting him,[55] are hardly designed to persuade. Luther was simply poking fun at Erasmus as he wrote, 'when a man does not take this subject seriously and feels no personal interest in it, never has his heart in it and finds it wearisome, chilling, or nauseating, how can he help saying absurd, inept, and contradictory things all the time, since he conducts the case like one drunk or asleep, belching out between his snores.'[56] This, Luther must have known, would entertain his readers (I confess to being amused myself) but it would never win over his adversary. In extolling grace he had, we might say, neglected graciousness. *The Lord's servant must not be quarrelsome but kind to everyone, able to teach, patiently enduring evil, correcting his opponents with gentleness*, said the Apostle (2 Timothy 2:24-25).[57] And yet Luther was heard to say, 'I vehemently and from the very heart hate Erasmus', while mere mention of his name could send him into a 'paroxysm of loathing.'[58] If it is true to say that 'Erasmus set out to win a debate [but] Luther sought to comfort and rescue the lost'[59] then he failed with at least one significant

---

[54] B. Hägglund, *History of Theology* trans G. J. Lund (St. Louis: Concordia, 2007), 223.

[55] A prominent feature of Luther's rhetoric from around page 180 onwards of *Bondage of the Will*. 'Madam Diatribe' occurs first on page 191.

[56] Luther, *The Bondage of the Will*, 179.

[57] Roger Nicole has written helpfully about such disagreements between Christians. He cites the 'Golden Rule' of Matthew 7:12 as a key principle to remember in such circumstances and, quoting 2 Timothy 2:24-26 as I have done above (and which Luther does for another reason on page 140!), reminds us that, 'A Christian in carrying on discussions with those who differ should not be subject to the psychology of the boxing ring where the contestants are bent upon demolishing one another.' See 'How to Deal with Those Who Differ from Us' at http://thirdmill.org/how-to-deal-with-those-who-differ-from-us-part-one (last accessed 20th January 2017).

[58] See Marius, *Martin Luther*, 442 who cites TR 1, number 818.

[59] Forde, *Captivation*, 25.

lost sheep. Indeed, they often misunderstood and argued past each other, failing fully to engage in the other's argument.[60]

Luther, however, was also concerned more widely that others would not be distracted from the gospel or from true reform by Erasmus's sortie into theology. This explains why he was so passionate and bold—Erasmus had touched a raw nerve. Luther 'always assumed that the crux of the Reformation was a struggle for right doctrine; the Reformation was not a silly issue over loose living or superstition, as if Lutherans were holier than Catholics. It was a question of what the Christian religion really is, and that question is so serious that it holds human salvation in the balance.'[61] So the German Hercules was surprisingly indifferent to many of the issues which exercised the Rotterdam Rottweiler, since '[t]o him the corruption of the Papacy lay deeper, in its loss of the Gospel... We should not, therefore, give our attention to the wicked lives of the Papists so much as to their impious doctrine' he declared.[62] As always, it is important to remember that even if immorality in the church can be censured or prevented, our doctrine could still be unhealthy.

Luther himself considered *The Bondage of the Will* his best work, because it so effectively addresses these issues. Writing in July 1537 to Wolfgang Capito he confesses, 'Regarding [the plan] to collect my writings in volumes, I am quite cool and not at all eager about it because... I acknowledge none of them to be really

---

[60] See Lohse, *Martin Luther's Theology*, 163 and Kolb, *Bound Choice*, 28. Kolb also shows, for example, on pages 24-25 how different definitions of 'will' were at work in the debate, while Packer, 'Luther Against Erasmus', page 111 discusses the inadequacies of sixteenth century concepts of 'will' generally.

[61] B. Thompson, *Humanists and Reformers*, 409. See also Packer, 'Luther Against Erasmus', 118-119 who claims this debate, 'established once and for all that the Reformation conflict was not primarily about obscurantist superstitions and ecclesiastical abuses, matters over which humanists like Erasmus and theologians like Luther might under certain circumstances have made common cause; but that it was essentially concerned with the substance of the Gospel.'

[62] Gerrish, *Grace and Reason*, 165. See also Bainton, *Here I Stand*, 191 who writes, 'All along he had declared that the contest was over the faith and not over the life, and that if the morals were amended the teaching would still be unsound.'

a book of mine, except perhaps the one *On the Bound Will* and the *Catechism*.'[63]

So let us now turn to examine the content of Luther's counter-blast, under two headings which summarise his primary concerns as they arise in the course of the book: first the clarity of Scripture, and then the bondage of the will and salvation by grace alone.

The Clarity of Scripture

Instead of launching straight into a rebuttal of Erasmus's exegesis and doctrinal formulation, Luther begins by questioning the humanist's whole frame of mind on the issue. Erasmus claimed to dislike 'assertions' (echoing the title of Luther's response to the Papal Bull which had excommunicated him) and wished he had liberty to be a skeptic and not have to take sides on the issue of free will.[64] He preferred 'to compare opinions, look for consensus, put forward an opinion that seemed most probable – that process is actually the technical meaning of the word Diatribe.'[65] To this Luther replies with some warmth, 'it is not the mark of a Christian mind to take no delight in assertions... The Holy Spirit is no Skeptic.'[66] God did not reveal his word to us in order for us to take a scholarly and detached view on basic questions, as Erasmus had done.

Luther then proceeds to take Erasmus to task for his assertions (!) about the obscurity of Scripture, and the apparently needless debates which Christians had had for centuries over issues of

---

[63] LW 50:172-173.

[64] Erasmus, *The Freedom of the Will*, 37.

[65] D. MacCulloch, *Reformation: Europe's House Divided 1490-1700* (London: Penguin, 2004), 151 referring to a Greek word in the full Latin title of Erasmus's work *De libero arbitrio diatribē sive collatio*. See also Lohse, *Martin Luther's Theology*, 161 and Kolb, *Bound Choice*, 24 on diatribe as a genre.

[66] Luther, *The Bondage of the Will*, 105, 109. See also Oberman, *Luther*, 215.

biblical interpretation.[67] Luther claims any obscurity in the Bible is merely provisional and contingent, having to do with our current ignorance of its vocabulary or grammar. 'Truly it is stupid and impious,' he writes, 'when we know that the subject matter of Scripture has all been placed in the clearest light, to call it obscure on account of a few obscure words... It is true that for many people much remains abstruse: but this is not due to the obscurity of Scripture, but to the blindness or indolence of those who will not take the trouble to look at the very clearest truth.'[68]

Erasmus would rather not have certain doctrines openly discussed before the 'common herd' or 'untutored multitude.'[69] Luther is vehemently opposed to such self-censorship from preachers: 'Truth and doctrine must be preached always, openly, and constantly, and never accommodated or concealed... If, therefore, God has willed that such things should be openly spoken of and published abroad without regard to the consequences, who are you to forbid it?'[70] God had a saving purpose in revealing the truth about the human will in Scripture: 'It is thus for the sake of the elect that these things are published, in order that being humbled and brought back to nothingness by this means they may be saved.'[71]

Luther sees in Erasmus's attack on the clarity of Scripture a typically Roman ploy. In the kingdom of the Pope, he says, 'nothing is more commonly stated or more generally accepted than the idea that the Scriptures are obscure and ambiguous, so that the spirit to interpret them must be sought from the Apostolic See of Rome.' This was a devilish conspiracy to trample

---

[67] Erasmus, *The Freedom of the Will*, 39-40.

[68] Luther, *The Bondage of the Will*, 110-111.

[69] Erasmus, *The Freedom of the Will*, 40.

[70] Ibid., 132, 135. See, however, P. Althaus, *The Theology of Martin Luther* trans. R. C. Schultz (Philadelphia: Fortress Press, 1966), 285 on Luther's view of appropriate timing when it comes to drinking the strong drink of teaching on predestination.

[71] Luther, *The Bondage of the Will*, 137.

down the Bible.[72] In response, Luther set out his understanding of the internal and external clarity of Scripture. By *internal* clarity he meant an appreciation of Scripture located in the understanding of the heart: 'If you speak of internal clarity, no man perceives one iota of what is in the Scriptures unless he has the Spirit of God. All men have a darkened heart, so that even if they can recite everything in Scripture, and know how to quote it, yet they apprehend and truly understand nothing of it... For the Spirit is required for the understanding of Scripture.'[73]

As for the *external* clarity of Scripture, this concerns a judgment to be made by the public ministry of the word and is the chief concern of leaders and preachers. He proves that Scripture has the ability to act as a clear guide for the church from those places in Scripture itself where it is appealed to, for example, as an arbiter of disputes (Deuteronomy 17:8), a light for the eyes and the path (Psalm 19:9; 119:105), and a shining lamp in the darkness (2 Peter 1:19).[74] 'The apostles,' he avers, 'like Christ himself, point us to the Scriptures as the very clearest witnesses to what they themselves say... In short, if Scripture is obscure or ambiguous, what point was there in God's giving it to us? Are we not obscure and ambiguous enough without having our obscurity, ambiguity, and darkness augmented for us from heaven?'[75]

Erasmus had claimed he willingly submitted to 'the inviolable authority of the Holy Scriptures and... the decrees of the Church.[76] Luther on the other hand would not permit the Church to have such authority on its own account. Far from requiring the Pope's authoritative interpretation of Scripture, then, each congregation had the power to ensure it had correct teaching from the word. This was the conclusion he had reached in 1523

---

[72] Ibid., 158-159.

[73] Ibid., 112.

[74] Ibid., 159-161.

[75] Ibid., 162.

[76] Erasmus, *The Freedom of the Will*, 37.

when writing (at their request) to the villagers of Leisnig in electoral Saxony:

> [W]herever there is a Christian congregation in possession of the gospel, it not only has the right and power but also the duty – on pain of losing the salvation of its souls and in accordance with the promise made to Christ in baptism – to avoid, to flee, to depose, and to withdraw from the authority that our bishops... and the like are now exercising. For it is clearly evident that they teach and rule contrary to God and his word... it is a divine right and a necessity for the salvation of souls to depose or to avoid such bishops... and whatever is of their government.[77]

Luther's hero Augustine had also said something similar, writing, 'We should not obey those bishops who have been duly elected, if they commit errors, or teach or ordain any thing contrary to the divine Scripture', a quotation which appears in the *Augsburg Confession*.[78]

This of course is a pertinent word for today in so-called 'mixed denominations,' where the tyranny of the centre and 'ongoing conversations' between opposing factions can act as a barrier to the rule of God's word. Synodical discussions in mainline denominations are often predicated on the idea that Scripture is not clear, and so we must use the magical tools of hermeneutics to unlock the truth for today — which so often turns out to be very different from the faith once and for all delivered to the saints, but surprisingly similar to the spirit of the age. Erasmus' urbane approach of comparing opinions and searching for consensus can

---

[77] 'That a Christian Assembly or congregation has the right and power to judge all teaching and to call, appoint, and dismiss teachers, established and proven by Scripture' in LW 39:308-309.

[78] Augustine, *Ad Catholicos Fratres Liber Unos*, chapter 28, CSEL 52:264. I am grateful to Peter Sanlon for the correct source of this quotation, which is wrongly attributed in the *Augsburg Confession* Article 28 to Augustine's epistle against Petilian.

sometimes be dangerous to the integrity of the gospel, and the safety of the soul.

Luther's most powerful point on the clarity of Scripture is that if the Bible is not clear then he may as well return to Rome and to the safety of the Pope's 'infallible' interpretations. If Erasmus was permitted to call into question the Bible's clarity on important doctrinal matters then this would ultimately be the death knell for the Reformation project. This is why great care must be taken in a supposedly 'post-modern' context when handling discussions of hermeneutics, which can so easily undermine the authority of the word and leave people baffled and confused. In such a climate the clearer but less biblical notes being sounded by Rome (or indeed, Mecca) will be far more attractive to those seeking truth and guidance. If Scripture is ambiguous then it makes perfect sense for Rome to anathematize those who do not agree with 'holy mother Church, whose duty it is to judge regarding the true sense and interpretation of the Holy Scriptures.'[79] This is ultimately part of the reason why Erasmus considered the Roman Church to be, so to speak, the best boat to fish from.

Is the Bible clear today? For Erasmus it was certain issues of doctrine which were unclear, but biblical morality remained 'most plainly evident.'[80] Not so today. Christians can be discouraged by modern trends in confusing interpretations which appear to make the Bible say things at odds with its plain meaning, especially in the field of ethics. As Mark Thompson explains, 'An argument that the meaning of Scripture is unclear, or irrelevant because of its location amidst the historical particularities and thought world of antiquity, has featured in debates over gender relationships (especially over how these are reflected in church life), human sexuality (especially over the acceptability or otherwise of homosexual behaviour) and the sanctity of yet unborn human

---

[79] *Decretum de editione et usu sacrorum librorum*, Council of Trent, Session IV, 8 April 1546 as cited in M. D. Thompson, *A Clear and Present Word: The Clarity of Scripture* NSBT 21 (Nottingham: Apollos, 2006), 150 footnote 28.

[80] Erasmus, *The Freedom of the Will*, 40.

life.[81] Indeed, while I was first researching this chapter, US Presidential hopeful Barak Obama, basing his endorsement of homosexual civil unions on the Sermon on the Mount, rejected other biblical injunctions which spoke against it because they occurred in 'an obscure passage in Romans.'[82] As one blogger commented at the time, 'Our public discussion of Scripture has become so degraded that someone like Obama can say that Romans is 'obscure,' and the overall reaction is not a horse laugh, but rather a shrug accompanied with a non-committal 'that's a point of view, certainly.' The central problem with this is that Scripture is the inspired Word of God, given to us in order to serve as a light in a dark place.'[83] This seems to me to be an excellent modern expression and application of Luther's sentiment.

The Bondage of the Will and Salvation by Grace Alone

We move on from Luther's prolegomena on the subject of Scripture to discuss the heart of his contention with Erasmus. The book was called not *The Clarity of Scripture*, after all, but *The Bondage of the Will*. The Latin title *De Servo Arbitrio* was taken (not coincidentally) from a saying of St Augustine in a classic anti-Pelagian treatise.[84] So it was clearly Luther's intention to defend the Augustinian doctrine of sin, nicely summed up by a phrase Luther used previously at Heidelberg: 'Free will without

---

[81] M. D. Thompson, *A Clear and Present Word*, 161.

[82] http://www.christianitytoday.com/gleanings/2008/march/obama-cites-sermon-on-mount-for-his-support-of-civil-unions.html (last accessed 20th January 2017).

[83] http://dougwils.com/s7-engaging-the-culture/why-we-should-rather-not-become-an-obama-nation.html (last accessed 20th January 2017).

[84] Lohse, *Martin Luther's Theology*, 163 says 'By using this title Luther intended to make clear that he understood himself as defender of the Augustinian doctrine of sin and grace against Pelagians old and new.' See Augustine's *Contra Julianum* 2.8.23.

grace has the power to do nothing but sin.'[85] This one sentence summary is oft quoted in *The Bondage of the Will*,[86] and was the essential starting point for the affirmation that salvation must, therefore, be entirely the work of God's grace alone, and the source of Luther's confidence that 'Augustine… is entirely with me.'[87]

Some historians have seen the key to Reformation, and to Protestant theology in general, as being justification by faith alone. This was indeed spoken of by the Reformers in glowing terms, most famously when Luther himself declared that if the article of justification stands, the church stands but that if it falls, the church falls,[88] while John Calvin called justification 'the main hinge on which religion turns.'[89] Yet this exalted language of central importance can also be heard in *The Bondage of the Will* concerning free will, sin, and grace. 'What I am after in this dispute,' he stated boldly, 'is to me something serious, necessary, and indeed eternal, something of such a kind and such importance that it ought to be asserted and defended to the death, even if the whole world had not only to be thrown into strife and confusion, but actually to return to total chaos and reduced to nothingness.'[90] Near the end of the book, Luther praises Erasmus not only for his 'eloquence bordering on the miraculous' but most of all for his insight:

[85] Augustine, *The Spirit and the Letter* 3.5 as quoted in Lull's text of 'The Heidelberg Disputation' (*Martin Luther's Basic Theological Writings*, 40), but translated as 'A man's free-will, indeed, avails for nothing except to sin, if he knows not the way of truth' in P. Schaff (ed.), *Nicene and Post-Nicene Fathers*, First Series, Volume 5, Saint Augustine: *Anti-Pelagian Writings* trans. P. Holmes, R. E. Wallis, and B. B. Warfield (Peabody MA: Hendrickson, 1999), 84-85.

[86] E.g. on page 265 as 'free choice avails for nothing but sinning.'

[87] Luther, *The Bondage of the Will*, 145.

[88] WA 40 III. 352.3 *'quia isto articulo stante stat Ecclesia, ruente ruit Ecclesia.'*

[89] J. Calvin, *Institutes of the Christian Religion* (Philadelphia: Westminster Press, 1960), III.xi.1, page 726.

[90] Luther, *The Bondage of the Will*, 128.

I praise and commend you highly for this also, that
unlike all the rest you alone have attacked the real
issue, the essence of the matter in dispute, and have
not wearied me with irrelevancies about the papacy,
purgatory, indulgences, and such like trifles (for
trifles they are rather than basic issues), with which
almost everyone hitherto has gone hunting for me
without success. You and you alone have seen the
question on which everything hinges, and have
aimed at the vital spot.[91]

Such was the vital and absolutely fundamental significance of
teaching the enslaved will. Luther had been formulating and
defending his thoughts on it since at least his *Disputation on
Scholastic Theology* in 1517.[92] It functioned as a critical defining
issue, distinguishing him and his Reformation movement over
against the humanism of Erasmus, the Catholicism of Rome, and
the radical reformation of the Anabaptists. Concerning the latter,
German/Moravian Anabaptist leader Balthasar Hubmaier wrote
two pamphlets against Luther's theological anthropology in 1527
precisely because, explains Steinmetz, he saw very clearly 'that the
doctrine of the bondage of the will undercut the Anabaptist
understanding of conversion, baptism, the nature of the Church,
and Christian morality.'[93] Even more importantly, this
Augustinian doctrine of sin and grace was likewise held with
equal fervency by Zwingli, Bucer, Calvin and others. As Warfield
rightly states, 'the material principle of the Reformation… was
not at first known by the name of justification by faith alone, but
it was from the first passionately embraced as renunciation of all
human works and dependence on the grace of God alone for
salvation… There are two foci around which this gospel revolves:
the absolute helplessness of man in sin; the sole efficiency of grace

---

[91] Ibid., 333.

[92] Article 5 of the *Disputation* for example states, 'It is false to state that man's
inclination is free to choose between either of two opposites. Indeed, the inclination is
not free, but captive. This is said in opposition to common opinion.' Lull, *Martin
Luther's Basic Theological Writings*, 13.

[93] Steinmetz, *Luther in Context*, 59.

in salvation... All else that Protestantism stood for, in comparison with this, must be relegated to the second rank.'[94]

Erasmus, on the other hand, recoiled from such a pessimistic anthropology and the insistence on grace *alone* as being capable of saving and transforming human beings. As we have seen above, he insisted that the warnings, exhortations, and commands of Scripture must imply an ability in human beings, however puny and feeble, to comply. Since Erasmus banged this drum so many times in his own work, Luther (whose book is essentially a point by point refutation of what Erasmus had written) comes back with tedious frequency to the same counterargument: such passages of Scripture 'show not what men can do but what they ought to do.'[95] Indeed, 'it is Satan's work to prevent men from recognizing their plight and to keep them presuming that they can do everything they are told.'[96]

Luther makes his case from the Scriptures, refuting Erasmus's exegesis point by point and showing that he often makes the text prove too much; where he wanted to prove only such free choice as can will nothing good without grace, he ends up 'proving' by his inferences a freedom and ability to keep *everything* God commands.[97] Logically, Luther also insists that if God is omnipotent and has unerring foreknowledge then there cannot be such a thing as free will.[98] This is the first point in his summary conclusion: 'if we believe it to be true that God foreknows and predestines all things, that he can neither be mistaken in his foreknowledge nor

---

[94] Warfield, 'The Theology of the Reformation', 465, 473, 476. MacCulloch, *Reformation*, 151, from a different theological angle to Warfield, similarly writes that Luther's view 'that human beings could expect nothing but condemnation, and had nothing to offer God that would merit salvation [was] the very heart of the Reformation's reassertion of the darkest side of Augustine.'

[95] Luther, *The Bondage of the Will*, 188. See also pages 189, 190, 195, 196, 205 and many other places. Luther himself claimed, with a glint in his eye no doubt, that 'Diatribe' wanted him 'to die of unrelieved boredom while she keeps on discoursing' (page 290).

[96] Ibid., 193.

[97] E.g. ibid., 202.

[98] The force of the section covering pages 239-246.

hindered in his predestination, and that nothing takes place but as he wills it (as reason itself is forced to admit), then on the testimony of reason itself there cannot be any free choice in man or angel or any creature.'[99]

It should be recognised, however, that Luther (rightly or wrongly) does leave room for a certain kind of human freedom. 'Free choice,' he admits, 'is allowed to man only with respect to what is beneath him and not what is above him... On the other hand in relation to God, or in matters pertaining to salvation or damnation, a man has no free choice, but is a captive, subject and slave either of the will of God or the will of Satan.'[100] This is an often repeated distinction in his *Table Talk*: 'we are not able to do anything that is good *in divine matters*.'[101] Or as he puts it elsewhere, 'he that will maintain that man's free-will is able to do or work anything in spiritual cases, be they never so small, denies Christ... [yet] I confess that mankind has a free-will, but it is to milk kine, to build houses, &c., and no further.'[102] Marius is sarcastically critical at this point and considers the idea of 'freedom in what is beneath us' to be ultimately nonsensical because seemingly mundane choices can lead to much greater effects: 'we may assume we have free choice in spreading jam or marmalade on our toast in the morning... We may also choose freely whether to be a lawyer or a monk, since our vocations seem to be a part of the freedom Luther grants to things below. Yet if we become a monk who rebels against monasticism and becomes a great prophet of God, our free choice in the beginning might

[99] Ibid., 332.

[100] Ibid., 143.

[101] Kepler, *The Table Talk*, page 91 (number 226).

[102] Ibid., pages 93-94 (number 229).

seem to be part of God's providence.'[103] Ultimately, Luther would recognise, even this free agency must submit to the over-arching providential rule which ensures that not even a sparrow falls to the ground without the Father's say so (Matthew 10:29).

The main thrust of Luther's rebuttal of Erasmus, however, is simple. As R. C. Sproul has it, 'Luther is driving Erasmus where Erasmus does not want to go, straight into the arms of Pelagius.'[104] Indeed Marius, again taking a controversial and provocative line, says, 'I suspect that Erasmus would have found himself in substantial agreement with Pelagius had the two been able to transcend time and the demands of orthodoxy to sit down over a good cask of wine to have a long talk about God, humankind, and morals.'[105] Erasmus was firmly anchored in semi-Pelagian patterns of thought and religious practice, but Luther would not recognise the legitimacy of a middle way between Augustine and Pelagius, since to give an inch to free will was to take everything from God's glory and to lose the best of both systems (if indeed there can be anything good about Pelagius). The question of the freedom or bondage of the will, therefore, 'was in no way irreverent, inquisitive, or superfluous; instead, it had to do with the central issue of the Christian faith: what does God do in salvation, and what does man do?'[106] Luther's answer was straightforward: we are by nature children of wrath, slaves to sin and to Satan (Ephesians 2:1-3), so that if we are to be saved it must be by grace alone. It is possible to please

---

[103] Marius, *Martin Luther*, 462. Cf. Forde, *Captivation*, 49-50 and H. J. McSorley, *Luther: Right or Wrong? An Ecumenical-Theological Study of Luther's Major Work, 'The Bondage of the Will'* (New York: Newman Press, 1969), 143-159. There is a similar use of Luther's own story to illustrate a point in this debate, in Scott Christensen, *What About Free Will? Reconciling our Choices with God's Sovereignty* (Phillipsburg: P&R, 2016), 148.

[104] R. C. Sproul, *Willing To Believe: The Controversy Over Free Will* (Grand Rapids: Baker, 1997), 100.

[105] Marius, *Martin Luther*, 454.

[106] Brecht, *Martin Luther*, 227.

God only once he has freed us. In that sense, the 'answering echo to *The Bondage of the Will* is *The Freedom of the Christian*.'[107]

Conclusion: Lessons for Today's Reformers

On the major ecclesiological and ethical issues of the century, Reformers and humanists shared much common ground, just as today evangelicals often share common concerns with other Christians on headline issues such as sexuality, gender, and the family. We may find common cause with old theological enemies and conservative secularists alike, but it would be a mistake to see this as building a platform for the gospel. Antipathy to the gospel of grace alone continues beneath the pragmatic expedience of contemporary ecclesiastical alliances. Co-belligerence has its uses, but it also has its limitations. Luther's run-in with Erasmus on the issue of the will should make us aware of that. We must be wary, then, of confusing 'the big issue' of the day with the gospel.[108] Erasmus and Luther both stood against abuses in the church, but for fundamentally different reasons and in a way that eventually saw them poles apart theologically. We must be alert to the danger that we may be losing our grip on the gospel if the name 'orthodox' becomes the label we use merely for those who happen to agree with us on, say, issues of human sexuality, while issues of human salvation are sidelined or neglected.

Reform of the church today needs to aim, as Luther aimed, at a recovery of the gospel and nothing less. Our interest ought not to be just in sweeping away abuses, or placing of power in evangelical hands, or returning to an apparently golden age when all was supposedly well (whether 2000, 500, or 50 years ago). Surely if Luther's insistence on grace alone—even against a potentially powerful ally like Erasmus—shows us anything, it is

---

[107] T. George, *The Theology of the Reformers* (Leicester: Apollos, 1988), 77.

[108] See Carl Trueman's insightful and amusingly titled editorial in *Themelios* 29.2 (April 2004), 'Why You Shouldn't Buy The Big Issue.'

that reform is not simply about getting the right people onto the right committees, or changing the ethos of a denomination, but recovering and preaching the gospel.

Moreover, if there is to be a new Reformation, it must recognise that our view of sin is not a secondary issue but an essential evangelical tenet. To retain the power of Luther's gospel we must be defined not just by our attachment to 'Bible, cross, and mission', but by a view of human nature which sees its only hope as the utterly unmerited favour of God who must work in us to will and to work for his good pleasure (Philippians 2:13). In a context where much of modern evangelicalism still (as J. I. Packer and O. R. Johnston wrote in 1957) has semi-Pelagianism in its blood,[109] and is tempted to gloss over doctrinal differences for the sake of a united front against secularism, to be heirs of the Reformation will mean upholding this unpopular and much-maligned truth, against all-comers. If we still prize the name Protestant and wish to be known as Reformational churches we cannot ignore this core Reformation doctrine or its implications for our evangelism, social action, and ecclesiological engagement.

Space prohibits a consideration of other important aspects of Luther's thought as expressed in *The Bondage of the Will*, such as his controversial assertions regarding the hidden and revealed God,[110] and his hermeneutics. Enough has been said, however, to make it clear that an engagement with this ancient debate between Erasmus and Luther is of vital and dynamic interest to the modern church. Yet we should not forget the historical and personal situation which brought such powerful ideas to the fore. Sadly for Luther, the publication of the book we have been examining came at a very difficult time. He faced, recounts Bainton, 'the pope implacable, Henry VIII railing, Duke George

---

[109] J. I. Packer & O. R. Johnston, *Martin Luther on the Bondage of the Will* (1957), 58. The conclusion of the translators' introduction to this edition remains a perceptive and sober challenge to the modern church after nearly 60 years.

[110] On which, I have found it stimulating to compare the treatments of R. C. Doyle, *Eschatology and the Shape of Christian Belief* (Carlisle: Paternoster, 1999), 175-181 and Althaus, *The Theology of Martin Luther*, 20-24, 274-286.

raging, Erasmus refuting, Staupitz dead.'[111] Many in the Wittenberg circle would not hold on to his pioneering formulations in *The Bondage of the Will* for very long.[112] The later debate between Bellarmine and Whitaker may be seen as a 'significant extension of the Luther-Erasmus debate'[113] and the issues would continue to be fought over for at least another century after Luther's death.

Perhaps the subject is handled better by Calvin, the great systematiser of the second generation. In *Institutes* book 2 chapters 2-5 he proves to be a more assiduous interpreter of the patristic evidence, a more persuasive exegete, and a more judicious systematic theologian than his great German hero. But he was also immensely conscious that he was standing on the shoulders of giants, not least Martin Luther. Luther's treatment in *De Servo Arbitrio* was somewhat rough, given its occasional and polemical nature and the pressures the author was under at the time. We might also say that he was at the vanguard of experimenting with appropriate ways of articulating the biblical message. As Kolb so gracefully puts it, 'Luther was constructing a new theological paradigm, and that effort inevitably drew him into trying out new vocabulary. He learned from such experiments even when they failed to produce satisfactory results.'[114] He may not be as clipped and precise as Chapter 1 section 7 of the *Westminster Confession of Faith* in his definition of the clarity of Scripture. But there is nothing to beat his raw energy, power, and wit on every subject he touches. One does not often come away from reading a section of Calvin's *Institutes* with a smile, a giggle, or a belly-laugh. Yet Luther manages somehow to entertain as well as edify, even when (as we have said above) his manners are not always worthy of emulation.

---

[111] Bainton, *Here I Stand*, 198.

[112] See Kolb, *Bound Choice*, 271-290 and Nestingen in Forde, *Captivation*, 19. See also the excellent monograph by Gregory B. Graybill, *Evangelical Free Will: Philipp Melancthon's Doctrinal Journey on the Origins of Faith* (Oxford: Oxford University Press, 2010).

[113] M. Thompson, *A Clear and Present Word*, 150.

[114] See Kolb, *Bound Choice*, 27. See also pages 2, 10, and 26-27.

Erasmus attempted to make Luther's insistence on the bondage of the will appear unbalanced and somewhat cranky. Luther in turn exposed the fatal flaws in the Erasmian 'middle way.' Sometimes truth is not a blend of two components, like grace and free will, but is to be found in an unadulterated purity. A mere drop of poison is sufficient to ruin a perfectly good drink; as the old rhyme says, 'Johnny was Erasmian. But Johnny is no more. What Johnny thought was H_2O, was H_2SO_4.' So, as Luther suggests, 'We must therefore go all out and completely deny free choice, referring everything to God; then there will be no contradictions in Scripture, and the difficulties, if not cured, can be endured.'[115]

So as he prayed, 'may the Lord, whose cause this is, enlighten us and make us vessels for his honour and glory. Amen.'[116]

---

[115] Luther, *Bondage of the Will*, 291.

[116] Ibid., 334 alluding to Romans 9:19-24.

The Inexhaustible Fountain of All Good Things: Union with Christ in Calvin on Ephesians

This chapter is a modified and expanded version of an article first published in Themelios 34.2 (2009) and lectures given at the European Leadership Forum and Cambridge University. I wish to thank Mark Garcia for arousing my interest in the subject, and Richard Rex for his stimulating and provocative insights, which made me think hard about how to improve this.

> We should be satisfied with the benefits of our Lord Jesus Christ, and that when we are grafted into his body and made one with him by belief of the gospel, then we may assure ourselves that he is the fountain which never dries up, nor can ever become exhausted, and that in him we have all variety of good things, and all perfection.[1]

For many the mention of the acclaimed French Reformer John Calvin immediately calls to mind an image of a stern, bearded systematician whose compassionless logic and doctrine of predestination represent all that is bad about theology. Yet those who have spent any time getting to know Calvin's work first-hand will hardly recognise this clichéd caricature (apart from the fact that he did have a beard). The man whose most famous work, the *Institutes*, claims to contain 'almost the whole sum of piety' and

---

[1] J. Calvin, *Sermons on the Epistle to the Ephesians* (trans. A. Golding; Edinburgh: Banner of Truth, 1973), 355.

begins by extolling the value of knowing God, was a devout and passionate man with a touchingly pious personal motto: 'My heart I offer you, O Lord, promptly and sincerely.' It is a shame that this sentiment is not the first thing that comes to mind when we remember this great servant of God.

Whilst election is not, of course, an unimportant theme in Calvin's work, the subject of this chapter—union with Christ—is a much more pervasive one. It is undoubtedly the key idea in his teaching on the way we receive the grace of Christ. While refuting Osiander, one of his German Lutheran opponents, Calvin says, 'that joining together of Head and members, that indwelling of Christ in our heart—in short, that mystical union—are accorded by us the highest degree of importance.'[2] Calvin's application of the gospel is summed up in what he says about union with Christ. Here more than anywhere we hear the heartbeat of the preacher who is committed not to cold abstract theologising but a personal, passionate, and pious relationship with his Lord and Saviour.

We could do a lot worse than return to Calvin's biblical emphasis on the believer's union with Christ to encourage us in presenting a Christ-centred gospel to the alienated and relationally-hungry inhabitants of the twenty-first century. In the process, we will also find a doctrinal resource of immense value in refuting false teaching, both ancient and modern.

The title of this chapter reflects Calvin's lovely and oft-repeated emphasis on Christ as the inexhaustible fountain of all good things, from whom—by means of our union with him—we draw our life, our righteousness, and our sanctification.[3] Though this language may be common in Calvin, it was, however, no common or merely conventional thing for him. He is amazed by it —indeed he says that union with Christ 'ought to ravish our

---

[2] J. Calvin, *Institutes of the Christian Religion* (ed. J. T. McNeill; trans. F. L. Battles; Philadelphia: Westminster, 1960), 737 (3.11.10).

[3] He is fond of alluding to Colossians 1:19 and 2:3 (e.g. *Sermons*, 118, 380, 396), but his own 'fountain' image is pervasive (e.g. *Sermons*, 124, 169, 220, 320, 355, 402, 404, 606, 616, 703). There is a mixture of the two ideas in *Institutes of the Christian Religion: 1536 Edition* (ed. and trans. F. L. Battles; London: Collins, 1986), 57.

minds in astonishment,'[4] and the vocabulary he uses to describe it is accordingly rich and varied.[5] So we dive in expecting to be seduced by what Calvin says about our intimate relationship with Christ. We will listen to what he says under three headings: the necessity of union with Christ, the benefits of that union, and the importance of 'closing the gap' between us and God (which has particular reference to the pastoral and doctrinal errors addressed by this doctrine).

We will particularly concentrate on Calvin's work on Ephesians, as seen in his commentary and sermons on that book.[6] The Apostle Paul's letter itself contains the 'in Christ' formula several times, and more than one *locus classicus* for the doctrine of union (such as Ephesians 5:28–32). This furnishes Calvin with many exegetically warranted opportunities to discuss union with Christ. It also furnishes us with over 850 pages of opportunities to examine his regular pastoral use of it, his exegetical workings, and the links he makes between union and other doctrinal loci.

While many may know him just as a systematic theologian, Calvin's commentaries and sermons take up far more space in his collected works than the *Institutes*. As a biblical commentator, he was 'unique and extremely illuminating... an endlessly fresh and eye-opening interpreter.'[7] Yet when Calvin reviewed his life's work on his deathbed, 'he talked more about his sermons than anything.'[8] Between 1541 and 1564 he is estimated to have preached around 4,000 sermons about thirty-five to forty minutes

---

[4] *Sermons*, 615.

[5] E.g. in his *Commentary*: spiritual union (324), fellowship (262), intercourse (262, 323), and gathered together in Christ (271). In his *Sermons*: communication (511), engrafting (615), head-members relation (291), clothed with him (194), partakers of him (205), joined to him (222), cleaving to him (227), made one with him (282), he dwells in us in a secret union (290), we live in him (615), we put on Christ (333), incorporated into him (501), linked to him (595), and God has conjoined himself with us (616).

[6] The commentary is *Commentaries on the Epistle of Paul to the Ephesians in Calvin's Commentaries* (vol. 21; trans. W. Pringle; Grand Rapids: Baker, 1993).

[7] J. Haroutunian, ed., *Calvin: Commentaries* (Philadelphia: Westminster, 1958), 15.

[8] J. D. Currid, *Calvin and the Biblical Languages* (Fearn, Ross-Shire: Mentor, 2007), 11.

long, without notes but not without preparation, twice on Sundays and once or twice midweek.[9] The forty-eight sermons on Ephesians were first preached ten years after his commentary was published, on Sundays from May 1558 to March 1559.[10] In contrast to the mere thirty or so references to union doctrine in the commentary,[11] around ninety percent of the sermons mention and make use of it in some way.[12] It seems to be one of his default ways of speaking about the blessings and benefits of the gospel.[13]

It is significant that these sermons were preached at the same time as Calvin was revising the *Institutes* for the very last time. Richard Muller suggests that 'significant editing sometimes occur[s] in strata of the *Institutes* that follow a series of sermons.'[14] The same effect can be observed as a result of Calvin's work on his commentaries.[15] In my view, a good case can be made that union language becomes much stronger and more important in the final 1559 edition of the systematic work precisely because

---

[9] Currid, *Calvin and the Biblical Languages*, 22–26.

[10] Published in French (1562) and English (1577). De Greef, *The Writings of John Calvin*, 112–14, gives the date of the first sermon as May 15, 1558; the English edition claims May 1 (*Sermons*, viii). See R. C. Zachman, *John Calvin as Teacher, Pastor, and Theologian* (Grand Rapids: Baker, 2006), 147–72.

[11] For the most developed, see *Commentary*, 220–25 (Ephesians 2:1–7), 322–25 (Ephesians 5:28–33). Calvin often passes over a union text without comment: in *Commentary*, 207 (1:13), he supplies a verb which removes a possible reference to union, and on 235 (2:13), 245 (2:22), 309 (5:8), and 334 (6:10), he declines to comment on it, despite significant textual warrant.

[12] Only five of forty-eight sermons fail to mention it (4:31–5:2; 5:11–14, 15–18; 6:1–4, 10–12).

[13] See where the text does not itself utilise union language, e.g. *Sermons*, 181, 205, 240, 313, 438, 640.

[14] R. A. Muller, *The Unaccommodated Calvin: Studies in the Foundation of a Theological Tradition* (Oxford: Oxford University Press, 2000), 115.

[15] On the relationship between Books 1 and 2 and Calvin's commentaries on the Gospels and Old Testament historical books, see S. Edmondson, 'The Biblical Historical Structure of Calvin's Institutes' (SJT 59 [2006]: 1–13). On Book 3 and the 1556 Romans commentary, see M. A. Garcia, *Life in Christ: Union with Christ and Twofold Grace in Calvin's Theology* (Carlisle: Paternoster, 2008), 90.

Calvin was preaching on Ephesians.[16] Certainly we can say that near the end of his life the mature Calvin held the doctrine of union with Christ to be both vital and exceedingly precious.

1. The Necessity of Union

We begin, then, by looking at our need of union with Christ, as Calvin expounds it. In the *Institutes* he begins Book 3 by saying Christ's work is 'useless and of no value for us' if we are separated from him: 'all that he possesses is nothing to us until we grow into one body with him.'[17] Yet the situation outside of Christ is much worse than merely missing out on blessings proffered to us as a result of his suffering. Calvin sees things much more radically. Preaching on 'you have put off the old man' in Ephesians 4:22, he says,

> For we know that there are (so to speak) two fountain-heads of mankind, that is to say, Adam and our Lord Jesus Christ. Now with regard to our first birth we all come out of the fountain of Adam and are corrupted with sinfulness, so that there is nothing but perverseness and cursedness in our souls. It is necessary for us then to be renewed in Jesus Christ, and to be made new creatures.[18]

Fundamental to Calvin's thought regarding our need for union with Christ is our preexisting union with Adam. It is true that 'while we are out of Christ, all is under the dominion of Satan,[19] yet more importantly it is this relationship with Adam (nowhere mentioned by name in Ephesians itself) which separates us from

---

[16] A separate chapter would be needed to prove this hypothesis. But note Ephesians quotations in 2.12.5 (added in 1559), as well as the major new section in 3.1.1 concerning union in which the first scriptural allusion is Ephesians 1:22 (or 4:15). See also the note on 340 of the Battles translation (2.6.1) on how soteriology is introduced in a new chapter by 'this radical *in Christo* passage.'

[17] *Institutes* 3.1.1.

[18] *Sermons*, 426. See *Commentary*, 294–95.

[19] *Commentary*, 309.

God and renders us liable to his judgment. This makes renewal 'in Christ' an absolute necessity for us. As Calvin says in the very next sermon on Ephesians 4:23–26, again utilising the fountain motif,

> [W]hen our father Adam was once fallen, and had become alienated from the fountain of life, he was soon stripped stark naked of all good. For being separated from God, what could he be but utterly lost and hopeless? Can we find either life, or righteousness, or holiness, or soundness, or uprightness out of God?[20]

Note that we are implicated in Adam's fall and our nature is affected by it, just as Calvin establishes in *Institutes* 2.1 (followed by the Reformed tradition generally).[21] Hence Calvin sees the human plight from the angle of separation from God which makes us devoid of all good, both righteousness and holiness, and also from the angle of our union with Adam. He goes on to prescribe the remedy for such separation in terms of union with Christ, saying, 'just as Adam ruined us and plunged us with himself into the abyss of death, so we are new created by God in the person of our Lord Jesus Christ... we must rise again in him if we would live indeed... we must be new[ly] created in Jesus Christ.'[22] As Edmondson rightly summarises, for Calvin, 'Adam's fall and the resultant alienation of humanity from God form the primary context for speaking of Christ as Mediator,'[23] so also does

---

[20] *Sermons*, 436. See *Commentary*, 220, and Ephesians references in 3.24.10.

[21] On this see John Murray, *The Imputation of Adam's Sin*, reprinted in *Justified in Christ: God's Plan for Us in Justification* (ed. K. Scott Oliphint; Fearn, Ross-shire: Mentor, 2007), 203–94 (esp. 219–20 for criticism of Calvin and 223–41 on two ways of conceiving union with Adam).

[22] *Sermons*, 436–37. See Adam-Christ contrasts on 153, 194, 206, 334, 508, 601; *Commentary*, 198, 225, 229.

[23] S. Edmondson, *Calvin's Christology* (Cambridge: Cambridge University Press, 2004), 30.

it form the primary context for speaking of our need for union with him.[24]

The same basic idea of our desperate spiritual need for union with Christ is also communicated in other ways throughout the *Sermons*, without reference to Adam. So preaching on 'they were at that time without Christ' in Ephesians 2:11, Calvin declares, 'since we can have neither life, nor soul health, nor righteousness, nor anything else that is allowable, except in Jesus Christ, it is just the same as saying that we have nothing but utter wickedness and perdition in ourselves.'[25] Again, in his sermon on Ephesians 6:19–24, he asks, 'what is the reason that we are so corrupted in our nature that we are void of all goodness and filled with all kinds of vices, and in short, we are altogether detestable, except that we are utterly estranged from our Lord Jesus Christ who is the fountain of all goodness?'[26] Our evil works and nature in God's sight are due to our estrangement from Christ and necessitate a reunion as the only way to regain what was lost. Not only does separation from God equate to spiritual death,[27] but it also ruins any physical blessings we may possess: 'they would all be converted to evil, if we were not members of our Lord Jesus Christ.'[28]

Interestingly, Calvin also sees that God himself has a need, in some way, for union with us. Commenting on the church as Christ's 'fullness' in Ephesians 1:23, Calvin boldly asserts that it is 'the highest honour of the Church, that, until he is united to us, the Son of God reckons himself in some measure imperfect... not

---

[24] See also 1 Cor 15:22 in *Sermons*, 601.

[25] *Sermons*, 172. See *Commentary*, 219.

[26] *Sermons*, 702–3. Calvin does not hold to the common medieval notion that sin is a mere privation, that is, that sin has no ultimate metaphysical reality. If he did, as a Roman Catholic friend of mine pointed out, his sayings here that we are 'void of all goodness' would mean we are void of all being! He is not asserting that. On his dissatisfaction with the 'subtlety' of privation theory, see his *Concerning the Eternal Predestination of God* translated by J. K. S. Reid (London: James Clarke), 169 and Barbara Pitkin, 'Nothing but Concupiscence: Calvin's Understanding of Sin and the Via Augustini' in *Calvin Theological Journal* 34 (1999), 347-369.

[27] *Sermons*, 128.

[28] *Sermons*, 571.

until we are along with him, does he possess all his parts, or wish to be regarded as complete!'[29] Not that this strictly challenges his self-sufficiency or aseity as such, but rather it is 'as if a father should say, "My house seems empty to me, when I do not see my child in it." A husband will say, "I seem to be only half a man when my wife is not with me."'[30]

So in summary, Calvin teaches that as spiritual descendants of Adam we are estranged from God. To escape his curse and be renewed with all spiritual life and health we must be united to God by Christ. Until that union is achieved with all his people, Christ regards himself as being without his fullness; yet this must be a gracious, unmerited impetus on his part since in our natural state we show no inclination towards him.

2. The Benefits of Union

Lane G. Tipton argues biblically that 'Jesus Christ, as crucified and resurrected, contains within himself—distinctly, inseparably, simultaneously and eschatologically—every soteriological benefit given to the church' and that 'there are no benefits of the gospel apart from union with Christ.'[31] That is certainly the view that Calvin espouses in his work on Ephesians.

To begin with, Christ received all good things from his Father for us, 'with the condition that if we are truly members of his body, all things that he has belong to us.'[32] Not only so but 'the Father has not given him some particular portion only, but in such a way that all of us may so draw from his plenitude that we can

---

[29] *Commentary*, 218.

[30] *Sermons*, 123. Brief comments in *Commentary* become a fuller exposition in Sermons. On God's aseity and 'absolute independence' and 'glorious all-sufficiency', see Calvin's commentary on Psalm 50:9 (cf. Acts 17:25), and Garry J. Williams, *His Love Endures For Ever: Reflections on the Love of God* (Nottingham: IVP, 2015), 90-98. Calvin had lost both his wife and an infant son a few years previously.

[31] L. G. Tipton, 'Union with Christ and Justification,' in *Justified in Christ: God's Plan for Us in Justification* (ed. K. Scott Oliphint; Fearn, Ross-shire: Mentor, 2007), 32, 34.

[32] Calvin, *Sermons*, 116–17.

not lack anything, for he is the fountain that can never be drained dry.'[33] Later Reformed emphases chime in well with this: Geerhardus Vos insists, for instance, when discussing union with Christ and the *ordo salutis*, 'There is no gift that has not been earned by Him.'[34] Michael Horton, when outlining the covenant of redemption, similarly concludes, 'The mutual giving between the persons of the Trinity extends outward *ad extra* to their acts of giving to creatures: gift-giving between them is the ground for the gifts from them to us.'[35]

Yet according to Calvin what we are offered is not merely gifts but Christ himself. God 'has joined himself to us in the person of our Lord Jesus Christ, and in him we are made partakers both of him and all his benefits.'[36] Indeed, as he goes on to note later when speaking of 'growing up into Christ' (Ephesians 4:15–16), 'we cannot possess the good things of our Lord Jesus Christ to take any profit from them, unless we first enjoy him. And that is the very reason why he gives himself to us.'[37] Thus, at the end of one sermon Calvin arrestingly presents Christ as inviting his hearers, 'I am yours, possess ye me.'[38]

Moreover, this is not something to be, as it were, hoarded by the congregation alone; such union is part of the grace which Calvin regularly prays will be given 'not only to us but also to all peoples' as he concludes many of his sermons.[39] Christ offers us,

---

[33] *Sermons*, 704.

[34] G. Vos, 'The Doctrine of the Covenant in Reformed Theology,' in *Redemptive History and Biblical Interpretation: The Shorter Writings of Geerhardus Vos* (ed. R. B. Gaffin; Phillipsburg, NJ: Presbyterian & Reformed, 1980), 248.

[35] M. S. Horton, *Covenant and Salvation: Union with Christ* (Louisville: Westminster John Knox, 2007), 138.

[36] *Sermons*, 289.

[37] *Sermons*, 403, 401. See *Commentary*, 240, 262; *Institutes* 3.2.24. See also H. Bavinck, *Our Reasonable Faith* translated by H. Zylstra (Grand Rapids: Eerdmans, 1956), 399 who concludes that the benefits cannot be separated from Christ's person.

[38] *Sermons*, 404.

[39] *Sermons*, 21. See 475, 505, 591 for links to future consummated union. See also 49, 126, 184, 241.

in union with himself, all that we need for perfect happiness, all we can wish for, everything necessary for our joy and contentment.[40] He has all power and strength in him and can give it to us, as Calvin points out when Paul refers to that key Ephesian theme of power in 1:19 and 6:10.[41] Indeed, all Christ's possessions belong to us in faith-union, in such a way that 'once we are possessed of our Lord Jesus Christ, we may well give up all other things as superfluous and profitless.'[42]

2.1. Benefits Together

There has sometimes been controversy about the relation of union with Christ to justification in the *ordo salutis* (order of salvation). Some have conceived of justification as the basis for union; Richard Gaffin, Lane Tipton, and Peter Lillback have all convincingly shown that this is not in keeping with Calvin's particular way of relating the benefits of union. They also go further and claim that this has traditionally been a more Lutheran move.[43] As Garcia summarises it, 'the Lutheran and Reformed strands of the Reformation… adopted distinguishable understandings of the justification/sanctification relationship.'[44] John Fesko has cast significant doubt on these wider claims about the Reformed and Lutheran traditions as a whole,[45] though they do at least seem to accurately reflect the teaching of Calvin himself.

---

[40] *Sermons*, 73, 267, 269.

[41] *Sermons*, 108, 653.

[42] *Sermons*, 76, 249.

[43] Gaffin, 'Biblical Theology and the Westminster Standards,' 173; Tipton, 'Union with Christ and Justification,' 42–45; P. A. Lillback, 'Calvin's Development of the Doctrine of Forensic Justification: Calvin and the Early Lutherans on the Relationship of Justification and Renewal,' in *Justified in Christ: God's Plan for Us in Justification* (ed. K. Scott Oliphint; Fearn, Ross-shire: Mentor, 2007), 51–80.

[44] Garcia, *Life in Christ*, 252.

[45] See J.V. Fesko, *Beyond Calvin: Union with Christ and Justification in Early Modern Reformed Theology* (1517-1700) (Göttingen: Vandenhoeck and Ruprecht, 2012), 34-52. Space precludes an assessment of these important claims since my focus here is narrowly on Calvin and his teaching, not whether his view is normative for all Reformed theology or whether the latter speaks with one voice on the subject.

So it is surprising to find some, such as Michael Horton, arguing for what Garcia and others would call the more Lutheran conception as if it were Calvin's. Horton writes that justification 'is the forensic basis of union with Christ' and 'the forensic origin of our union with Christ, from which all of our covenantal blessings flow.'[46] Continuing the theme, he goes on to say that 'Christ alone is the basis for justification and union, but the act of justification is logically prior to union.'[47] He cites Berkhof in support of what he calls the 'classic Reformed interpretation' of the relationship between union and justification,[48] but also claims the patronage of Calvin himself:

> Regardless of whether union temporally preceded justification, Calvin is clear that the latter is the basis for the former: 'Most people regard partaking of Christ (*Christi esse participem*) and believing in Christ as the same thing. But our partaking of Christ (*participation quam habemus cum Christo*) is rather the effect of believing (*fidei effectus*)....Forensic justification through faith alone is the fountain of union with Christ in all of its renewing aspects.[49]

Since he is quoting from Calvin's commentary on Ephesians 3:17 here (and utilising the fountain metaphor too, no less) it is especially important for us to assess this claim. Horton appears to me to have inverted Calvin's teaching, missing the fact that for Calvin justification is a benefit of union with Christ and not the basis for it. As the quotation he uses from Calvin says, it is faith which effects our partaking of Christ, not justification (which is not mentioned in the quotation he gives, or its context, or the text

---

[46] Horton, *Covenant and Salvation*, 129, 138–39.

[47] *Covenant and Salvation*, 147.

[48] *Covenant and Salvation*, 147–48, citing L. Berkhof, *Systematic Theology* (rev. ed.; Grand Rapids: Eerdmans, 1996), 452.

[49] *Covenant and Salvation*, 143; quoting Calvin, *Commentary*, 262.

being commented on).[50] To say that one of the benefits of union with Christ is the basis for the union itself, or that it is logically prior to the union in and through which it is received does not seem to make good sense of Calvin. Perhaps the clearest expression of this is in *Institutes* 3.16.1, which Horton himself quotes:

> Although we may distinguish them [justification and sanctification], Christ contains both of them inseparably in himself. Do you wish, then, to attain righteousness in Christ? You must first possess Christ; but you cannot possess him without being made partaker in his sanctification, because he cannot be divided into pieces. Since, therefore, it is solely by expending himself that the Lord gives us these benefits to enjoy, he bestows both of them at the same time, the one never without the other. Thus it is clear how true it is that we are justified not without works yet not through works, since in our sharing in Christ, which justifies us, sanctification is just as much included as righteousness.[51]

Both this and the preceding paragraph in Calvin make it clear that justification and sanctification are both received at the same time. Moreover it is explicitly our 'sharing in Christ' which is said to justify us (*quoniam in Christi participatione, qua iustificamur*). For Horton's interpretation to be accurate that would have to be the other way around—'our justification, which unites us to Christ.' This, however, would not only prove a point about the relationship of union and justification but also (in the context of that sentence) confound justification and sanctification, which Calvin is always extremely careful to avoid. Of course justification

---

[50] Justification is mentioned once in the *Commentary* (230). The verb 'justify' does not occur in the theological sense, while 'justified' and 'justifies' occur once each (outside quotations of 1 Cor 6:11 and Rom 8:30). None of these have any relevance to the point at hand.

[51] *Institutes* 3.16.1. See *Covenant and Salvation*, 142.

is important — 'the main hinge on which religion turns'[52] — but that does not mean it is prior to or more basic than union theologically.[53] Luther himself declared that if the article of justification stands, the church stands but that if it falls, the church falls;[54] and yet for him 'the question on which everything hinges' was the bondage of the will, as we have seen in chapter 1 above.[55] We need not always read such language absolutely.[56]

For Calvin then, justification and sanctification are distinct yet inseparable, and simultaneously bestowed on us in union with Christ by faith.[57] In Christ, the sun, we have both light and heat, justification and sanctification, distinguishable but together.[58] Union with him can be said to justify us or, indeed, to be the fountain of our justification, but not vice versa. We can also see this illustrated in Calvin's work on Ephesians. The term 'righteousness' can often be used interchangeably with 'justification,' especially in forensic contexts.[59] So when Calvin says that 'out of Christ there is no righteousness' and that righteousness 'is offered to us in Christ by the gospel,' we see here that a right standing with God is one of those blessings offered to us in union with Christ.[60] If justification is taken to be synonymous with

---

[52] *Institutes* 3.11.1.

[53] See R. B. Gaffin, 'Justification and Union with Christ,' in *A Theological Guide to Calvin's Institutes: Essays and Analysis* (ed. D. W. Hall and P. A. Lillback; Phillipsburg, NJ: Presbyterian & Reformed, 2008), 257.

[54] *D. Martin Luthers Werke* (90 vols.; Kritische Gesamtausgabe; Weimar: H. Böhlau, 1883–), 40:3.352.3. Hereafter abbreviated to WA.

[55] E.G. Rupp and P.S. Watson, *Luther and Erasmus: Free Will and Salvation* (Philadelphia: Westminster, 1969), 333.

[56] Calvin even refers to *faith* as the chief of all spiritual benefits in *Sermons*, 28. I am grateful to Dr Horton, whom I greatly admire and respect, for friendly email and face-to-face discussions on all this.

[57] Garcia calls this a *unio Christi-duplex gratia* soteriology (*Life in Christ*, 3).

[58] *Institutes* 3.11.6.

[59] Calvin takes 'righteousness' in Ephesians 4:24 as ethical rather than forensic, and he rules out an imputed righteousness sense in 6:14.

[60] *Commentary*, 223, 228.

forgiveness of sins then perhaps Ephesians 1:7 itself could convince us that this is a blessing obtained *in* Christ and not something upon which that union is based.[61] Other synonyms and antonyms for justification are also used by Calvin in relation to union.[62]

This would seem to imply very strongly that for Calvin justification, the imputation of righteousness, does not take place *prior* to union, but is in fact one of the manifold blessings obtained in union itself.[63] As he says in his refutation of Osiander, 'Just as one cannot tear Jesus Christ into pieces, so also these two are inseparable since we receive them together and conjointly in him, namely, righteousness and sanctification.'[64] Indeed, as Gaffin has suggested by examining the structure of Book 3 of the *Institutes*, 'the relative '*ordo*' or priority of justification and sanctification is indifferent theologically' to Calvin.[65] Precisely because both are given simultaneously in union with Christ it does not matter if one treats sanctification before justification (as Calvin so startlingly does) or vice versa: neither has logical or temporal priority on his model. In Christ by faith we obtain both a new life

---

[61] See *Sermons*, 295, for the equation of justification and forgiveness. See also the citation of similar passages (Phil 3:8–9; 2 Cor 5:19–21; 1 Cor 1:30) by D. A. Carson, 'The Vindication of Imputation: Of Fields of Discourse and Semantic Fields,' in *Justification: What's at Stake in the Current Debates?* (ed. M. Husbands and D. J. Treier; Leicester: Apollos, 2004), 72.

[62] *Sermons*, 44, 172, 380.

[63] See *Sermons*, 220, for our righteousness as flowing only from 'the fountain of all good' in Christ, and 559 for several benefits obtained 'in our Lord Jesus Christ' including 'full righteousness.'

[64] *Institutes* 3.11.6, from Garcia, *Life in Christ*, 2n3 (a slightly different translation from Battles, 732).

[65] Gaffin, 'Biblical Theology and the Westminster Standards,' 177.

and a new legal status. Christ is the source of both; the legal change does not create the life, or vice versa.[66]

2.2. Benefits to Come

In another sense, the benefits received in union with Christ are not perfected at the point of faith. Ephesians itself bases imperatives upon the doctrine of union: in Ephesians 4:25 Paul exhorts his readers to speak the truth *for we are members one of another*. This presupposes the existence of a spiritual unity among believers in the church which binds them to one another even as it binds them to Christ (Ephesians 1:10; 4:1). In the same way, Calvin often bases exhortations upon the union of Christ with his people: 'Seeing that we are members of our Lord Jesus Christ, it is fitting that we should link together in true unity, or else we shall, as much as in us lies, tear his body in pieces.'[67]

Calvin also often links union with Christ to rule by Christ, to make it clear that cleaving to him requires submission to his governance: 'we must learn to allow ourselves to be ruled and to be held in check by the hand of the Lord Jesus Christ, that thereby we may show ourselves to be true members of his body.'[68] We also can be said to submit to him *in order that* we might partake of his benefits,[69] and be motivated to mortification by our union with him.[70] Conversely, we are warned that sin cuts us off

---

[66] The fascinating study of Fesko, *Beyond Calvin: Union with Christ and Justification in Early Modern Reformed Theology (1517-1700)*, 29-30 does speak of 'The priority of justification over sanctification' in Reformed theology, and finds causal language more prominent 'beyond Calvin' in the tradition, claiming from a wider study that 'the hallmark of an early modern Reformed doctrine of union with Christ is according theological priority to justification over sanctification, or the priority of the forensic over the renovative… a person can say, 'I am sanctified because I am justified.' But he cannot say, 'I am justified because I am sanctified.' Cf. pages 381-382.

[67] *Sermons*, 333. Note Calvin's standard image of tearing Christ in pieces. For other exhortations see *Sermons*, 293, 326, 443.

[68] *Sermons*, 119. See 595 for the related idea of following Jesus and 292, 357, and 705 for the indwelling Spirit who reigns over us (through the word); 327 links 'joined together' language with Christ reigning over us.

[69] E.g. *Sermons*, 572, 573 of wives.

[70] E.g. *Sermons*, 575, 673.

from Christ, our ungodliness threatening and hindering our union.[71]

In addition, although believers are already said to be joined to and incorporated in Christ by their present faith, there remains a future aspect to our union with Christ. We do not have the full enjoyment of all the riches in Christ which are communicated to us, yet one day we shall be filled to the full 'when he has joined us perfectly to him.'[72] This is something for which Calvin occasionally prays at the end of a sermon. So, for instance, at the end of the sermon on Ephesians 2:8–10, he prays that God would increase his grace in us 'until he takes us away out of this world and joins us with our Lord Jesus Christ, who is the fountain of all perfection, that we may also be perfect in him.'[73] That future consummated union with God is seen as a godly aspiration: 'having him as our Head, we all reach out to God, and aspire to him, desiring nothing but to be one with him.'[74] Yet the future is assured precisely because of our present union with Christ by the Spirit.[75]

The question naturally arises, 'Why does God not join us to himself in perfection immediately?' Calvin's reflection on this in the sermon on Ephesians 4:6–8 is that God designs by this delay to teach us humility and dependence on him, and yet also to show us that we ought to value other people within the body.[76] This latter emphasis is a reminder that God 'sends forth his spiritual benefits and good among us by such channels as he thinks good,'[77] for as he says elsewhere, 'faith cannot be without humility,

---

[71] *Sermons*, 360, 495.

[72] *Sermons*, 109–10. See 403.

[73] *Sermons*, 168–69. See prayers on 316, 475, 505.

[74] *Sermons*, 336. See *Institutes* 3.2.24.

[75] See *Sermons*, 154, 468.

[76] *Sermons*, 339–40.

[77] *Sermons*, 120. See 402 and *Commentary*, 288.

and God tests it in making mortal men to be the means by which he communicates himself to us.'[78]

3. Closing the Gap in Union

3.1. Roman Catholic Errors

We now turn to another controversial aspect of union with Christ, the way in which union closes the gap between God and us. This will bring us into areas of conflict with Lutheran and Roman Catholic theologies particularly. Calvin's doctrine was a matter of some controversy in his own time of course, and he always wrote and preached with that in mind. The most palpable polemical context for his sermons is, naturally, the ongoing battle with Roman Catholicism. He will often write or speak against 'papist' doctrines or practices,[79] but his big issue with Roman doctrine is the distance it puts between Christ and his people. He inveighs against 'the folly of popedom in conceiving patrons, advocates, and mediators towards God'; 'the papists have,' he says, 'imagined themselves to be separated from our Lord Jesus Christ, not knowing that he has become our brother in order that we might have intimate access to him.'[80] Calvin was not the first to make these connections between Christ as the font or fountain of life and his sole mediation; John Wyclif had done so too in the fourteenth century, for example, writing:

> [M]any think it would be helpful if Christ alone among men was worshipped, because He is the greatest mediator and intercessor... So he would be a fool who sought some other intercessor... it is not fitting for Him to mediate in company with other saints... It is madness, then, to leave this font of all

---

[78] *Sermons*, 215. See the idea that God sends blessings 'from the inexhaustible fountain of his liberality' to us through people 'as rivulets' ('Catechism of the Church of Geneva,' in *Calvin, Treatises on the Sacraments* [trans. H. Beveridge; Fearn: Christian Heritage, 2002], 70–71).

[79] E.g. *Sermons*, 204.

[80] *Sermons*, 113.

ability behind in favour of a sluggish and remote rivulet, especially when the faith does not teach that such a stream has its source in this font of life.[81]

Calvin preaches this aspect of union with Christ winsomely and persistently. So rather than viewing God as standing afar off and remaining aloof from us so that we must run to patron saints or to Mary, 'we must go straight to our Lord Jesus Christ,' or in effect we are saying 'Jesus Christ is nothing to us, neither do we have access or approach to him.'[82] Ironically, Calvin presents the doctrine of union with Christ as the only true way to be united with the saints of old, who together with us are conjoined to Christ by faith. Angels, patriarchs, prophets, and holy kings are our companions in union with Christ, as well as other living Christians.[83] This emphasis on union with Christ as our link to the saints of old can be seen in the Anglican Collect for All Saints Day too:

> Almighty God, which hast knit together thy elect in one communion and fellowship, in the mystical body of thy Son Christ our Lord: Grant us grace so to follow thy holy Saints in all virtues, and godly living, that we may come to those unspeakable joys, which thou hast prepared for all them that unfeignedly love thee; through Jesus Christ.[84]

---

[81] Wyclif, *Trialogus*, 189 (III.30).

[82] *Sermons*, 119, 123.

[83] See *Sermons*, 113, 117, 120, 223–24.

[84] *The Book of Common Prayer* (1549).

This is very different to Roman Catholic prayers, which plead for the intercession and help of the saints.[85] For Calvin and other Reformed theologians, to interpose the saints somehow in between Christ and his living people was, however, simply to deny that a true, vital union existed between them. We have direct access to the ever-flowing fountain of life.

3.2. Protestant Errors

One of the main areas of contention between the Reformers and Rome was always the sacraments. Yet interestingly, Calvin's main argument on this score in the Ephesians work is not against transubstantiation but against the sacramentology of other Protestants (such as Lutherans and those who held the Supper to be a mere commemoration) because of their concomitant errors regarding our supposed distance from Christ. The link between union and the sacraments is of course the operation of the Spirit as the bond of our union with Christ,[86] and to speak of the Spirit brings the Trinitarian nature of Calvin's doctrine into view. Union with Christ is union with the Father in Christ by the Spirit.[87] The distance between each member of the Trinity and the church has been closed: the Father dwells in us by the Spirit,[88] and Christ comes to us by his (the Spirit's) power.[89] All three members of the Trinity are at work in union since 'it is by the power of the Spirit, and not by the order of nature, nor in any common fashion, that we are of the bone and of the flesh of our Lord Jesus Christ. And

---

[85] Contrast Cranmer's Anglican Collect with Roman Catholic prayers, e.g. 'Angels, Archangels, Thrones, Dominions, Principalities, Powers, heavenly Virtues, Cherubim and Seraphim; all Saints of God, holy men and women, and especially my patrons: intercede for me that I may be worthy to offer this Sacrifice to almighty God, to the praise and glory of His name, for my own welfare and also that of all His holy Church. Amen' (From the *Roman Missal*) or 'Father, All-Powerful and ever-living God, today we rejoice in the holy men and women of every time and place. May their prayers bring us your forgiveness and love. We ask this in the name of Jesus Christ our Lord. Amen' (from the *Liturgy of the Hours*).

[86] See *Institutes* 3.1.1.

[87] See *Commentary*, 205, and union with the Father on 220, 235.

[88] *Sermons*, 333. See *Commentary*, 270.

[89] *Sermons*, 291, 355, 579–81, 603. See *Commentary*, 262, 291.

the reason why we are members of his body is that God his Father has ordained and established him as our Head.'[90] The role of both the Father and the Spirit is to ensure that any gap between us and Christ is closed.

The link between pneumatology and sacramentology in Calvin's thought appears numerous times, quite apart from explicit discussion of the sacraments themselves. So on several occasions he comments that the Spirit's dwelling in us enables us to live by Christ's substance, that his body and blood flow to us by the Spirit's power.[91] In John 6:56 Christ says, *Whoever feeds on my flesh and drinks my blood abides in me, and I in him* making this a key passage for the doctrine of union. It has often been seen as referring to the Lord's Supper directly,[92] and for Calvin there is certainly a link. Yet it is at the level of union with Christ that the connection is seen: 'in the sixth chapter of John, [Christ] discourses copiously and professedly on that mystery of sacred conjunction of which He afterwards held forth a mirror in the sacraments.'[93] That is, for Calvin John 6 is not about the sacraments *per se*,[94] but both John 6 and the sacraments are about union with Christ; and the way that he sees the eating and drinking to be taking place in both is through the Spirit. Through his instrumentality we live by Christ's substance, so that he is anything but distant and detached from us: 'the supper ought to serve as a ladder in the search for our Lord Jesus Christ. It is

---

[90] *Sermons*, 602.

[91] See the idea of living by Christ's 'substance' in *Sermons*, 356, 360, 404. See *Commentary*, 324.

[92] See the helpful discussions in L. L. Morris, *The Gospel according to John* (2nd ed.; NICNT; Grand Rapids: Eerdmans, 1995), 331–33, and D. A. Carson, *The Gospel according to John* (Pillar New Testament Commentary; Leicester: Inter-Varsity, 1991), 277–78.

[93] Quoted in R. S. Wallace, *Calvin's Doctrine of the Word and Sacrament* (Edinburgh: Scottish Academic, 1995), 198. See *Commentary*, 323 and *Sermons*, 578, 614.

[94] See on John 6:53 in *Commentaries on the Gospel according to John* in *Calvin's Commentaries*: Volume XVII (trans. W. Pringle; Grand Rapids: Baker, 1993), 265.

meant to confirm us in the assurance that he dwells in us and that we are made one with him.'[95]

This means that Calvin has no time for mere commemorationism. In 1539 he added a section to the *Institutes* concerning the sense in which Christ's body is life-giving, and it is full of references to Ephesians: 'the flesh of Christ is like a rich and inexhaustible fountain that pours into us the life springing forth from the Godhead into itself,' he says, quoting in support Ephesians 1:23; 4:15–16; 5:30, 32.[96] He makes reference to a 'commemoration only' view in his commentary also, labelling it 'egregiously mistaken.'[97] Many of the references on this point are to passages in Ephesians 5, which Calvin held to be important not just for understanding marriage but also for grasping the Lord's Supper.[98] It is interesting to note that when concerned theologically with our potential isolation from Christ, Calvin should find such riches in a passage about marriage which was itself instituted precisely because *it is not good that the man should be alone* (Genesis 2:18).

Not only is Calvin against mere memorialism but he also writes and speaks against a Lutheran sacramentology/Christology.[99] This again is raised in connection with the distance of Christ from his people. For example, he comments on Ephesians 4:10, 'When we hear of the ascension of Christ, it instantly strikes our minds that he is removed to a great distance from us; and so he actually is, with respect to his body and human presence. But Paul reminds

---

[95] *Sermons*, 581. See also 403. Baptism is not so prominent, though see *Sermons*, 193, 330.

[96] *Institutes* 4.17.9. He quotes the passages themselves. We cannot rely on citations of biblical texts found in modern translations of the Institutes since the majority do not appear in Calvin's originals. See Muller, *Unaccommodated Calvin*, 141.

[97] *Commentary*, 323.

[98] Calvin was not alone in ascribing great importance to Ephesians 5. See H. Zanchius, *Of the Spirituall Marriage betweene Christ and the Church, and every Faithfull Man* (Cambridge: John Legate, 1592). Interestingly Zanchius speaks similarly to Calvin, 'God has set and established all good things in Christ alone the Mediatour, so that unless they be communicated, and come from Christ as from the fountaine, none can be made partaker of them' (132–33).

[99] See Garcia, *Life in Christ*, 149–95.

us, that, while he is removed from us in bodily presence, he fills all things by the power of his Spirit.'[100] In the sermon on this same passage, he says, 'Jesus Christ is not so locked up in any one place but that we may feel him present, and that he dwells in us, and that he fills all things [but] not with his body as some have crudely imagined.'[101] He has some pastoral sensitivity to the reasons why some may feel the need of such a doctrine, namely the felt remoteness of Christ. This gulf is bridged by his doctrine of union, carefully stated to guard against the Lutheran doctrine of the ubiquity of Christ's body: 'He is gone up to fill all things,' he preaches, 'not with his body, but with his benefits and gifts. For however great the distance may be between our Lord Jesus Christ and us, as far as heaven and earth are concerned, yet nevertheless he does not cease to dwell in us, but will have us also to be one with him.'[102]

3.3. The Incarnation

There is another sense in which Christ has closed the gap between us and God, yet not in an inherently salvific way. Calvin also speaks, of course, about the incarnation itself as a union of Christ with us. So as he begins to speak about Ephesians 5:28 and how we are of the flesh and bones of our Lord, he says that Jesus 'has taken a nature that is common to us, by which he has made himself intimate with us.' In that sense he is bone of our bones.[103] It could sound as if Christ has saved us in the incarnation itself when Calvin preaches, 'we are all knit together in the person of our Lord Jesus Christ. That is because he took our nature upon him and by that means abolished and took away the malediction that was in Adam.'[104] So writes Trevor Hart:

---

[100] *Commentary*, 276.

[101] *Sermons*, 353 (emphasis mine), 355.

[102] *Sermons*, 346 (emphasis mine). See also 357 and *Institutes* 4.2.24.

[103] *Sermons*, 600–601.

[104] *Sermons*, 206. See also 391.

The Incarnation is the Atonement. God and man have been reconciled in their personal union in Christ. The relationship between them has been restored and renewed. 'Atonement' is not simply a consequence of something that Christ does, which pertains to us individually and independently of him. Nor is the Incarnation to be considered a mere prerequisite of some atoning act or other. The two things stand and fall together, for they are one and the same.[105]

Yet this union of two natures in Christ, when Calvin unpacks it further elsewhere, is definitely not inherently salvific; God and man have not been reconciled by incarnation but by the atonement as a distinct (yet inseparable) act of God. Calvin makes this patently clear in his exposition of Ephesians. In the commentary, for example, he unpacks Ephesians 5:30–31 by saying, *We are bone of his bone, and flesh of his flesh*, (Gen. ii.23) not because, like ourselves, he has a human nature, but because, by the power of his Spirit, he makes us a part of his body, so that from him we derive our life.'[106] In his preaching on Ephesians 5:28–30 he unravels these things further. He says of Christ: 'he could not be the mediator between God and us, unless he had been of our nature.' Why not?

For he could not have atoned for the offences through which we were bound to endless damnation, unless he had clothed himself with our body... so it was necessary for our Lord Jesus Christ to be our flesh in our body... However, there is another matter to note... it is not intended that we should be so bold as to think to approach Jesus Christ, *as though we were linked to him of ourselves and of our own nature,*

---

[105] T. Hart, 'Humankind in Christ and Christ in Humankind: Salvation as Participation in Our Substitute in the Theology of John Calvin,' SJT 42 (1989): 83–84. See also J. B. Torrance, 'The Incarnation and 'Limited Atonement,' *Scottish Bulletin of Evangelical Theology* 2 (1984): 32–40.

[106] *Commentary*, 323–324 (emphasis mine).

but that is done in the power of his Holy Spirit, *and not in the substance of his body*.[107]

The point here is that Christ's mere possession of a human nature like ours (Christmas) does not enable us to approach him or link us to him savingly. Yet it was a necessary prerequisite to our salvation (Easter), something he had to do in order to make atonement for us. The saving union by which we obtain all his benefits is not a merely natural thing, but a sovereign act of God's Holy Spirit. As Calvin goes on to say, 'it is by the power of the Spirit, and not by the order of nature, nor in any common fashion, that we are of the bone and of the flesh of our Lord Jesus Christ... [it] is done specially when he so works by the power of his Holy Spirit that he is our Head, and we are gathered together in him and have a heavenly status.'[108]

So, to put it pithily, Christ takes our flesh and bones so that we might become bone of his bones and flesh of his flesh. Christ unites himself with humanity physically, in order to redeem his elect completely. Or in other words, faith union for Calvin is like marriage, and 'Between a man and his wife there is a far closer relation; for they not only are united by a resemblance of nature, but by the bond of marriage have become one man.'[109] One can, after all, marry only someone who shares one's nature, and not a dog or a cat (in England, for now, at least). Yet one does not, obviously, marry everyone who shares one's nature! So a shared human nature does not in and of itself constitute a marriage, just as (*contra* Hart) the incarnation is not the atonement or the resurrection or the ascension. Yet it is a necessary step towards those events in the *historia salutis* which make possible our incorporation in Christ in the *ordo salutis*. So to conclude, the pastoral application of the incarnation and union doctrine Calvin outlines is related again to the idea of closing the gap between God and man.

---

[107] *Sermons*, 601 (emphasis mine).

[108] *Sermons*, 602.

[109] *Commentary*, 322.

4. Conclusion: Bringing Christ Close to People

We have seen then that Calvin's work on Ephesians contains much of great interest and usefulness regarding the doctrine of the believer's (and the church's) union with Christ. What is latent in the commentary is often made patent in the sermons, which in turn had an effect on Calvin's more systematic presentation in the *Institutes*. Union with Christ is presented as an essential part of our salvation, made necessary by our natural and damning union with fallen Adam. It encourages us to flee to Christ, the fountain of all perfection and goodness, to drink deeply from his blessings and benefit from all his riches which are ours distinctly, inseparably, and simultaneously in him. In its pastoral application we see that, for Calvin the scholar-pastor, to speak of our marriage to Christ by faith was a powerful and effective means of bringing Christ close to his people that they might be guarded from false teaching and encouraged to cleave to him who was the source of their life—their wisdom, righteousness, sanctification, and redemption (1 Corinthians 1:30).

For those seeking a way to present the good news to a new generation, for whom the jargon of the institutional church is a foreign tongue, this emphasis in Calvin is something worth recovering and exploring in our own ministry. We have often said that Christianity is about relationship and not religion, and everybody understands relationships. While not everything can be squeezed into this mould, Calvin's use of the doctrine of union with Christ shows it can be an immensely rich and useful way of expressing the truths of the gospel and working through theological problems. Neglecting it can lead to some serious errors both doctrinally and practically. Yet getting it right helps tremendously in making the connections between what Christ has done in history and what he can do for us (at both individual and corporate levels), connections we often find difficult to make in a way that is both biblically accurate and comprehensible to our peers. For Calvin, who wished the grace of the gospel to be granted 'not only to us but also to all peoples,' it would be a fine legacy if his teaching on union were to aid us in playing our part in that great commission.

Justified Hesitation?
J.D.G. Dunn and The Protestant
Doctrine of Justification

This chapter is a modified and updated version of an article first published in Churchman 115/1 (2001). I wish to thank Professor Dunn for interacting with my original dissertation on this subject, despite the fact that we had to agree to disagree on my conclusions, as well as David G. Peterson and Mike Ovey for their wisdom on constructing my argument.

For the last few decades, the so-called 'New Perspective' has revolutionized Pauline studies. The impact has been most noticeable in studies of 'the Law' and of 'justification.' The first thing to note, however, about the 'new perspective on Paul' is that the name is a misnomer. There is no single 'New Perspective on Paul' but many new perspectives. What they share is a common starting point in the work of E.P. Sanders on Palestinian Judaism.[1] This itself is not 'new' as such, but a re-working of a hypothesis about the nature of Judaism by G.F. Moore.[2] It was J.D.G. Dunn who coined the term 'The New Perspective on Paul' in his Manson Memorial Lecture of 1982,[3] and it has since entered into popular use to refer to the work of scholars such as Sanders, Dunn, and N.T. Wright.

---

[1] See his *Paul and Palestinian Judaism* (London: SCM, 1977).

[2] Especially his 'Christian Writers on Judaism' HTR 14 (1921).

[3] Reprinted as chapter 7 of J.D.G. Dunn, *Jesus, Paul, and the Law: Studies in Mark and Galatians* (Louisville: Westminster, 1990).

On justification, criticism has been levelled by these scholars particularly against Martin Luther. Advocates of the 'New Perspective' such as Sanders, Dunn, and Wright claim that Luther significantly misunderstood Paul's teaching on this point.[4] All subsequent Protestant teaching on justification is assumed to be 'guilty by association' or 'guilty by descent' of this same fault: as Dunn says, 'Luther's line of thinking began to go astray — and *so also the Protestant doctrine of justification* which stemmed from Luther.'[5] Dunn goes on to claim that his New Perspective undercuts 'the traditional debates of post-Reformation theology... and leaves much of the dispute pointless.'[6]

In the light of such sweeping statements Christian preachers and teachers may find themselves hesitating. 'Can I still preach the old doctrine,' they ask themselves, 'when the weight of such scholarship seems to be against it?' To accuse Luther and the other Reformers of misreading Paul on justification is a serious and weighty allegation. Have we been misled all these years? Have Luther and the Reformers led us astray into thinking that justification means something it never did to Paul? The problem is more acute when it is realized just how important the old doctrine was seen to be by our Protestant forebears. A few citations will quickly show its perceived confessional importance:

Luther declared that if the article of justification stands, the church stands but that if it falls, the church falls.[7] Calvin called this doctrine 'the main hinge on which religion turns,'[8] while one of his successors at Geneva, Francis Turretin (1623-1687), declared that it is 'of the greatest importance... the principal

---

[4] See, for example, E.P. Sanders, *Paul and Palestinian Judaism*, 492 footnote 57; Dunn, *Jesus, Paul, and The Law*, pages 185-187; N.T. Wright, *The Climax of the Covenant* (Minneapolis: Fortress, 1993) 258-9.

[5] Dunn in J.D.G. Dunn and A.M. Suggate, *The Justice of God* (Carlisle: Paternoster, 1993), 13 (emphasis added). Cf. the similar comment on page 14.

[6] J.D.G. Dunn, *The Theology of Paul the Apostle* (Cambridge: Eerdmans, 1998), 344.

[7] WA 40 III. 352.3 *'quia isto articulo stante stat Ecclesia, ruente ruit Ecclesia.'*

[8] J. Calvin, *Institutes of the Christian Religion* (Philadelphia: Westminster Press, 1960), III.xi.1, page 726.

rampart of the Christian religion... This being adulterated or subverted, it is impossible to retain purity of doctrine in other places.'[9] More recently, Reformed theologian Robert Reymond has written of justification that it is 'the heart and core of the gospel' and that consequently, 'great care must be taken in teaching this doctrine lest one wind up declaring 'another gospel' which actually is not a gospel at all.'[10] Similar assertions are made by many other Protestant theologians including Thomas Cranmer, John Frith, John Foxe, John Owen, George Whitefield, John Wesley, and Jonathan Edwards.[11] What is more, 'New Perspective' scholars are also aware of how important justification is; Dunn himself speaks of 'its central significance for formulating the gospel [and] testing theology.'[12]

If justification is really this important, then we need to be sure we have got it right. Yet with widespread doubts about the traditional formulations and debates circulating in commentaries, books, and articles it would not be surprising if we were to hesitate before preaching justification. The question is, are we justified in hesitating? Having become convinced of the traditional understanding of the doctrine of justification by grace alone through faith alone, must we relinquish it under the barrage of attacks from 'the New Perspective'? It is not my aim to examine all the exegetical minutiae of 'the New Perspective' case here. Nor is it my aim to show that the traditional Protestant understanding of justification is correct. This chapter is not intended as an exercise in confrontational polemics. More modestly, I aim to show that at least one New Perspective scholar, J.D.G. Dunn, has not proven his case against the traditional doctrine. If this can be

[9] F. Turretin, *Institutes of Elenctic Theology* (3 vols.), (Phillipsburg NJ: Presbyterian & Reformed, 1992), 2:633 .

[10] R.L. Reymond, *A New Systematic Theology of the Christian Faith* (Nashville: Thomas Nelson, 1998), 740.

[11] For citations see P.H. Eveson, *The Great Exchange* (Bromley: Day One, 1996), 174-77. Cf. also G.J. Spykman, *Reformational Theology: A New Paradigm for Doing Dogmatics* (Grand Rapids: Eerdmans, 1992), 490-491.

[12] *The Theology of Paul the Apostle*, 340.

done then we should have fewer mental reservations about preaching and teaching the traditional Protestant doctrine.[13]

Has Dunn Read Luther (Properly)?

Dunn's major statements on justification are found primarily in his magnum opus *The Theology of Paul The Apostle*, but also in an important article and book.[14] In his mind (as revealed by his writing) there is a clear link between Luther and 'all subsequent Protestants.'[15] He declares that, 'However we understand Paul's conversion... it was not a conversion like Luther's. Consequently, it follows that an interpretation of Paul's teaching on justification by faith should not be predicated on the assumption that it was.'[16] The implication is that 'all subsequent Protestants' have made just this mistake, and based their teaching on the faulty assumptions of Luther and the other magisterial Reformers. The negative side of their emphasis on justification, Dunn claims, is:

> [A]n unfortunate strain of anti-Judaism... As Luther had rejected a medieval church which offered salvation by merit and good works, the same, it was assumed, was true of Paul in relation to the Judaism of his day. Judaism was taken to have been the antithesis of emerging Christianity: for Paul to react as he did, it must have been a degenerate religion, legalistic, making salvation dependent on human effort, and self-satisfied with the results.[17]

---

[13] Others have interacted with N. T. Wright in great detail on this subject. One recent and readable assessment of his work in this area can be found in Thomas Schreiner, *Faith Alone: The Doctrine of Justification* (Grand Rapids: Zondervan, 2015), especially pages 239-261.

[14] Dunn, *The Theology of Paul the Apostle*; 'The Justice of God: A Renewed Perspective on Justification by Faith' in JTS 43.1 (1992); *The Justice of God* (with A.M. Suggate).

[15] *The Theology of Paul the Apostle*, 335; cf. 'The Justice of God', 13-14.

[16] 'The Justice of God' JTS 43.1 (1992), 4.

[17] Dunn, *The Theology of Paul the Apostle*, 336-337.

There are several problems with this statement; the biggest problem is that it is not backed up with any evidence from the primary sources on Luther. In the footnote for the paragraph above, there is no reference to any of Luther's writings, only to citations found in the work of M. Saperstein. This might be forgivable if it could be demonstrated from elsewhere that Dunn was familiar with Luther at first-hand. All of Dunn's information about the Reformer appears, however, to be from second-hand sources. A search of his other writings reveals that every time Dunn quotes Luther he has gleaned the quotation (or opinion) indirectly from another writer, rather than from Luther's works themselves.[18]

There are only two possible exceptions to this. The first two famous lines of Luther's *The Freedom of a Christian* are quoted directly in Dunn's book *Christian Liberty*: 'A Christian is a perfectly free lord of all, subject to none. A Christian is a perfectly dutiful servant of all, subject to all.'[19] Another is an allusion (not a quotation) in Dunn's commentary on Romans,[20] but this is also

---

[18] See for example:

1. The citation of *On the Jews and Their Lies* in 'The Justice of God: A Renewed Perspective On Justification By Faith' JTS 43.1 (1992), 5 (attributed to M. Saperstein);
2. The quotation from *The Preface to James* in *Unity and Diversity in the New Testament*, 425 footnote 7 (attributed to Kümmel);
3. The comments from *The Preface to the Revelation of St. John* in 'The Authority of Scripture According to Scripture Part II', 222f footnote 70 (attributed to Kümmel).

Apart from the books and articles mentioned already, I searched for references to / by / about Luther in the following works by Dunn: *Jesus, Paul, And The Law: Studies in Mark and Galatians* (Louisville: Westminster, 1990); *Christology in the Making* (London: SCM, 1989); *Unity and Diversity in the New Testament* (London: SCM, 1977, 1990); 'The Authority of Scripture According to Scripture' Parts 1 & 2 *Churchman* 96.2 & 96.3 (1982); *Romans 1-8* (Dallas: Word, 1988); *Romans 9-16* (Dallas: Word, 1988); *The Epistle to the Galatians* (Peabody: Hendrickson, 1993); *1 Corinthians* (Sheffield: SAP, 1995); *The Epistles to the Colossians and to Philemon* (Paternoster: Carlisle, 1996).

[19] *Christian Liberty: A New Testament Perspective* (Grand Rapids: Eerdmans, 1993), 3-4. The quotation is, he tells us, 'Accessible e.g. in J. Dillenberger, *Martin Luther: Selections from his Writings*' (Footnote 3) although this is not one of the standard scholarly sources.

[20] Dunn, *Romans 1-8* (Dallas: Word, 1988), 247.

indirectly attributed to Harrisville. Since there are twenty-five references to Harrisville and only one to Luther in the whole two-volume commentary, it is at least possible that the Luther quotation was gleaned from Harrisville. Even so, it is safe to say that Dunn does not demonstrate a great familiarity with Luther's own works. His knowledge of other Reformers also appears to be meagre and second-hand.[21]

This lack of footnotes referring to primary sources on the people and positions he attacks is all the more surprising since Dunn is normally an assiduous writer of footnotes: in thirty-five pages of his articles for *Churchman* in 1982, for example, there are 118 footnotes referring to 160 other sources.[22] The fact that he does not interact sufficiently with Luther and his other Reformation opponents leaves him open to the charge of building 'straw men' — something which he has been accused of before when addressing doctrinal issues.[23] This lacuna in his workings makes it very difficult indeed to check his reading of Luther, Calvin, and what he calls 'all subsequent Protestants.' In other words, it is impossible to verify, from his published work at least, whether Dunn has actually grappled with the traditional Protestant teaching on justification.

This is disappointing given the two pages of Bibliography and 224 footnotes in his chapter on justification in *The Theology of Paul the Apostle*. He has certainly not indulged in a careful reading or point-by-point refutation of Luther, or indeed of any classic Protestant writer on justification. Indeed, after the original version of this chapter was published, Professor Dunn did admit after

---

[21] Knowledge of Luther's contemporary Melanchthon for example: cf. the five words quoted from *Apology of the Augsburg Confession* in *Theology of Paul the Apostle*, 336 (attributed to Reumann). Five words from Calvin's *Institutes* 1.7.4 are quoted (out of context) in footnote 99 on page 431 of *Theology of Paul the Apostle* while the same words are alluded to (and the citation given as *Institutes* 1.7.4-5) in Dunn's *Romans 1-8*, 454.

[22] 'The Authority of Scripture According to Scripture' Parts 1 & 2, *Churchman* 96.2 & 96.3 (1982).

[23] The *Churchman* articles (above) seek to refute Warfield, yet Dunn only cites his (minor) work seven times! Cf. R. Nicole, 'The Inspiration and Authority of Scripture' *Churchman* 97.3 (1983), 199.

citing my comments that 'there is some justification for these critical comments since my early formulations were not sufficiently refined... I freely admit that I am no expert on Luther'. However, he then seems to reinterpret or neglect to remember some of his more startling comments on this subject, in what appears to me to be a rather disingenuous defence.[24]

Contrary to Dunn's assertion, he has not proven that Luther or other Protestant theologians thought of first-century Judaism as a 'degenerate religion.'[25] Nor has he shown that they generally thought of Luther's experience as precisely parallel to Paul's; rather, he seems to simply assume it.[26] If Dunn can prove the veracity of these assertions then he has failed to do so by providing references to the relevant works. 'Luther's line of thinking began to go astray — and *so also the Protestant doctrine of justification* which stemmed from Luther,'[27] he tells us. But 'Luther and those who joined him,'[28] remain innocent until proven guilty, and the case against them has not been made.

Romans 7 and the 'Introspective Conscience'

Some of the references Dunn makes are either incorrect or misleading. In a discussion of Romans 7, for example, he writes:

> Paul's conversion was understood as the climax to a long, inward, spiritual struggle, during which Paul

---

[24] See J.D.G. Dunn, *The New Perspective on Paul* (Wissenschaftliche Untersuchungen zum Neuen Testament 185; Tübingen: Mohr Siebeck, 2005), 16-22. I note with amusement that on page 17 note 76 I am accused of being more moderate than Carl Trueman.

[25] In Luther's works (LW 47:283) there is one reference to 'degenerate Jews', but it is a reference to the Jews of Luther's day who refused to hear the story of Jesus, explicitly contrasted to those of the first century. That is not to say Luther was incapable of the most inexcusably anti-Semitic comments.

[26] He states this most forcefully in 'The Justice of God' in JTS 43.1 (1992), 3-4.

[27] Dunn in J.D.G. Dunn and A.M. Suggate, *The Justice of God* (Carlisle: Paternoster, 1993), 13 (emphasis added). Cf. the similar comment on page 14.

[28] 'The Justice of God', 3.

had wrestled with the pangs of a troubled conscience — just like Luther... The cries of self-perplexed anguish in Rom. 7:14-25, 'I do not do what I want, but I do the very thing I hate' (7:15), 'Who will deliver me from this body of death?' (7:24), could be drawn in as the self-confession of the pre-Christian Paul. Like Luther and Augustine before him, it could be assumed that Paul had found justification by faith to be the answer to his own spiritual torment, the peace with God which flows from the recognition that God's acceptance is not dependent on human effort.[29]

Here Dunn builds on the work of K. Stendahl to undermine the presentation of justification as the answer to a plagued conscience.[30] Paul, he says, never had this crisis of conscience before he was a Christian, and so it would be wrong to read Paul as if Romans 7 were about pre-Christian angst to which justification was the answer. The problem is, although Luther compares his former zeal as a monk with Paul's zeal as a Pharisee,[31] not once in his own account of his 'tower experience' does he compare Paul's conversion to his own.[32] His understanding of justification by faith has nothing whatsoever to do with reading his own experience into Paul. Dunn may think that it is 'no wonder that Luther and those who joined him should assume that Luther's discovery had first been Paul's',[33] but I have yet to find any evidence that he or they ever did make this assumption.

---

[29] 'The Justice of God', 3.

[30] K. Stendahl, 'The Apostle Paul and the Introspective Conscience of the West' HTR 56 (1963).

[31] Cf. Luther, 'Lectures on Galatians 1-4' (1535) in LW 26:68.

[32] Cf. Luther, 'Preface to the Complete Edition of Luther's Latin Writings' (1545) in LW 34:336-338. Whether his famous 'reformatory discovery' can really be called his 'conversion' is a debatable point, but it is to this experience that Dunn refers in 'The Justice of God.'

[33] Dunn, 'The Justice of God', 3.

Luther and Augustine (as cited by Dunn) do not in fact agree on the interpretation of Romans 7. Augustine does apply Romans 7 to himself immediately before what he saw as his conversion in *Confessions* 8:5. As he narrates his own conversion he seems to suggest that before he was a Christian he was troubled like the 'wretched man' of Romans 7:

> I had now no longer my accustomed excuse that, as yet, I hesitated to forsake the world and serve thee because my perception of the truth was uncertain. For now it was certain. But, still bound to the earth, I refused to be thy soldier; and was as much afraid of being freed from all entanglements as we ought to fear to be entangled. Thus with the baggage of the world I was sweetly burdened, as one in slumber, and my musings on thee were like the efforts of those who desire to awake, but who are still overpowered with drowsiness and fall back into deep slumber... On all sides, thou didst show me that thy words are true, and I, convicted by the truth, had nothing at all to reply but the drawling and drowsy words: 'Presently; see, presently. Leave me alone a little while.' But 'presently, presently,' had no present; and my 'leave me alone a little while' went on for a long while. In vain did I 'delight in thy law in the inner man' while 'another law in my members warred against the law of my mind and brought me into captivity to the law of sin which is in my members.' For the law of sin is the tyranny of habit, by which the mind is drawn and held, even against its will. Yet it deserves to be so held because it so willingly falls into the habit. 'O wretched man that I am! Who shall deliver me from the body of this death' but thy grace alone, through Jesus Christ our Lord?'[34]

---

[34] *Confessions* 8:5.

This is the text that Dunn footnotes as a classic example of the kind of retrospective reading he is against.[35] Augustine states quite clearly elsewhere, 'The man described here is under the Law, prior to grace; sin overcomes him when by his own strength he attempts to live righteously without the aid of God's liberating grace.'[36] Paul could not, therefore, be speaking of himself as an Apostle and a Christian: Romans 7 seems here in Augustine to be understood as pre-Christian experience. Far from agreeing with this position, however, Luther takes issue with Augustine on precisely this point, saying, 'There are some, and among them St. Augustine, who denied that the Apostle here [in Romans 7] speaks of his own person... But the whole passage shows very clearly a strong hatred against the flesh and a sincere love for the Law and all that is good. No carnal man ever does this.'[37]

So, according to Luther, Romans 7 is *not* about the carnal man, the preconversion existence of a Christian. Indeed, Augustine himself changed his mind, and in his major work against the Pelagians he says:

> And it once appeared to me also that the apostle was in this argument of his describing a man under the law. But afterwards I was constrained to give up the idea by those words where he says, 'Now, then, it is no more I that do it.'... And because I do not see how a man under the law should say, 'I delight in the law of God after the inward man;' since this very delight in good, by which, moreover, he does not consent to evil, not from fear of penalty, but from love of righteousness (for this is meant by 'delighting'), can only be attributed to grace... The apostle is rightly understood to have signified not,

---

[35] Dunn, 'The Justice of God', 3 footnote 4.

[36] Following a quotation of Romans 7:15-16 in *Propositions from the Epistle to the Romans 44.2; Augustine on Romans*, translated by P. F. Landes (Chico, CA: Scholars Press, 1982) 17.

[37] Luther, *Commentary on the Epistle to the Romans* (Grand Rapids: Zondervan, 1960), 96 (on Romans 7:9ff).

indeed, himself alone in his own person, but others also established under grace.[38]

Luther is aware that Augustine changed his mind, and quotes him extensively on the subject. On Romans 7:7f in his lectures on Romans, he writes:

> From this passage on to the end of the chapter the apostle is speaking in his own person and as a spiritual man and by no means merely in the person of a carnal man. St. Augustine first asserted this extensively and repeatedly in his book against the Pelagians. Hence in his *Retractations*, I, 23, taking back a former explanation of this passage he says, '… I was absolutely unwilling to understand this passage as referring to the person of the apostle who was already spiritual, but I wanted to refer it to him as a man placed under the Law and not yet under grace. This is the way I first understood these words, but later, after I had read certain interpretations of the divine words by men whose authority impressed me, I considered the matter more carefully and saw that the passage could also be understood of the apostle himself.'[39]

So Luther followed the later Augustine, and did not read his own conversion experience into Romans 7. A footnote in one of Dunn's books from 1975 might indicate that he was once aware of Luther's interpretation of Romans 7,[40] yet he does not make this clear in his later work on the 'New Perspective,' which appears to indict Luther alongside 'those who joined him' for reading Paul retrospectively.[41]

---

[38] Augustine, *Against Two Letters of the Pelagians* I.x.22 and 24; *Nicene and Post-Nicene Fathers* (Grand Rapids: Eerdmans, 1971), Volume 5, 384. See the whole discussion of Romans 7 from I.viii.13ff as well as his statements in *Retractations* I.xxiii.1 and II.i.1 and *Contra Julianum* Book II (3.7 and 4.8).

[39] LW 25:327, 335.

[40] See *Jesus and the Spirit* (London: SCM, 1975), 444 footnote 57.

[41] See again that statement in 'The Justice of God' 3: 'no wonder that Luther and those who joined him should assume that Luther's discovery had first been Paul's.'

Did those who joined Luther make this mistake? As Packer rightly states, 'In the sixteenth century, confronted by theologies that referred this whole passage to preconversion experience... Luther, Calvin, and all the magisterial Reformers except Bucer and Musculus invoked the passage as exegeted by [the later] Augustine to show that there is sin in the best Christians' best works.'[42] The traditional Reformed position reads Romans 7 in the same way as Luther and Calvin. For instance, Melanchthon, Beza, B.B. Warfield, Charles Hodge, Louis Berkof and John Murray, as well as puritans such as Owen, Charnock, and Goodwin all read it this way as, it seems, do the *Heidelberg Catechism*, the *Belgic Confession*, and the *Westminster Confession of Faith*. [43]

There may be some in this tradition who read it differently and fall into the trap which Dunn warns us against. Theirs, however, is a self-confessed minority view, and Dunn does not name a single proponent of it in support of his contention. He claims that 'it was not until the end of the third decade of this century [the twentieth century] that Werner Kümmel effectively undermined the more traditional interpretation of Rom. 7 and prevented it from being used as a piece of pre-Christian autobiography.'[44] Yet the idea that Romans 7 is 'a piece of pre-Christian autobiography' was actually undermined so effectively by Luther, Calvin, and others that it *cannot* be called the 'traditional interpretation' at all. Dunn's allegation that Luther's preconversion experience has been habitually read back into Paul is thus seen to be without support.

This is important because Dunn is claiming that Luther and other Protestants have incorrectly stated the doctrine of justification precisely because of this misunderstanding of Paul.

---

[42] 'The Wretched Man Revisited: Another Look at Romans 7:14-25' in S. K. Soderlund & N. T. Wright, *Romans and the People of God* (Cambridge: Eerdmans, 1999), 71.

[43] See Packer, ibid., plus his earlier 'The 'Wretched Man' in Romans 7' in *Keep in Step with the Spirit* (Leicester: IVP, 1984), 263-270 and A. B. R. Clark, *Delight for a Wretched Man: Romans 7 and the Doctrine of Sanctification* (Darlington: Evangelical Press, 1993), 16-18. Hodge's position is clear from his commentary, *Romans* (Crossway Books: Wheaton, 1993), 218-225 where he describes it as the 'ordinary interpretation.'

[44] Dunn, 'The Justice of God' pages 3-4.

Yet the Reformed tradition does not, as Dunn claims, read Luther and Augustine's experience of justification back into the New Testament. Assumptions about Luther's 'introspective conscience' affecting his reading of Paul are without foundation, because Luther does not make all the links Dunn claims he does.[45] He does not 'assume that [his] discovery [of justification] had first been Paul's.'[46]

If the traditional doctrine of justification is to be indicted alongside Luther's, as Dunn suggests it can be, then at least the case against Luther has to prove solid. It does not, however, stand up to close scrutiny. Dunn not only misrepresents the traditional Reformation position, but he fails to demonstrate an acquaintance with the primary sources. Dunn's case for abandoning the traditional doctrine of justification rests heavily upon this point, but it is evident that from the start that his attack has not been made with sufficient strength or integrity to cause us to hesitate in preaching it.

The Background to Paul's Doctrine

A further aspect of Dunn's case against the traditional doctrine of justification revolves around his understanding of the relationship between covenantal nomism and medieval soteriology.

> Most insidious of all, was the way this reading of Paul's teaching on justification by faith in the light of Luther's experience reinforced the impression that Judaism, and not least the Judaism of Paul's time, was *a degenerate religion.* Luther had striven to please God by his acts of penitence and good works. The Church of his day taught that salvation could be gained by merit, the merit of the saints, that the time spent in purgatory could be diminished by the purchase of indulgences. That was what the discovery

---

[45] See G. Bray, 'Justification: The Reformers and Recent New Testament Scholarship' *Churchman* 99 (1995), 103-106 for further rebuttal of points against Luther.

[46] Dunn, 'The Justice of God', 3.

of justification by faith had freed him from. It was all too easy to read Paul's experience through the same grid. What Luther had been delivered from was also what Paul had been delivered from. As the medieval church taught salvation by merit and good works, so must the Judaism of Paul's day.[47]

Following Sanders, Dunn is convinced that first-century Judaism was in fact not a religion of works, but one of grace. Sanders came up with the label 'covenantal nomism' to describe first-century Jewish religion: that is, one got into the covenant by grace, not by works, and that works only played a role after this initial salvation by grace. Dunn argues that Luther and others misunderstood what Paul was trying to say about justification because they thought that Paul was arguing against a legalistic system like medieval Catholicism.

At this point, Dunn distorts medieval soteriology. Although merit and good works were thought by medieval theologians to play a part in salvation, and even of justification, their soteriology was far more nuanced than 'salvation by works' or 'salvation by merit.' In theory at least, all the medieval schools of thought on justification would have defended the concept of grace,[48] in much the same way as Dunn (following Sanders) defends the concept of grace in Judaism.[49] The diluted value of the words 'mercy' or 'grace' (so often *not* defined as unconditional) in both medieval Catholicism and Judaism must be recognized.[50] As Seifrid avers, 'In contradiction to Sanders' assumptions [which Dunn follows] ... an

---

[47] 'The Justice of God', 6-7.

[48] See A.E. McGrath, *Iustitia Dei: A History of the Christian Doctrine of Justification* (Cambridge: CUP, 1998), 190 on the anti-Pelagian structure of the doctrine throughout its history, especially the medieval period.

[49] Dunn, *Theology of Paul the Apostle*, 338.

[50] See the critique of Sanders in R. Smith, 'A Critique of the New Perspective on Paul' RTR 58.2 (1999), 101.

emphasis on 'mercy' did not necessarily exclude the idea that obedience was a prerequisite to salvation in early Judaism.'[51]

A very real synergism was present in both systems, according to works an indispensable role in salvation, even if technically speaking it was still said to be by 'grace.' Judaism may not have been legalistic, but neither did the Reformers assume that the religion of their day was purely legalistic. Calvin was conscious that in the Catholicism of his day, 'a great part of mankind imagine that righteousness is composed of faith *and* works.'[52] Opponents of the traditional Protestant doctrine did not dispute the fact that salvation began with grace. It was the place given to works *alongside* grace that was in contention: 'This is the pivotal point of our disputation,' says Calvin, 'For on the beginning of justification there is no quarrel between us and the sounder Schoolmen.'[53] The doctrine of Luther and others was polemically directed not against legalism per se, as Dunn suggests, but against theologies which, while they spoke of grace in theory, were in practice as 'covenantally nomistic' (semi-Pelagian?) as 'New Perspective Judaism.' Peter O'Brien's conclusion that, 'many advocates of the newer reading of Paul have failed to wrestle with the character of the Reformation debate' is spot on.[54]

Dunn's argument against the traditional doctrine of justification is specifically based on what he sees as Luther's illegitimate equation of Jewish and Roman Catholic soteriology. Having apparently proved that Judaism was not offering salvation by merit, Dunn's conclusion is that Luther was faulty in his understanding and application of Paul's theology of justification. He does not substantiate the existence of such a direct link in Luther's thought; the evidence he provides in the footnote, while

---

[51] M.A. Seifrid, *Justification By Faith: The Origin and Development of a Central Pauline Theme* (Leiden: E.J. Brill, 1992), 133.

[52] *Institutes*, 3.11.13 (emphasis added).

[53] *Institutes*, 3.14.11.

[54] P.T. O'Brien, 'Contemporary Challenges to the Doctrine of Justification By Faith' in R.J. Gibson (ed.), *Justification and Christian Assurance (Explorations 10)*; Adelaide: Openbook Publishers, 1996), 19.

containing some quotations from Luther, does not make the point unless his own interpretive comments in the note are read in quotation marks and attributed directly to Luther.[55] If it were possible to provide such evidence he could conceivably argue that subsequent formulations of the doctrine of justification have suffered because of this weak link. Yet once it is seen that covenantal nomism and medieval *semi*-Pelagianism have much in common, including a common denial of 'salvation by good works,' and that the Reformation doctrine was not aimed at straightforward 'salvation by works' anyway, the basis of Dunn's criticism disappears. There is, therefore, no cause for hesitation here when it comes to preaching the traditional doctrine.

Dunn's 'New Perspective' begins by attacking Luther and the other Reformers. We have seen that, first, his attack is not backed up with citations from the primary sources, and that he in fact seems to misunderstand Luther and others on the points in question. Second, we see that he misunderstands and misrepresents the Reformation debate. That debate wasn't against a simple 'justification by works' theology as he claims, and the New Testament wasn't interpreted as if it addressed mere legalism either.

These things alone should cause us to doubt whether Professor Dunn has a good case against the traditional Protestant understanding of justification. On the basis of the evidence so far, we would be justified in hesitating to go further with Dunn's re-reading. But there are some other causes for doubt about the veracity of his arguments too.

The Terminology of Justification

It is surprising that Dunn relies on a dubious linguistic argument to make his terminological assertions. He claims that, "'righteousness' is a good example of a term whose meaning is

---

[55] See *Theology of Paul the Apostle*, 337 footnote 7. It is not just a printing error since the same interpretive comments appear with no quotation marks in 'The Justice of God' (page 7 footnote 19).

determined more by its Hebrew background than by its Greek form. The point is that the underlying Hebrew thought in both cases [with 'righteousness' and 'to justify'] is different from the Greek."[56] To back up his conclusions on the alleged 'Hebraic' character and relational meaning of *dikaiosune* he cites 1 Samuel 24:17 as his sole biblical example: *Saul said to David, 'You are more righteous than I; for you have repaid me good, whereas I have repaid you evil.'*[57] This, however, is clearly one of the uses of *dikaios/tsadiq* which has by no means been ignored by Protestant theologians but which is normally classified as comparative, a very rare use of a term which is normally forensic/legal in its meaning.[58]

Dunn here follows the work of a scholar from the nineteenth and early twentieth century named Hermann Cremer in 'realigning the debate on 'righteousness' to its Hebrew background with the resulting emphasis on relationship.'[59] What Dunn doesn't say is that Cremer's approach came under severe attack at the turn of the century, but most decisively in 1961 from James Barr. Barr's seminal work, *The Semantics of Biblical Language*, ruthlessly undermined any attempt to appeal to an absolute dichotomy between 'Hebrew thought' and 'Greek thought,' a dichotomy that Cremer and Dunn posit.[60] That this distinction cannot be easily and simply made is a recognized axiom of lexical semantics,[61] and is

---

[56] *The Theology of Paul the Apostle*, 341.

[57] *Theology of Paul the Apostle*, 341. The reference is 1 Samuel 24:18 in the LXX and Hebrew.

[58] See Turretin, *Institutes*, 2:634 for example, who lists Ezekiel 16:51-52 and Jeremiah 3:11 as other examples of the comparative use.

[59] *Theology of Paul the Apostle*, 341-2 footnote 27; See the even more direct reliance on Cremer in 'The Justice of God' in JTS 43.1 (1992), 16. Cremer's work is *Die Paulinische Rechtfertigungslehre im Zusammenhange ihrer geschichtlichen Voraussetzungen* (Gütersloh: Bertelsmann, 1900).

[60] J. Barr, *The Semantics of Biblical Language* (Oxford: OUP, 1961). See especially chapters two, three and eight, where the concept itself and Cremer specifically, are refuted.

[61] See M. Silva, *Biblical Words and Their Meaning: An Introduction to Lexical Semantics* (Grand Rapids: Zondervan, 1994). Cremer is especially criticised in the section running from pages 18-28.

discouraged in basic exegetical handbooks. As Don Carson says, 'If one mentions titles like *Hebrew Thought Compared with Greek* in a room full of linguistically competent people, there will instantly be many pained expressions and groans... one should be suspicious of all statements about the nature of the 'Hebrew mind' or 'the Greek mind' if those statements are based on observations about the semantic limitations of words of a language in question.'[62]

Yet Dunn freely, and without qualms or reservations, contrasts the 'Greek worldview' with 'Hebrew thought'[63]—'Hebrew thought' and 'the Graeco-Roman concept.'[64] Although this may not always be the precise fallacy so comprehensively attacked by Barr, it is certainly too simplistic a presentation of the linguistic arguments. It also compares very unfavourably with the detailed work on the meaning of justification which can be found in the writings of people like Calvin and Turretin, or in the more recent publications of John Murray,[65] or Mark Seifrid.[66] At the very least, Dunn's linguistic understanding of the key terms in the debate on justification must be questioned because it is not very thorough.

On the basis of this linguistic argument, Dunn quickly dismisses Protestant-Roman Catholic disputes over the meaning of *dikaioo* as 'either-or exegesis.' He claims that:

> The recognition of the essentially relational character
> of Paul's understanding of justification also speaks
> with some immediacy to the traditional debates of

[62] D.A. Carson, *Exegetical Fallacies* (Second edition; Grand Rapids: Baker, 1996), 44.

[63] *Theology of Paul the Apostle*, 341.

[64] 'The Justice of God' 16.

[65] The Appendix on the meaning of the terms in Murray's recently reprinted commentary on Romans is called 'the finest available in English' by Robert Reymond (Reymond, *New Systematic Theology*, 743 footnote 49).

[66] See his *Christ, Our Righteousness* (Leicester: Apollos, 2000) and 'Righteousness language in the Hebrew Scriptures and early Judaism: Linguistic considerations critical to the interpretation of Paul' in D. A. Carson (ed.), *Justification and Variegated Nomism 1: The Complexities of Second Temple Judaism* (Tübingen & Grand Rapids: Mohr Siebeck, 2001).

post-Reformation theology. In fact, it largely undercuts them and leaves much of the dispute pointless. The debate on whether 'the righteousness of God' was subjective or objective genitive, 'an activity of God' or 'a gift bestowed by God,' can too easily become another piece of either-or exegesis. For the dynamic of relationship simply refuses to conform to such analysis... The other dispute, as already noted, was whether the verb *dikaioo* means '*make* righteous' or '*reckon as* righteous.' [o]nce again the answer is not one or the other but both.[67]

Protestant theologians generally conclude that the verb 'to justify' means 'to reckon as righteous' whereas the Catholic position is that it means 'to make righteous.' According to Dunn, it means both, and the debate itself is pointless. Space forbids an examination of exactly why this distinction has been made historically. It is certainly illegitimate, however, to write off centuries of 'either-or exegesis' with the simple answer that both sides were right. It is not as if no-one has ever tried to find a mediating position between Protestant and Catholic doctrine until now! Dunn claims that he does not want to set aside the Reformation doctrine, that 'there is no call to set aside the often penetrating insights of Reformation and Protestant restatements of the doctrine' and he only wishes to 'restate a more rounded and richer and more biblical doctrine of justification.'[68] What his redefinitions mean though is that the Reformers actually got it wrong, for their positive assertions always go hand in hand with negative denials. They do not say that *dikaioo* means 'reckon as righteous.' What they say is that it means 'reckon as righteous' and definitely not 'make righteous'—the negative always accompanying the positive.

---

[67] *The Theology of Paul the Apostle*, 344.

[68] 'The Justice of God', 21; cf. *The Theology of Paul the Apostle*, 367.

87

Works of the Law

There is also cause for doubt over Dunn's understanding of the phrase 'works of the law.' Paul's insistence that 'works of the law' cannot justify (Romans 3:20) sounds strange in the light of Sanders' reconstruction of Judaism. If the law was not, and never had been, a way of 'getting in' as far as Judaism was concerned, what was Paul opposing? Dunn suggests that 'works of the law' ought to be understood as the Law of Moses as it operated *socially*. In other words, they are those works which particularly separate Jews from Gentiles in society: circumcision, the food laws, and the Sabbath.[69] 'Works of the Law' were not works done to earn God's favour, but distinctive works done by those already inside the covenant community: they were not for 'getting in' but 'staying in'—or as Dunn puts it, "'Works of the Law' is the Pauline term for 'covenantal nomism.'"[70]

This is a reasonable and thoroughgoing attempt to reconcile Sanders' New Perspective with what Paul actually says. Dunn denies that the phrase refers *only* to circumcision, the food laws, and the Sabbath. What he says is that 'in a context where the relationship of Israel with other nations is at issue, certain laws would naturally come more into focus than others.'[71] Yet, if 'works of the law' really does refer to works which separate Jew from Gentile then why does he only highlight ceremonial aspects of the Law? Why not the moral and ethical precepts of the Law, such as those which forbade homosexuality for example? Jews and Gentiles were certainly distinct as regards their accepted sexual ethics.

In any case, Dunn's suggestion about the meaning of 'works of the law' is by no means a new suggestion, as he appears to think. The traditional doctrine of justification often interacts with a view (sometimes identified as Roman Catholic) that sees 'works of the

---

[69] *The Theology of Paul the Apostle*, 354-359 especially page 356.

[70] ibid., 355.

[71] *The Theology of Paul the Apostle*, 358.

law' as referring only to works of the ceremonial law, or to distinctly 'Jewish' works.[72] This view can be traced back to Pelagius, who argued that ceremonial works are excluded by Paul, but not moral works, thus relying on that old distinction between civil, ceremonial, and moral law.[73] The purpose of this in Pelagius is to reintroduce some element of works into justification: to allow moral works to count before God while explaining Paul's allergy to 'works of the law.' Calvin calls this view 'an ingenious subterfuge' which, regardless of its long pedigree is 'utterly silly.' He spends some time discussing it but concludes: 'Even schoolboys would hoot at such impudence. Therefore, let us hold as certain that when the ability to justify is denied to the law, these words refer to the whole law.' Calvin tries to explain why Paul speaks occasionally of 'works of the law' instead of 'works' generally: even legalists, he says, would only give such weight to works which had the 'testimony and vouchsafing of God' behind them (i.e. those written in God's own law).[74] Calvin is also not unaware of the fact that these ritual-ceremonial laws functioned as 'badges' to exclude the Gentiles.[75]

Turretin also interacts with this view of 'works of the law' which Dunn suggests. He points out that if the socially-excluding ceremonial law alone was to be excluded, then justification would have been ascribed to the moral law, which it never is. Using the New Testament he shows that ceremonial works brought with them the obligation to fulfil the *whole* Law of Moses—and so Paul had opposed them because of this larger implication. Other

---

[72] See the discussion in Calvin, *Institutes*, 3.11.19-20; Turretin, *Institutes*, 2:641; C. Hodge, *Systematic Theology* Volume 3 (London: Thomas Nelson: 1873), 134-135. See also the comments of Musculus, Gwalther, and Wigand on Galatians 2:15-21 in G. Bray (ed.), *Galatians-Ephesians* (Reformation Commentary on Scripture; Downers Grove, Illinois: IVP Academic, 2011), 72-73.

[73] John Owen, *Works*, 5:285-286 outlines a threefold division of the law based on different Hebrew terms for law, but the distinctions are also traceable through Aquinas (e.g. *Summa Theologiae*, 2/1, Q.99) at least as far back as Pelagius (see footnote 36 on page 749 of the Westminster Press edition of Calvin's *Institutes*). Cf. D.A. Carson, *The Sermon on the Mount* (Grand Rapids: Baker, 1992), 35.

[74] Quotations from Calvin, op.cit., 749-750 (*Institutes*, 3.11.19-20).

[75] See *Institutes* II.vii.17 for example.

people interact with this sort of view as well, including James Buchanan[76] and John Owen, who claims to show 'the vanity of that pretence.'[77] The Reformed consensus on the subject is that 'works of the law' includes all works generally.[78] This is not a mere *assumption* but a well thought-through conclusion reached in dialogue with an opposing opinion which saw 'works of the law' as specifically ceremonial or distinctively 'Jewish.' Professor Dunn appears to be sadly unaware of just how much thinking has been done on this precise issue over the past few centuries.

As G.K. Chesterton says somewhere: 'You can find all the new ideas in the old books; only there you will find them balanced, kept in their place, and sometimes contradicted and overcome by other and better ideas. The great writers did not neglect a fad because they had not thought of it, but because they had thought of it and all of the answers to it as well.'[79] Dunn may be right to draw our attention to the historical background of Paul's writings on justification, but his new perspective on 'works of the law' is not actually very new at all, and the issues he raises have not been ignored over the centuries. The reasons for considering them may have changed, but many of the answers were thought of long ago. Dunn cannot therefore use what he sees as a new insight to undermine the old doctrine. As John Barclay points out in his own impressive survey of the historical discussion, 'Without a long perspective, one can hardly comprehend, let alone contribute to, contemporary debates on such historically charged topics.'[80]

---

[76] J. Buchanan, *The Doctrine of Justification* (Edinburgh: Banner of Truth, 1997), 66ff, 349ff.

[77] Cf. John Owen, *The Doctrine of Justification By Faith*, 278-282 in *The Works of John Owen* edited by W.H. Goold (Edinburgh: Banner of Truth, 1998) volume 5. The quote is from page 282.

[78] Cf. Hodge, op.cit., 137; Reymond, op.cit., 749.

[79] See 'On Reading' in G.K. Chesterton, *The Common Man* (New York: Sheed and Ward, 1950), 23.

[80] John M.G. Barclay, *Paul and the Gift* (Grand Rapids: Eerdmans, 2015), 186. Note also his exposure of the inadequacy of Dunn's grasp of Reformation reception of Paul, on page 159. 'Good Protestant doctrine' was never as simplistic as some of its opponents have made out.

All of which is quite apart from the fact that in his sizeable new commentary on Romans, Richard Longenecker dismisses Dunn's treatment of 'works of the law' as misconstruing Paul, not understanding what he said about the Jews and his attitude to mainline Judaism, and as riding 'roughshod' over Paul's whole argument in Romans 2:17-3:20.[81]

Conclusion: Preaching Without Hesitation

To conclude then, are we justified in hesitating to preach the traditional Protestant doctrine of justification by grace alone through faith alone because of the work of Christ alone? Is this doctrine, as is traditionally held, the answer to the question, 'How can a sinner be saved?' or must we redefine the question and the answer as Dunn suggests? I think that on the evidence provided here, we have no need to hesitate. We must still be convinced somehow that the traditional doctrine is biblically faithful and theologically consistent. If that is so, however, there is no need to pause too long on account of Dunn's New Perspective.

Professor Dunn's contributions to New Testament scholarship have been weighty, learned, and highly stimulating. His great skill as a communicator comes across in everything he writes. Yet, as I have tried to show, while his knowledge is deep it may not always be broad enough to be reliable in areas outside of modern (twentieth-century) Pauline scholarship. His contributions to the complex and fast-moving debates on the 'New Perspective' are essential reading, particularly for those with an interest in the doctrine of justification (such as all Christian ministers). The historical and doctrinal conclusions which he comes to, however, should be handled with great care. His indictment of Luther and 'all subsequent Protestants' for misunderstanding Paul's theology of justification has been demonstrated to rely on second-hand evidence and (in places) fallacious logic and exegetical technique. Some of his ideas are not as new as the name 'New Perspective'

---

[81] See Richard N. Longenecker, *Romans* (NIGTC; Grand Rapids: Eerdmans, 2016), 362-370.

would suggest. So, therefore, there is no need to hesitate on Dunn's account in preaching the gospel of justification by faith alone, as we have received it.

The Ordinary Instrument of Salvation: Edmund Grindal on Preaching

This is a modified version of the 2013 St Antholin Lecture, first published by Latimer Trust. I wish to thank Clifford Swartz, former chaplain of St. Bees School, founded by Grindal, for the chance to consider some of the modern applications of the great Archbishop's example at that school's Speech Day.

Those who have heard the story of Archbishop Thomas Cranmer and how he was martyred cannot fail to be moved by his courage as he faced the wrath of Henry VIII's daughter, Queen Mary. The fires of persecution which she lit under the faithful took the lives of many leading Protestants, who sealed with their blood and ashes the glorious Reformation doctrines of grace. Some people speak of a new persecution of Christians in the West today, and whether this is a sober assessment of the direction our society is moving in or whether it is over-dramatising things, we must be grateful that it is highly unlikely we will ever be forced to go to a literal stake for the true profession of the gospel in our age. Though Cranmer initially caved in to the pressure of interrogation and recanted his beliefs, as he approached the fiery gateway to eternity his dying words reaffirmed all that he had written and taught in defence of the Reformed faith.[1]

Yet opposition to the good news of Jesus Christ comes in many forms. Sticks and stones—as well as the gallows and the executioner's axe—may break our bones, but words are an equally effective weapon in the war against truth. Derision, scorn, caricature, and marginalisation have often been deployed in an effort to silence those who preach the word. Resisting the tempting lure of self-censorship, which such tactics implicitly hope to enforce, can be difficult and often costly. Some would find going out in a blaze of glory far easier to cope with temperamentally. It may be less heroic than a martyrdom, but it is no less noble to stick one's neck out, to speak against those in power, to voice the unpopular opinion, to draw a line and make a stand. To those who are called to the less tangible pain of this sort of resistance, God gives not the spirit of timidity and cowardice, but of power and love and self-control (2 Timothy 1:7). Such was the path set before Archbishop Edmund Grindal, one of Cranmer's successors at Canterbury, who chose to go head-to-head with Henry VIII's other daughter, Queen Elizabeth I.

Grindal's Career

Grindal's story is less well known than it ought to be amongst evangelicals. He was born in 1516 or 1520 (our sources are conflicting) on the coast of west Cumberland in the north of England. He escaped his impoverished northern environment by, as Patrick Collinson puts it, 'climbing an educational ladder into an ecclesiastical career in the more prosperous south.'[2] He studied at Cambridge and rose to become President of Pembroke College there in 1549, the year Cranmer released the first edition of *The Book of Common Prayer*. The master of St Catherine's College at

---

[1] I have explored Cranmer's inspiring example a little further in Lee Gatiss (ed.), *Confident and Equipped: Facing Today's Challenges in the Church of England* (London: Lost Coin, 2014), 23-24.

[2] Patrick Collinson, 'Grindal, Edmund (1516x20–1583)', in *Oxford Dictionary of National Biography* (Oxford: Oxford University Press, 2004).

the time was his close friend, from the very same small village, Edwin Sandys, who rose to be Vice Chancellor of the University and later Archbishop of York. Having been influenced theologically by the Swiss Reformer, Heinrich Bullinger, Grindal was also strongly influenced at Cambridge by the German Reformer Martin Bucer, who was appointed Regius Professor of Divinity there. Indeed, Grindal spent much of his enforced exile during the days of 'Bloody Mary' in Bucer's city of Strasbourg, and was greatly indebted to Bucer's vision of pastoral care and discipline.[3] He was also a close friend of Peter Martyr Vermigli, the Italian Reformer who fled to Strasbourg too, having been Regius Professor at Oxford until Mary came to the throne.[4]

Nicholas Ridley noted Grindal's theological, polemical, and administrative gifts and he was soon brought to the attention of the movers and shakers in Edwardian England, including William Cecil, who was to be Secretary of State under both Edward VI and Elizabeth. He became a chaplain to the young King, Precentor of St Paul's Cathedral, and a Prebendary of Westminster Abbey. All these preferments were lost when he fled the Roman Catholic backlash in 1554, of course, but he was now

---

[3] Patrick Collinson, *Archbishop Grindal 1519-1583: The Struggle for a Reformed Church* (London: Jonathan Cape, 1979), 56 notes Grindal's underlining of certain passages in his copy of Bucer's *De Regno Christi*. Bucer's influence over Grindal has been disputed, however, by Basil Hall, 'Martin Bucer in England' in David F. Wright (ed.), *Martin Bucer: Reforming Church and Community* (Cambridge: Cambridge University Press, 1994), 157 who provocatively asks whether the only close connection between the writings of the two men is actually their dislike of excessive bell-ringing. This is too hasty a judgment, based on a lack of mere verbal parallels. I will note some of the significant parallels in what follows, but I think it is safe to say that Grindal and Bucer were on the same page theologically, sharing many concepts and programmatic concerns. This can be seen even in those parts of *De Regno Christi* which Grindal did not annotate, e.g. Book 2 chapters 4-5, 7, and 13 on salvation via preaching, and the restoration of impropriations to ecclesiastical use as key to revival (English translation in Wilhelm Pauck, *Melanchthon and Bucer* (Louisville: Westminster John Knox Press, 1969), 269-306).

[4] On these continental influences on English Protestants, see Patrick Collinson, 'England and International Calvinism 1558-1640' in Menna Prestwich (ed.), *International Calvinism 1541-1715* (Oxford: Clarendon Press, 1985), 197-223 and Anthony Milton, 'Puritanism and the Continental Reformed Churches' in John Coffey and Paul Lim (eds.), *The Cambridge Companion to Puritanism* (Cambridge: Cambridge University Press, 2008), 109-126.

a public figure. During his exile, he worked closely with John Foxe on his *Acts and Monuments*, or as we know it, Foxe's *Book of Martyrs*, which inspiringly narrates the details of what was going on back in England.[5] Indeed, Grindal played a key role in acquiring the last writings and trial records of both Ridley and Cranmer for inclusion in that volume, so it is perhaps partly due to him that we know about their famous martyrdoms. He also tried to persuade the more Presbyterian-minded parties in the British diaspora not to abandon English ways but to retain the effect and substance of the 1552 *Book of Common Prayer*.[6]

Grindal arrived back in England the day that Elizabeth I was crowned, and within a few months he was installed as Bishop of London. He is on record as saying that he consented to being made a bishop in order to prevent 'semi-papists' and other time-servers from filling such posts.[7] Others saw in him the maturity and character to handle the temptations of preferment without losing the passion to reform or the backbone to resist intimidation. In the ensuing negotiations he attempted to make fewer concessions to traditional 'Catholic' religious practices than were eventually enshrined in the Elizabethan Settlement. He fought hard behind the scenes for the re-establishment and further perfection of the Protestant Reformed constitution, particularly arguing against images, crosses, and altars which some, including the Queen herself, were keen to reinstate. He had an excellent relationship to the foreign churches in London, as their superintendent, and a firm alliance with John Calvin who was of course influential over the French church there. Grindal's was the English face of Calvinism. He oversaw the ordination of hundreds of new clergy in the capital, representing a massive influx of Reformed Protestant exiles into the restored Church of England.[8]

---

[5] Collinson, *Archbishop Grindal*, 80.

[6] Collinson, *Archbishop Grindal*, 73-78.

[7] DNB, s.v.

[8] The quality of many people ordained at this time was, however, dubious according to Collinson, *Archbishop Grindal*, 112.

When the Queen initiated a clampdown on clergy who didn't wear the surplice, Grindal was put into a very difficult situation.[9] He was not exactly enthusiastic about such clerical vestments himself,[10] but it was his job to enforce conformity on those — now labelled puritans — who broke the rules and were stubbornly recalcitrant.[11] It has been suggested that it was precisely because he was somewhat soft on Puritanism that he was soon 'kicked upstairs' to become Archbishop of York.[12] Yet that appointment was consistent with a clear government policy to begin Protestantizing the north more effectively. Archbishop Grindal began to make inroads against the superstitious remnants of medieval folk religion and Roman Catholicism in the dark corners of the land. His injunctions reveal an increasing focus on the preaching of the word of God as the principal means by which these hindrances to spiritual flourishing would be removed and replaced.[13] In an area without many preachers,[14] he also managed to import about forty learned preachers into the diocese

---

[9] On the controversy over vestments, and the Admonition of 1572, see the St Antholin Lecture by Andrew Cinnamond, *What Matters in Reforming the Church? Puritan Grievances under Elizabeth I* (Latimer Trust, 2011).

[10] Grindal was reported, in an *ex parte* account of his examination of some presbyterian puritans, as saying, 'You see me wear a cope or a surplice in Paul's. I had rather minister without these things, but for order's sake and obedience to the prince.' See William Nicholson (ed.), *The Remains of Edmund Grindal* (Cambridge: Cambridge University Press, 1843), 211.

[11] On the changing meaning of the word 'puritan' see Lee Gatiss, '1662 and All That' in *Truth at All Costs: Papers Read at the Westminster Conference 2012* (Stoke-on-Trent: Tentmaker, 2013), 13-14.

[12] DNB, s.v.

[13] See Nicholson (ed.), *Remains*, 127, 137, 146-147, 152, 160-161, 165. Vicars under 40 were to memorise a chapter of Paul's epistles every day, or be removed, ibid., 149! See also Irvonwy Morgan, *The Godly Preachers of the Elizabethan Church* (London: Epworth Press, 1965), 66.

[14] In 1535, the Archbishop of York had estimated that there were less than a dozen preachers in the whole diocese and many benefices were so poor that no learned man would take them. See Henry Ellis (ed.), *Original Letters Illustrative of English History*, 3rd Series, ii (London, 1846), 338. Nicholson (ed.), *Remains*, 325-326 and Hastings Robinson, *The Zurich Letters*: Volume 1 (Cambridge: Cambridge University Press, 1842), 259-260.

of York during his six year tenure there, targeting market towns such as Hull as well as remote Pennine parishes.

When Matthew Parker died in 1575, Grindal was appointed to succeed him as Archbishop of Canterbury. It was hoped that he would solidify the anti-Roman Catholic front, reform church discipline, and improve the standard of ministry across the country. His appointment was welcomed by moderate puritans though Grindal himself was conflicted about whether to accept or not, possibly because he knew some of the difficulties of trying to walk a fine line at court, pursuing a reformist agenda while staying on the right side of the Queen. He made his way to Lambeth Palace, and began his work.

Grindal's Clash with the Queen

It was not long before the storm broke. In June 1576 news reached court that there was disorder in parts of the midlands involving 'exercises of prophesying.'[15] These were, in essence, local gatherings of ministers very much like those we might now call fraternals or 'preaching groups', to hear sermons from fellow clergy, critique one another, pray and encourage each other in the work. This was a form of in-house training, also used in places such as Zurich, designed to refine the preaching ministry and improve standards, though lay people would often be in attendance too, to hear and learn. They were usually led by a senior minister, and approved by the local bishops. They were not, however, approved of by the Queen. On 12th June, she ordered her new Archbishop to suppress these exercises. Grindal had introduced the exercises into the dioceses of London and York

---

[15] On the prophesyings, see Patrick Collinson, *The Elizabethan Puritan Movement* (Oxford: Clarendon Press, 1967), 168-176. Cf. Morgan, *Godly Preachers*, 68-74. It should be pointed out that some at the time disliked the use of the word 'prophecy' or 'prophesying' here, and the link to 1 Corinthians 14, thinking that this referred to a gift of the apostolic age, now ceased. Such people preferred to call the meetings 'exercises' or 'conferences.'

himself, from which key centres they spread more widely, so this was a cause very close to his heart.[16]

Grindal went back to his office to commission a survey and do some research. He wrote to all his bishops asking for reports on what prophesyings were happening in their dioceses, and their opinion of such meetings. The vast majority of replies were warmly favourable towards them.[17] He then also began, with the help of his chaplains, to compose a learned treatise in defence of the practice,[18] as well as some sensible rules for their better regulation.[19] Six months later, he returned to court fully briefed and ready to argue his case, but the Queen was intransigent and incensed. She ordered him not only to stop the prophesyings from happening, but to slim down the number of preachers generally. Clergy could read the set, pre-approved Anglican homilies each Sunday. But three or four preachers per county writing their own sermons and expounding the scriptures each week was quite enough, she declared. She wanted tight control over the supply and content of sermons, and claimed that since all this was *adiaphora*, a secondary matter, she could command suppression.[20]

---

[16] Patrick Collinson, 'The Prophesyings and the Downfall and Sequestration of Archbishop Edmund Grindal (1576-1583)', in M. Barber, S. Taylor & G. Sewell (eds.) *From the Reformation to the Permissive Society: A Miscellany in Celebration of the 400th Anniversary of Lambeth Palace Library* (Woodbridge, Suffolk: Boydell and Brewer, 2010), 39-41 reprints a document by Grindal or someone very close to him claiming he had first introduced the practice in England, though they were 'performed in the primitive church' and 'instituted in most of the best reformed and pure churches of our time.' It would be difficult for him to be 'the agent of their abolition.'

[17] On the bishops' letters, see Collinson, 'The Prophesyings,' 13-18.

[18] Lambeth Palace Library, MS 2014, folios 72-80 and MS 2007, folios 126-144. A synopsis of the four chapters may be found in LPL MS 2014, folio 72v. and further related notes in MS 2872 and MS 3470, folios 32.39v.

[19] Nicholson (ed.), *Remains*, 373-374.

[20] Grindal wrote a defence against this claim, containing arguments which according to Collinson, 'The Prophesyings', 25 'place him full-square on the 'puritan' side of this argument.' Cf. pages 26-29 which transcribes part of the manuscript. One of the things which this document says is not an 'article of fayth' but would not be a mere matter of indifference on which to yield to authority, would be 'the commaudment that a woman of synguler lerninge should preache' (page 27).

The Archbishop left this frustrating audience with the Queen and in response wrote to her the letter for which he is now most famous. In essence, it is an essay of about 5500 words explaining why she was wrong and should keep her nose out of the spiritual government of the church. There may have been many ways to quietly evade and thwart her wishes, but Grindal did not feel he could adopt that approach with this issue. He defended the true office of preaching, and the practice of 'prophesyings', before asking her to respect the proper and ancient separation of powers between the church and the godly monarch. And he offered to resign. It is a fabulous letter, and my purpose now is to take a closer look at what Grindal said, with an eye on how it might instruct and encourage us today.[21]

Defence of Preaching

Grindal began his letter to the Queen by confessing how upset he had been by her somewhat personal attack on him regarding this subject. He was 'exceedingly dismayed and discomforted' by her speeches 'concerning abridging the number of preachers, and the utter suppression of all learned exercises and conferences among the ministers of the church.' These speeches, he said, 'sounded very hardly against mine own person,' but he was more concerned that they would harm God's church and indeed not be very good for the Queen herself if he actually obeyed her strictly. He did not want to offend her, but he felt it was his duty as Archbishop to defend what he saw as the cause of God and truth. If he merely flattered her he would be judged by God for negligence, and would not be helping her either. He has in mind here the role of a minister to be a watchman, warning of judgment to come, such as we find in Ezekiel 33.

---

[21] What follows expounds the letter to the Queen as found in Lansdowne MS 23, number 12, folios 24-29 which is transcribed in Nicholson, *Remains*, 376-390, and an edited version of which (with Latin translations and source notes) I included at the back of *Edmund Grindal: The Preacher's Archbishop* (London: Latimer Trust, 2013), 24-40.

Grindal is courteous and respectful, and praises the Queen where he can. 'We have received by your government many and most excellent benefits,' he declares, 'as, among others, freedom of conscience, suppressing of idolatry, sincere preaching of the gospel, with public peace and tranquillity.' He was sure that she meant well, as many of the best monarchs did who made errors of judgment, 'yet they have not refused afterwards to be better informed out of God's word.' He compared himself here to the prophets of the Old Testament, but also to the fourth-century bishop, Ambrose of Milan, who had written to the Emperor Theodosius to persuade him against a particular course of action.[22] This was a somewhat ominous precedent to cite since Ambrose had been so bold as to even excommunicate the Emperor at one point![23] Grindal said that although he knew the Queen's piety was genuine, 'I cannot marvel enough, how this strange opinion should once enter into your mind, that it should be good for the church to have few preachers.'

> Alas, Madam! Is the scripture more plain in any one thing, than that the gospel of Christ should be plentifully preached; and that plenty of labourers should be sent into the Lord's harvest; which, being great and large, standeth in need, not of a few, but many workmen! [Matthew 9:35-38]

Solomon had used 150,000 men to build his temple, and 3,300 overseers, said Grindal, 'and shall we think that a few preachers may suffice to build and edify the spiritual temple of Christ, which is his church!' This was a pertinent point, since as Bishop of London a few years previously, Grindal had given a vast amount of money himself to help rebuild St Paul's Cathedral which had

---

[22] See Philip Schaff and Henry Wace (eds.), *Nicene and Post-Nicene Fathers*: Second Series. Volume 10 (Peabody, Massachusetts: Hendrickson, 1994), 440-445 for the text of Ambrose's letter concerning the restoration of the Jewish synagogue. See also the letter concerning the massacre at Thessalonica on pages 450-453.

[23] See Bucer's appropriation of Ambrose's interactions with Theodosius in Martin Bucer, *Concerning the True Care of Souls* (Edinburgh: Banner of Truth, 2009), 106-108, where he concludes, 'Note that when the true bishops governed the church, this was the seriousness with which action was taken in the church against those who had injured the church by public and heinous sins.'

been struck by lightning and partially destroyed by fire.[24] It is also a pertinent point for us today, as we consider the vast amounts of money often spent on similar ecclesiastical building projects in our generation, while it is often harder to raise money to put well-trained gospel workers into the field.

Grindal went on to quote from the example of Christ and the words of the apostle Paul to the effect that 'often and much preaching' was a prerequisite for New Testament religion to flourish. Titus 1:5 is especially important here. *Appoint elders in every town*, Paul wrote to Titus. And if the Holy Spirit expressly prescribes a preacher for every town, how can the Queen possibly think that three or four per county could possibly be sufficient?[25]

Grindal then wrote some of his most oft-quoted words on the subject of preaching: 'Public and continual preaching of God's word is the ordinary mean and instrument of the salvation of mankind.' You cannot get more significant and exalted than that! Preaching is the normal way that people get saved, but it also has a number of other very positive spiritual effects. 'By preaching of God's word,' writes Grindal, 'the glory of God is enlarged, faith is nourished, and charity increased. By it the ignorant [person] is instructed, the negligent exhorted and incited, the stubborn rebuked, the weak conscience comforted.' This is powerful rhetoric, exalting the preaching and proclamation of the word as a

---

[24] According to Collinson, *Archbishop Grindal*, 180 he contributed at least £1,100 to the repairs out of his own pocket (a little over a year's income from the see).

[25] The Greek word is πόλις, meaning a population centre without specific reference to size, and though it may be contrasted with κώμη, the word for a small village it does not mean an area as large as an English county. See Johannes Louw and Eugene Nida, *Greek-English Lexicon of the New Testament Based on Semantic Domains*: Second Edition (New York: United Bible Societies, 1989), 1.88 and 1.89. Grindal uses the Latin word *oppidum*, which usually has the same meaning, though in C. Julius Caesar, *Caesar's Gallic War* (New York: Harper & Brothers, 1869), 5.21 Caesar refers to the British use of this term as also including a fortified wood or forest. See Bucer's comment on this text in *Concerning the True Care of Souls*, 35-36.

vital instrument of spiritual growth.[26] But the shrewd Archbishop is also careful to add that 'By preaching also, due obedience to Christian princes and magistrates is planted in the hearts of subjects... So as generally, where preaching wanteth, obedience faileth.' Grindal cites here his experience in the North, where loyalty to the Tudor regime and to the Queen herself was often encouraged by preachers, and was sometimes under threat in areas without solid Protestant ministry.[27]

However, Grindal also notes that it is important to maintain standards in the ministry. Only those who are able and reliable should be allowed into the pulpit and licensed for such ministry. Ability is shown by knowledge of the Bible, and usually by a degree from one of the universities; reliability is shown by a good and godly life. Those who did not meet those requirements, even in a time when there was a dire need for clergy, should be removed and barred from the office of public teaching. But he is careful to qualify what is meant by ability in preaching: 'in our time,' he writes, 'many have so delicate ears, that no preaching can satisfy them, unless it be sauced with much finess and exornation of speech.' Unless preaching is ornamented and presented in pleasurable ways, some people will not listen. Or indeed, he adds, they simply use this as an excuse for their closed minds and hardened hearts which desire nothing more than to continue in their sin.

---

[26] Bucer also had this focus on the word as the instrument of pastoral work, e.g. *Concerning the True Care of Souls*, 167-171 where he says, 'all strengthening of the weak and ailing sheep depends on the word of God being faithfully set forth to them, and them being led to listen to it gladly and have all their joy in it.' He speaks of 'constant meditation in the law of God' drawing Christ's sheep away from worldliness, and how they are to be warned and corrected 'through God's word.' The weak, sick, disorderly, and negligent must be 'well instructed and reminded.' Cf. p 181, the gospel 'requires the most faithful, earnest and persistent teaching, instruction and admonition that anyone could ever employ', in public sermons and also privately. See also his treatise *De Ordinatione Legitima* in Whitaker, *Martin Bucer*, 180.

[27] See Christopher Hill, 'Puritans and 'the Dark Corners of the Land' in *Transactions of the Royal Historical Society*, Fifth Series, Vol. 13 (1963), 78-81 and R. L. Arundale, 'Edmund Grindal and the Northern Province', in *Church Quarterly Review*, clx (1959), 197-98.

I wonder if there is something of a challenge here to us? Do we have a similarly high view of preaching? It is true, as Richard Hooker would later write against certain puritans, that public reading of the word of God itself has power to convert and edify, as one of the ordinary means of grace: 'Sermons are not the only preaching which does save souls.'[28] Yet preaching has been under threat of late, from a variety of angles, particularly by those with seemingly less confidence in the power of the naked word of God. We are told that people no longer want to listen to the Bible being read or preached. Instead they want interactive groups, to ask questions and start 'conversations', not an instructive, edifying monologue from the Bible. They need jokes and PowerPoint and video clips or they will not listen. But could we ever say that PowerPoint is 'God's instrument for the salvation of mankind'? By ministerial anecdotes 'the glory of God is enlarged, faith is increased and charity increased'? Are questioning conversations, rich in cultural allusions but low on scriptural content, the way that the ignorant are instructed, the negligent exhorted, the stubborn rebuked, and the weak conscience comforted? I think probably not, and the impoverished biblical literacy of our generation is testimony to how poorly people have been served by a low estimate of preaching and its pastoral significance.

As several people have noted, 'sermonettes make Christianettes.'[29] Too many of our congregations are stuck on a milky five-minute homily when what they need is a more meaty half hour (at least). Yet they are not denied access to this essential spiritual nourishment by a stubbornly conservative Queen or a lack of published resources to help preachers or a dearth of literate,

---

[28] Richard Hooker, *Of the Laws of Ecclesiastical Polity* (A. S. McGrade, ed.; Oxford: Oxford University Press, 2014), 2:45, 57 (Laws V:19, 5:21). Hooker goes on to say that, 'So worthy a part of divine service we should greatly wrong, if we did not esteem preaching as the blessed ordinance of God, sermons as the keys to the kingdom of heaven, as wings to the soul, as spurs to the good affections of man, to the sound and healthy as food, as physic to diseased minds' (V:22, on page 58f).

[29] See John Stott, *I Believe in Preaching* (London: Hodder and Stoughton, 1982), 7, 294. The phrase can be attributed to Michael Green, John Stott, Campbell Morgan, or Stuart Holden. P. T. Forsyth said, similarly, 'A Christianity of short sermons is a Christianity of short fibre' in *Positive Preaching and the Modern Mind* (London: Independent Press, 1907), 109-110.

university-educated clergy, but by their own dulled spiritual appetites and the superficial short-sightedness of our consumer-driven entertainment culture. How many of our congregations have such 'delicate ears' that they cannot abide more than the most cursory unfolding of the Bible which, as Grindal says, 'is sweet and delectable' to all true Christians?

Elizabeth I replied to this sort of argument that the set, prescribed Homilies, written by men such as Cranmer, should be sufficient. Grindal conceded that they were indeed godly and beneficial, but they were by no means comparable to having a trained minister preaching a specially-composed sermon to a congregation he knew and loved personally. Grindal quotes from Matthew 24:45 to show that this is the sort of ministry which Christ himself anticipated in the Gospel: *Who then is the faithful and wise servant, whom his master has set over his household, to give them their food at the proper time?* That is, a wise preacher knows how to 'apply his speech according to the diversity of times, places, and hearers, which cannot be done in homilies: exhortations, reprehensions, and persuasions, are uttered with more affection, to the moving of the hearers, in sermons than in homilies.' Complaining of the sacrilegious use of impropriations,[30] he complains that only one in eight parishes can actually pay a sufficient stipend to support such a preacher. Since preaching God's word is 'the food of the soul', reading homilies is better than nothing ('better half a loaf than no bread'); but the best solution would be to restore tithes and ecclesiastical livings to the use of the church rather

---

[30] The right to appoint a minister in a parish (the advowson), and to the tithes from it (the living) were often improperly appropriated by private patrons, who used all or most of the money for their own benefit, with little going to pay for the spiritual nourishment of the parish itself. On campaigns against such impropriations and for puritan attempts to use the patronage system for evangelistic ends, see Lee Gatiss, 'The Grand Nursery of Puritanism: St Antholin's as a Strategic Centre for Gospel Ministry', in Lee Gatiss (ed.) *Preachers, Pastors, and Ambassadors: Puritan Wisdom for Today's Church* (London: Latimer Trust, 2011), 3-47.

than to allow private patrons and absentee Rectors to use the money for their own ends.[31]

This, we might apply in two ways. There has always been a steady trade in printed sermons. Nowadays we also have a steady trade in freely accessible mp3 downloads and online videos of other people's teaching. This can be edifying and good, if they are used well. On the other hand, if lazy or badly-trained ministers— or those who are not very good at prioritising their time—lean on such material too heavily in feeding their flocks, they have essentially abdicated their pastoral responsibilities, and are no better than those who in Elizabethan England simply read the set Homilies and considered their work done.

We might also see the relevance of what Grindal says to those who think they can be properly fed simply by listening to good talks on the internet, or to a preacher far away piped in on a big screen. Yes, we might find there some excellently clear and inspiring teachers. But they do not love us or know us. Even the greatest celebrity preachers can never apply the Bible in powerful and moving ways to me in the same way that somebody who knows me and my contexts well can do; and I am less likely to take note of the things they say than I am when the word is served up for me each week by preachers whom I, in turn, know and respect and can watch as they put flesh on their preaching by living it out. The personal, dynamic, existential nature of what is going on as we listen to live, freshly-prepared, locally-applied preaching is simply irreplaceable. Grindal knew that, and it is for this very thing that he put his neck on the line.

---

[31] As well as sharing this concern regarding impropriations, Martin Bucer was also against the 'mere written prescription' of set services and Homilies, saying, 'In some places the churches have only readers in the place of pastors and teachers: and in most of these they are men who do not even perform the office of reader properly... Now, when the Lord was instituting the sacred ministry of the church he did not say, 'Go into all the world and read the gospel and my teaching to the people', but he said, 'Preach the gospel and teach it to every creature...' See E. C. Whitaker, *Martin Bucer and the Book of Common Prayer* Alcuin Club No. 55 (Great Wakering: Mayhew-McCrimmon, 1974), 150.

Defence of Prophesyings

So Grindal's letter to the Queen begins with a defence of such preaching. But the second thing Grindal must defend is the idea of preaching conferences, those 'exercises for prophesying' as they were known. His defence is in four parts: they are well ordered and authorised; they are biblically sanctioned; they are useful for improving the standard of preaching; and without them there would be all kinds of negative consequences.

First, then, Grindal pointed out that the conferences were authorised by the diocesan bishops, who had proper legal and spiritual authority to arrange for such things.[32] This was important to stress, at a time when some believed that such meetings could herald the growth of an incipient presbyterianism. Their suspicions should not be taken lightly, even if they were not always warranted.[33] The prophesyings happened once a fortnight or once a month as the bishop allowed, he explained, before spending some time outlining the sort of things that were discussed at the meetings: a passage of scripture is read; the context of it is unpacked, along with the meaning of the words, with help from those who know the original languages where possible; there is discussion of the use and misuse of the text, and how to apply it doctrinally and practically. The whole was moderated by two or three of the senior clergy appointed by the bishop for the task, and although lay people were allowed to attend, they were not permitted to speak, nor was any 'controversy of this present time' to be brought up for debate. Those who broke the rules for seemly conduct in such assemblies were disciplined by the bishop. Finally, of course — and Grindal has to mention this! — 'The conclusion is, with prayer for your Majesty and all

---

[32] He told certain separatist Londoners who were hauled before him and other Ecclesiastical Commissioners in June 1567 for holding private religious meetings that, 'to gather together disorderly, to trouble the common quiet of the realm against the prince's will, we like not the holding of it.' Nicholson (ed.), *Remains*, 214. Cf. His Injunctions against 'secret conventicles, preachings, or lectures', in ibid., 144.

[33] Collinson, 'The Prophesyings', 5.

estates, as is appointed by the *Book of Common Prayer*, and a psalm.'

This may be a little different to the preaching groups some of us are part of today. Ours are perhaps less public affairs, and we keep the laity at arm's length somewhat, treating them as more of a professional gathering. This may be wise and sensible, though when the compromise of excluding lay people from these occasions was suggested to Grindal, he refused to support it.[34] I doubt many preaching groups these days end with a positive prayer for Her Majesty Queen Elizabeth II (or the appropriate Head of State) and a psalm, though it is possible, and would not be a bad thing. I would be more surprised, however, if such groups were convened and encouraged by diocesan bishops. Not only are most preaching groups and conferences today more ecumenical affairs, composed of evangelicals from across the spectrum of churchmanship, but our Anglican bishops are far too busy with other tasks I fear, while post-ordination training is, by all accounts, not exactly a masterclass in sermon improvement. A pastor today is expected to be so much more than a mere preacher; and while other aspects of a parish ministry are of course important, has evangelistic and edifying preaching slipped far too far down the list of priorities?

Second, Grindal outlined the ancient authority of such ministerial conferences. The prophet Samuel is his great example, as well as Elisha. The schools of the 'sons of the prophets' in their day gathered to study the scriptures and serve the church, and Grindal considers 1 Corinthians 14:29 to apply to such a meeting too. Prophecy was not about 'prediction,' but about 'the interpretation and exposition of the scriptures.' Some had been given the ability to do this 'by special miracle, without study', just

---

[34] Francis Bacon, who thought Grindal 'one of the greatest and gravest Prelates of this Land', considered the only problem with prophesyings to be that lay people were invited. Apart from that, they were in his opinion, 'the best way to frame and traine up Preachers to handle the Word of God as it ought to be handled, that hath been practised.' Francis Bacon, *Certaine considerations Touching the Better Pacification, and Edification of the Church of England* (London: 1604), E2. Cf. James Spedding, *The Letters and the Life of Francis Bacon*: Volume 1 (London: Longmans, Green, and Co, 1890), 88.

as some also had the gift of speaking with strange tongues; but now, he says, 'miracles ceasing, men must attain to the knowledge of the Hebrew, Greek, and Latin tongues, &c. by travail and study... So must men also attain by like means to the gift of expounding and interpreting the scriptures.' Preaching conferences were an ideal means of achieving this aim, and were in essence like the exercises used to train students in the universities except that the use of English (rather than academic Latin) allowed the prophesyings to be of use to the unlearned too.

Third, the Archbishop brings in as testimony the reports from his fellow bishops to testify to the advantages there are in permitting such exercises to continue. Ten bishops are singled out, which shows that the prophesyings were hardly just a puritan project. Six benefits were listed, namely:

1. Preaching conferences make ministers more skilful preachers.

2. They remove preachers 'from idleness, wandering, gaming, &c.'

3. They persuade the doctrinally dodgy to confess the truth.

4. They drive ignorant ministers to study harder.

5. They show lay people that the clergy are not lazy.[35]

6. They train up good preachers to 'beat down Popery.'

We may devise a slightly different list of advantages today, but this is a good start, and an interesting testimony from the bishops as to the state of the clerical profession in their day. But Grindal concludes with a somewhat dangerous line which may well have annoyed and angered his mistress: 'Only backward men in religion, and contemners of learning in the countries abroad, do fret against it [the idea of the exercises]; which in truth doth more commend it.' I think I might have advised him not to equate the Queen with those who are backward and anti-learning. That was hardly tactful or diplomatic. Martin Bucer had expressed the same desire more positively and perhaps more attractively in 1551, saying, 'People therefore who have at heart the welfare of the royal

---

[35] The joke that ministers 'only work one day a week' was obviously current in Elizabethan days too.

majesty and the whole kingdom, and have the means to make any contribution to this matter, should exert all their power and influence to secure that suitable and faithful ministers are found *and trained* and kept for each parish as soon as it can be done.'[36] Grindal may perhaps have had these programmatic words from his old friend ringing in his ears in the midst of the prophesyings crisis.

The Archbishop was concerned that suppressing the conferences would set back the cause and give succour and delight to the enemy. Just because a few disorderly souls may have abused a good institution that was no reason to close it down altogether. Therefore, since these meetings were so beneficial, he told Her Majesty, 'I am forced, with all humility, and yet plainly, to profess, that I cannot with safe conscience, and without the offense of the majesty of God, give my assent to the suppressing of the said exercises: much less can I send out any injunction for the utter and universal subversion of the same... Bear with me, I beseech you, Madam, if I choose rather to offend your earthly majesty, than to offend the heavenly majesty of God.' He would not gamble his soul for the prize of an Archbishopric.

One high church historian dismisses this as 'puritan crankiness.'[37] But it was nothing of the kind. These were brave words, and with them he offered to resign. Is it right at this point to call Grindal a puritan? Well, he was against the 'pure' form of presbyterian and separatist puritanism in his day, opposing Thomas Cartwright for example, but entirely Reformed theologically and sympathetic to those who found some ceremonial aspects of the Elizabethan settlement difficult. He says in his letter to the Queen that he allowed no-one to be admitted to the office of preaching 'that either professeth papistry or puritanism.' As Peter Lake argues, Grindal was the victim of 'an

---

[36] Whitaker, *Martin Bucer*, 151 (emphasis added). The printed edition of Bucer's *Censura* (from which these words are taken) was first published in 1577, at the height of the Grindal controversy, largely thanks to Grindal himself collecting Bucer's *Scripta Anglicana*.

[37] Walter H. Frere, *The English Church in the Reigns of Elizabeth and James I* (London: Macmillan, 1904), 192.

intensely ideological politics, conducted in and through the ideological codes of anti-popery and anti-Puritanism.[38] He finally refused to accept the idea that puritanism was the functional equivalent of popery in the mutating stalemate of the Elizabethan compromise, and rejected the use of 'scare tactics' against prophesyings. His stand is seen as even more courageous in this light, because he was not only taking a theological stand but refusing to play the sly politically-correct game that had enforced a seemingly stable consensus in Elizabeth's reign.

Separation of Powers

Grindal made two further pleas to Elizabeth as he closed his letter, which we would do well to note. They have relevance to us today in our discussions of 'establishment':

> The first is, that you would refer all these ecclesiastical matters which touch religion, or the doctrine and discipline of the church, unto the bishops and divines of your realm; according to the example of all godly Christian emperors and princes of all ages.

These things were to be judged in synods, not in palaces, he added (alluding again to Ambrose's letter to the emperor Theodosius). Judges and lawyers should determine questions of law, and economists should deal with the economy; likewise, theology and the church should be left to the bishops and theologians. The one contrary example he cites is when the son of Constantine the Great (272-337) started 'to judge of faith within the palace'. This,

---

[38] Peter Lake, 'A Tale of Two Episcopal Surveys: The Strange Fates of Edmund Grindal and Cuthbert Mayne Revisited,' *Transactions of the Royal Historical Society* (Sixth Series), 18 (2008), 155.

he said, led the emperor Constantius (317-361) into the heresy of Arianism—'a terrible example!'[39]

Second, Grindal spoke very plainly to the Queen about her mortality, and the fact that one day she would stand before the judgment seat of Christ to give an account of her actions. Therefore, 'when you deal in matters of faith and religion, or matters that touch the church of Christ, which is his spouse, bought with so dear a price, you would not use to pronounce so resolutely and peremptorily... but always remember, that in God's causes the will of God, and not the will of any earthly creature, is to take place.'

To conclude, he cautioned the Queen not to think that her reign was so blessed because she deserved it. Rather, the 'great felicity' of her reign was due to the rightness of the cause she stood for, that is, the Protestant Reformed religion, and the fervent prayers of godly people for her. The way he speaks in this final section indicates that he must have had real worries about her continued perseverance in this path: 'if ye turn from God, then God will turn away his merciful countenance from you,' he warned. Although God had many reasons to be angry with her and with England 'for our unfaithfulness', yet in response to her humility in this and for the sake of his own glory, the Lord would continue 'to shield and protect us under the shadow of his wings.'

Space precludes a detailed examination of the question of the relationship between the Church of England and the state. Suffice to say, the royal supremacy over the church, enshrined by the Tudors, has today in effect become a Parliamentary supremacy. Yet there are limitations on the authority that any state can be allowed over the workings of the church. The supremacy was designed to

---

[39] Constantius II is remembered as 'a heretic who arbitrarily imposed his will on the church' according to Arnold Jones, *The Later Roman Empire, 284–602: A Social, Economic and Administrative Survey* (Baltimore: Johns Hopkins University, 1986), 118. See Henry Bettenson and Chris Maunder (eds.), *Documents of the Christian Church: Fourth Edition* (Oxford: Oxford University Press, 2011), 20-21 and the Bishop of Cordova writing to Constantius, very much as Grindal wrote to Elizabeth, saying, 'Do not interfere in matters ecclesiastical, nor give us orders on such questions, but learn about them from us. For into your hands God has put the kingdom; the affairs of his Church he has committed to us.'

represent the laity of the church and give them influence alongside the clergy.[40] In a sense, by replacing the Pope this way, Cranmer set up the problem which Grindal and others have since had to face. Such delicate balancing acts between clergy and laity are now played out in the General Synod of the Church of England,[41] while Parliament is more representative not of the church but of an increasingly secular nation. What right that body can therefore have to dictate doctrinal policy to the church is a hotly debated point. Grindal's 'theoretical musings' on this subject, as Peter Lake calls them,[42] are an issue of very urgent pastoral relevance.

Parliament has threatened to force the church's hand most recently over the matter of women bishops, and may well do so again on issues to do with homosexuality (with which modern society has become so bizarrely obsessed). Although the situation is radically different, and more needs to be said, Grindal's warning surely remains pertinent: 'always remember, that in God's causes the will of God, and not the will of any earthly creature, is to take place... In God's matters all princes ought to bow their sceptres to the Son of God, and to ask counsel at his mouth, what they ought to do.' If matters of faith and Christian conduct begin to be decided within the Palace of Westminster, no doubt on the basis of what is desirable and acceptable for the man and woman down the pub, then a heresy no less pernicious than Arianism may soon

---

[40] Parliament exercised this role in 1928, for example, when it threw out the revised Prayer Book proposal that had been heavily sponsored by bishops and clergy. Indeed, Randall Davidson became the first Archbishop of Canterbury to succeed in resigning, when he stepped down because of this. In 1993, Parliament also insisted that proper provision be made for those who could not in conscience agree with women's ordination, and refused to allow the General Synod's proposed legislation to receive Royal Assent until such provision had been drawn up.

[41] For example, in November 2012 it was the House of Laity in General Synod which defeated the proposed legislation to allow women bishops without statutory provision for opponents, a proposal which clergy and episcopal representatives were overwhelmingly in favour of.

[42] Peter Lake, 'The Monarchical Republic of Queen Elizabeth I' (and the Fall of Archbishop Grindal) Revisited,' in John F. McDiarmid (ed.), *The Monarchical Republic of Early Modern England: Essays in Response to Patrick Collinson* (Aldershot: Ashgate, 2007), 143.

be upon us. For the glory of God and the good of England, it is sincerely to be hoped that the church can maintain control over its own doctrine and practice, and that those who hold sway in Synod will 'yield true obedience and reverence to the word of God.' For if we turn away from God...

The Impact of Grindal's letter

The Queen was furious with Grindal for refusing to do what she wanted. Despite many efforts to change his mind, he refused to yield. On May 7th 1577 he was essentially placed under house arrest in Lambeth Palace, and on her own authority she commanded bishops to suppress the prophesyings.[43] Brett Usher says what she did was 'the single most irresponsible decision that she ever took' with regards to the church.[44] Elizabeth wanted to go further and deprive Grindal, sack him in effect, but there was no obvious precedent for this. If you wanted to get rid of an Archbishop of Canterbury you usually had to call him a turbulent priest and have him assassinated or get him declared a heretic so he could be burned. Grindal was neither turbulent nor a heretic. But he was a man of principle, who despite reaching the very top after a glittering ecclesiastical career was willing to sacrifice it all. For the sake of what? For the sake of sound biblical preaching, the means and instrument of salvation. He was thrust to the margins of government, a victim of court intrigue and personal enmities as well as his own principles, because he cared more about the

---

[43] They did stop in many areas, but the idea and desire did not disappear. See Lee Gatiss, 'To Satisfy the People's Hunger for the Word: St. Antholin's as the Prototype Puritan Lectureship', in Lee Gatiss (ed.) *Pilgrims, Warriors, and Servants: Puritan Wisdom for Today's Church, St Antholin Lectures* (1991-2000) (London: Latimer Trust, 2010) and Patrick Collinson, J. Craig and B. Usher (eds.), *Conferences and Combination Lectures in the Elizabethan church: Dedham and Bury St Edmunds, 1582-1590, Church of England Record Society* (Woodbridge: Boydell Press, 2003), esp. xxvii. Purely clerical exercises would be encouraged under Grindal's more anti-Puritan successor, Archbishop Whitgift.

[44] Brett Usher, *William Cecil and Episcopacy* (Farnham: Ashgate, 2003), 152. Collinson, *Archbishop Grindal*, 249 says 'there was no more arbitrary exercise of the royal supremacy in the history of the Church of England than this.'

conversion and edification of England than he did for the prestige and power of Edmund Grindal.[45] He was the Preacher's Archbishop.

For six years the Church of England was denied its Archbishop of Canterbury, until Grindal finally died after a 'long Kafkaesque ordeal' in 1583.[46] His death was not as spectacular as Thomas Cranmer's had been twenty-seven years previously. His life and ministry have all but been forgotten. Yet he was a man of deep convictions who was willing to put his immense talents and opportunities at the service of Christ and to work towards the conversion of England. Like Cranmer, he had to make sacrifices and compromises, and survived many battles until he eventually fell afoul of the temper and religious proclivities of one of Henry VIII's feisty daughters.

Ours may well not be a day of giants and geniuses—or burnings—such as Cranmer was fated to see. But let us pray, in days when the preaching of God's word is downplayed and the evangelisation of our nation remains as urgent and difficult as ever, that we may be blessed with Grindals, who will grind away to prosecute a clear agenda of biblical teaching and reform wherever the Lord may place them. When many acquire the habit and reputation for jettisoning their principles for the sake of preferment and advance, let us hope to be inspired by those like Grindal, who are prepared to suffer professionally and politically when a clear but difficult stand becomes necessary.

---

[45] He did not want to be the sort of bishop who finds his place 'more at court than in the church', as Bucer, *Concerning the True Care of Souls*, 125 puts it.

[46] DNB, s.v. Collinson, 'The Prophesyings', points out that he was still kept busy with various tasks during his house arrest.

Shades of Opinion within a Generic Calvinism: The Particular Redemption Debate at the Westminster Assembly

This chapter is a modified and expanded version of an article first published in Reformed Theological Review 69.2 (August 2010), 101-118. I wish to thank Chad van Dixhoorn for his careful attention to detail and very useful interaction on the material in this and the following chapter, and Richard Muller for his kind encouragement.

The debate between Protestant theologians over 'particular redemption' was one of the most fraught in the seventeenth century, and continues to be 'one of the most controversial teachings in Reformed soteriology.'[1] Did Christ die for all indiscriminately? Did he die for the elect alone in particular? Or was there a middle way between these two options? I have entered the fray elsewhere with a whole book on the subject, and a more

---

[1] R. A. Blacketer, 'Definite Atonement in Historical Perspective' in C. E. Hill and F. A. James III (eds.), *The Glory of the Atonement: Biblical, Theological, and Practical Perspectives* (Downers Grove IL: InterVarsity, 2004), 304.

detailed examination of the Synod of Dort's deliberations.[2] The purpose of this chapter, however, is to examine a key public debate on this topic from seventeenth-century Britain, to note the variety of opinions about the atonement within the broadly Reformed camp and examine the biblical underpinnings of them.

There was intense interest in the subject of the particularity of the work of Christ from the beginning of the seventeenth century until near the end. The five-point Arminian Remonstrance and the subsequent Synod of Dort in 1618-1619 began several decades of passionate interchange. This arguably culminated in the *Formula Consensus Helvetica* of 1675, designed by its authors (including Francis Turretin) to exclude and condemn the Amyraldian 'middle way' between Arminianism and Calvinism. In between Dort and the Consensus comes the Westminster Assembly, a formative moment in Protestant creed-making which produced, according to B.B. Warfield, 'the most thoroughly thought out and most carefully guarded statement ever penned of the elements of evangelical religion.'[3] According to the surviving minutes of the Assembly, this august body of British divines discussed the issue of particular redemption in plenary session on at least one occasion whilst hammering out the wording of the *Confession of Faith*. That debate in the autumn of 1645 is the subject of our chapter here.

The debate began in the Jerusalem Chamber of Westminster Abbey on Wednesday morning, 22nd October 1645. Detailed work on the *Confession* had been ongoing for the Assembly of Divines since the summer of 1644, a year in the English Civil War which also saw crushing defeats for the Royalist armies at Nantwich and Marston Moor. As part of the discussion on 'God's

---

[2] See Lee Gatiss, *For Us and For Our Salvation: 'Limited Atonement' in the Bible, Doctrine, History, and Ministry* (London: Latimer Trust, 2012), and Lee Gatiss, 'The Synod of Dort and Definite Atonement' in D. Gibson and J. Gibson (eds.), *From Heaven He Came and Sought Her: Definite Atonement in Biblical, Historical, Theological & Pastoral Perspective* (Wheaton: Crossway, 2013).

[3] B. B. Warfield, 'The Significance of the Westminster Standards as a Creed: Address before the Presbytery of New York, November 8th, 1897' (New York: Charles Scribner, 1898), Section III.

eternal decree', Edward Reynolds' committee responsible for this section of the *Confession* brought a proposition for debate concerning 'Redemption of the elect only.'[4] The debate lasted for several days, possibly until 31st October, although only the first three days are well minuted.[5]

We will examine the debate here in two stages. First, we will see that far from being a black and white affair there were at least four different approaches at play in the discussion, which were brought out as the divines debated whether it was possible to dissent from the proposition without falling prey to Arminianism. Some have seen Amyraldianism as the main dissenting view, and we will examine this ultimately unsatisfactory analysis of the debate, underlining the differences between Dutch, French, and British versions of 'hypothetical universalism.'

Second we will examine how the debate moved on to look at God's intent in the atonement and the question of the universal offer of the gospel, noting the variety of exegetical approaches to this. This will reveal that at this stage there was no uniform defence against hypothetical universalism. In the next chapter we will then scrutinise the final product of the Assembly's deliberations to see how the *Westminster Confession* presents its teaching in the light of these discussions.

1. Is it Possible to Dissent from Particular Redemption Without Being an Arminian?

Scene one of the Westminster Assembly's debate revolved around the question of whether it is possible to dissent from particular redemption without being an Arminian. In the opening exchanges it is the Arminian question which is at the forefront of the delegates' minds. Edmund Calamy opens by attempting to distance himself from the Arminian view that Christ died indiscriminately for everyone. Clearly the proposition to be

---

[4] A. F. Mitchell & J. Struthers (eds.), *Minutes of the Sessions of the Westminster Assembly of Divines* (London and Edinburgh: William Blackwood, 1874), liv.

[5] Mitchell & Struthers, 160.

debated was asserting particular redemption (whether in the finally accepted form of words in WCF 3.6 or not is uncertain), and he was immediately concerned to speak against this. Yet he felt constrained to do so carefully: 'I am far from universal Redemption in the Arminian sense,' he began, 'but that that I hold is in the sense of our divines in the synod of Dort.'[6]

The next four entries in the minutes from Palmer, Reynolds, Calamy and Seaman all revolve around the Remonstrant (Arminian) view. Reynolds' statement is especially pertinent: he says of Calamy's view that it 'cannot be asserted by any that can say he is not of the Remonstrants opinion.'[7] In other words, he accuses Calamy of only a pretended distance between himself and the Arminians, averring that it is not actually possible to dissent from the 'redemption of the elect only' position without falling into Arminianism.

The Synod of Dort & James Ussher

The deliverances of Dort against the Dutch Arminian party were a key part of the immediate background to the Assembly's deliberations. The Arminians had asserted in their second of five articles, 'of universal redemption' that:

> Jesus Christ, the Saviour of the world, died for all men and for every man, so that he has obtained for them all, by his death on the cross, redemption and

---

[6] See C. Van Dixhoorn (ed.), *The Minutes and Papers of the Westminster Assembly 1643-1652: Volume 3. Minutes, Sessions 199-603* (1644-1646) (Oxford: Oxford University Press, 2012), 692. I have modernised the spelling in all quotations from the Minutes and other documents here, to make them easier to follow, and smoothed out capital letters and ellipses where necessary.

[7] Van Dixhoorn, *Minutes*, 692.

the forgiveness of sins; yet that no one actually enjoys
this forgiveness of sins except the believer.[8]

The drawing up of the canons of Dort in response had been 'a
complex and acrimonious affair.'[9] The rejection of Arminianism
was a foregone conclusion since no Remonstrant delegates were
permitted to vote; though they did attend and were interviewed
about their teaching, their defeat was 'predested'.[10] Yet the
Synod (like the Westminster Assembly) was far from
monochrome, with various shades of opinion expressed, not least
on the controversial second head of doctrine. Their final agreed
text replied to the Arminians with eight articles on the atonement
confirming the 'infinite price, and value' of the death of Christ
which was 'abundantly sufficient to expiate the sins of the whole
world', while also asserting that, 'God willed, that Christ by the
blood of his cross... should effectually redeem out of every people,
tribe, nation, and language, all them, and them only, who from
eternity were elected unto salvation, and given to him of the
Father.'[11]

This left several loose ends and unanswered questions. For
instance, as G.M. Thomas points out, 'an explicit link between
infinite sufficiency and indiscriminate preaching is avoided...
[and] no explanation is offered as to how the sufficiency of
Christ's death relates to the non-elect... As a result of the biggest

---

[8] P. Schaff, *The Creeds of Christendom volume 3: The Evangelical Protestant Creeds* (Grand Rapids: Baker, 1996 [1876]), 546. Note the slightly different Latin and English given in P. Heylyn, *Historia Quinquarticularis or, A DECLARATION of The Judgement of the Western Churches And more particularly Of the Church of ENGLAND in The Five Controverted Points Reproached in these Last times by the Name of ARMINIANISM* (London, 1660), 50-51.

[9] A. Milton (ed.), *The British Delegation and the Synod of Dort (1618-1619) Church of England Record Society volume 13* (Woodbridge, Suffolk: Boydell Press, 2005), 295-296.

[10] M. Dewar, 'The British Delegation at the Synod of Dort: Assembling and Assembled; Returning and Returned' in *Churchman* 106.2 (1992), 135.

[11] *The Judgement Of The SYNODE Holden at DORT* (London: John Bill, 1619), 22-24 (articles 3 & 8). See also the new edition of the papers from Dort in D. Sinnema, C. Moser, and H. Selderhuis (eds.), *Acta et Documenta Synodi Nationalis Dordrechtanae (1618-1619)* (Göttingen: Vandenhoeck and Ruprecht, 2015).

disagreement of the Synod, it was impossible to find an acceptable way of relating universal and particular aspects of the atonement in the final document.'[12] It is interesting then, back at Westminster, that Calamy alluded not only to the Synod but to the British delegation that had been sent to Dort. The British divines had submitted their views on the five controverted points in a document called *The Collegiat Suffrage*. On the issue of relating the universal and particular aspects of the atonement, this stated that:

> Christ therefore so died for all, that all and every one by the means of faith might obtain remission of sins, and eternal life by virtue of that ransom paid once for all mankind. But Christ so died for the elect, that by the merit of his death in special manner destinated unto them according to the eternal good pleasure of God, they might infallibly obtain both faith and eternal life.[13]

This is the same position taken by Calamy when he says in his opening statement that Christ 'did pay a price for all, absolute <intention> for the elect, conditional <intention> for the reprobate, in case they do believe.'[14] Hypothetically, then, all could be saved since provision had been made in the cross if only people would believe. Palmer also recognises this distinction, pointing out that the Arminians taught 'all equally redeemed', whereas others, presumably others holding a different form of 'universal' atonement, did not. Calamy was keen to distance his own view from that of the Remonstrants: 'The Arminians,' he said, 'hold that Christ did pay a price for this intention only: that all men should be in an equal state of salvation.' Clearly he did not agree with them about this, and stressed that his version of 'universality'

---

[12] G.M. Thomas, *The Extent of the Atonement: A Dilemma for Reformed Theology from Calvin to the Consensus* (Carlisle: Paternoster, 1997), 133.

[13] G. Carleton et al, *The Collegiat Suffrage of the Divines of Great Britaine, concerning the five articles controverted in the Low Countries* (London: Robert Milbourne, 1629), 47-48.

[14] Van Dixhoorn, *Minutes*, 692. The words in parentheses are written above the line in the text of the Minutes.

did not affect the doctrines of special election or special grace. That is, there was a further intention in the atonement: Christ died to actually save some. He would have agreed with Dort that special grace is reserved for only a part of mankind, that only the elect are effectually redeemed, although he would have been happy to say that all are redeemed in a different sense. The seventeenth-century usage of the word 'redeemed/redemption' allowed for such distinctions.[15]

What Calamy was saying is that Christ accomplished redemption for the elect and non-elect, but it was applied only to the elect. This position is not *mere* 'hypothetical universalism', which Clifford rightly says is 'a description more applicable to the Arminians', since it included an absolute redemption of the elect (which Arminianism did not).[16] To distinguish it from the Dutch Arminian position, then, it might more accurately be called Calvinist hypothetical universalism.

It is vitally important to note that this hypothetically universalist view had something of a heritage in Britain, being privately held by no less a man than the influential Irish Archbishop, James Ussher. In a letter dated March 3rd 1617, unpublished until after his death but widely copied, circulated, and talked about, he made the following distinction: 'The *satisfaction* of Christ, only makes the sins of mankind *fit for pardon*... The particular application makes the sins of those to whom that mercy is vouchsafed to be *actually pardoned*... By the virtue of this blessed Oblation, God is made *placable* unto our *nature*... but not *actually* appeased with any, until he hath received

---

[15] W. Cunningham, *Historical Theology: A review of the principal doctrinal discussions in the Christian church since the apostolic age Volume 2* (Edinburgh: Banner of Truth, 1960 [1862]), 327-328; A. A. Hodge, *The Confession of Faith: A Handbook of Christian Doctrine Expounding the Westminster Confession* (London: Banner of Truth, 1961 [1869]), 73, 154.

[16] A.C. Clifford, *Atonement and Justification: English Evangelical Theology 1640-1790 An Evaluation* (Oxford: Clarendon Press, 1990), 154. A. C. Troxel, 'Amyraut 'at' the Assembly: The Westminster Confession of Faith and the Extent of the Atonement' in *Presbyterion* 22/1 (1996), 46.

his son.'[17] He added that 'the universality of the satisfaction derogates nothing from the necessity of the special Grace in the application'[18] and that 'in one respect Christ may be said to have *died for all*, and in another respect *not* to have died for all.'[19]

It may therefore be noted that Calamy's approach to this issue is strikingly similar to Ussher's, and in fact Ussher is behind a great deal of the Calvinist hypothetical universalist case presented at Westminster. This can be seen with regards to the language of salvability used by Calamy and Seaman,[20] which echoes Ussher's on placability/fit for pardon. It can also be seen in the distinction Thomas Young makes between *pro natura Humana* [for human nature] and *electis* [for the elect ones],[21] which I presume, in the absence of elaboration in the Minutes, regards the question of the object of Christ's work (was it for human nature, or the elect?). This finds an echo in Ussher's language too when he writes that Christ 'intended by giving sufficient satisfaction to God's Justice, to make the *nature* of man, which he assumed, a fit subject for mercy', and that 'in respect of his mercy he may be counted a *kind of universal cause* of the restoring of our Nature.'[22]

Archbishop Ussher, however, was not one 'of our divines in the synod of Dort' with whom Calamy claimed doctrinal solidarity. Yet a copy of Ussher's private letter concerning his judgement on the extent of the atonement had, the epistle 'To the reader' at the start of the 1658 edition informs us, been carried to the Synod of Dort by 'a Member of it.' This editorial preface also tells us that 'not only in the forenamed subjects, but in the rest relating to the

---

[17] J. Ussher, *The Judgement of the late Archbishop of Armagh and Primate of Ireland, 1. Of the extent of Christs death and satisfaction* (London: for John Crook, 1658), 4-5.

[18] Ussher, *The Judgement of the late Archbishop*, 13.

[19] Ussher, *The Judgement of the late Archbishop*, 15. See the excellent study of Richard Snoddy, *The Soteriology of James Ussher: The Act and Object of Saving Faith* (Oxford: Oxford University Press, 2014), chapter 2.

[20] Van Dixhoorn, *Minutes*, 693, 694, 695.

[21] Van Dixhoorn, *Minutes*, 693.

[22] Ussher, *The Judgement of the late Archbishop*, 14-15, 28.

Remonstrants, the *Primate* concurred with *Bishop Davenant*, whose *Lectures De morte Christi*, & *prædestinatione & reprobatione*, he caused to be published.' So the chain of influence is revealed: as Moore makes clear,

> Without wanting to go into print with his concerns, [Ussher] counselled ministers through an extensive correspondence and sought through his immense personal influence quietly to win the next generation of theologians to a more balanced position... Davenant was Ussher's key convert.[23]

As the leader of the British delegation at Dort, John Davenant (later Bishop of Salisbury) was compelled to take a public stance on the issue and thus became a key figure in the development of a stream of Calvinist hypothetical universalism in Britain.[24] At Westminster, Calamy explicitly claims to stand in this tradition. Davenant's most famous work on the subject, written in 1627, was not actually published until 1650, after his death and after the Assembly's debate.[25] Yet his influence was felt not just through the legacy of his work as Bishop of Salisbury, but through the publication of the *Collegiat Suffrage* (Latin: 1626/English: 1629) and through other works which taught his approach to these questions, such as his 1641 book replying to Arminians Samuel Hoard and Henry Mason,[26] which Calamy's grandson called 'learned and peaceable... a book not valued according to its worth.'[27]

---

[23] J.D. Moore, *English Hypothetical Universalism: John Preston and the Softening of Reformed Theology* (Cambridge: Eerdmans, 2007), 212.

[24] Whether advocates of this position (ancient or modern) would revel in the acronym CHUB is a debatable point.

[25] J. Davenant, *Dissertationes Duæ: Prima De Morte Christi... Altera De Prædestinatione & Reprobatione* (Cambridge: Rogeri Danielis, 1650). See J. Davenant, *A Dissertation on the Death of Christ with an introduction by Dr Alan Clifford* (Weston Rhyn: Quinta Press, 2006), x and Moore, *English Hypothetical Universalism*, 187 n.70.

[26] J. Davenant, *Animadversions... upon a Treatise intitled God's love to Mankind* (Cambridge: Roger Daniel, 1641).

[27] Davenant, *A Dissertation on the Death of Christ*, xviii.

That Calamy's approach was the same as Davenant's can perhaps be seen in a small detail overlooked by other commentators on this debate. Palmer asks Calamy to clarify his position, regarding the conditional intention of the atonement for all 'in case they do believe'. Palmer says, 'I desire to know whether he will understand it *de omni homine* [of all people]' to which Calamy replies, '*De adultis* [of adults].'[28] This enigmatic exchange, on which further comment has not been preserved, could be explained by passages in Davenant's work on the atonement. In response to an objector, Davenant also 'refers to some difference to be observed in this matter between adults and infants' in terms of the conditional nature of universal grace.[29] It is 'foolish' he says, to assert that Christ died for all infants (in the universal sense) 'if they will believe', since 'they have not the use of reason and free will.' Yet the case is far different with adults, he concludes.[30] We can see, therefore, that at Westminster, Calamy takes a Davenantian position regarding an objection previously put to the hypothetical universalist case.

English Hypothetical Universalism and Amyraldianism

It should be noted that Calamy is not best labelled an Amyraldian, as many are in the habit of doing.[31] This may be understandable as a general label for Calvinist universalism, and

---

[28] Van Dixhoorn, *Minutes*, 693.

[29] J. Davenant, *A Dissertation on the Death of Christ* trans. Josiah Allport (London: Hamilton, Adams, and Co, 1832), 446.

[30] M. Fuller (ed.), *The Life, Letters, and Writings of John Davenant D.D.* (London: Methuen & Co, 1897), 199; Davenant, *A Dissertation on the Death of Christ* (Allport translation), 567.

[31] E.g. David P. Field, *Rigide Calvinisme in a Softer Dresse: The Moderate Presbyterianism of John Howe, 1630-1705* (Edinburgh: Rutherford House, 2004), 20; B. B. Warfield, *The Westminster Assembly and Its Work* (Grand Rapids: Baker, 2003 [1932]), 56, 142; Troxel, 'Amyraut 'at' the Assembly', 49-50; D. Blunt, 'Debate on Redemption at the Westminster Assembly' in *British Reformed Journal 13* (Jan-Mar. 1996), 2; strongly implied in R. T. Kendall, *Calvin and English Calvinism to 1649* (Carlisle: Paternoster, 1997 [1979]), 184 n.2 and Thomas, *The Extent of the Atonement*, 241.

Moïse Amyraut quickly became *the* name attached to 'universal redemption'.[32] Yet it is also inaccurate in some important ways, not least of which is that Amyraut's position depended on other distinctive theological commitments which were not shared by all hypothetical universalists. For example, his ordering of the decrees and his view on original sin and moral and natural ability found him on trial at Alençon in 1637.[33] He also held a unique and distinctive view on the Trinity which flowed from his understanding of redemption, but which was not shared by other universal redemptionists.[34] So 'Amyraldian' (or 'near-Amyraldian')[35] would certainly be an inappropriate anachronism for Davenant who learned his hypothetical universalism well before Amyraut had even begun to study theology.[36] It could also be inadequate and potentially misleading more widely. Mitchell refers to Calamy, Arrowsmith, Vines, and Seaman as 'disciples of Davenant',[37] and this they more likely were first, prior to any acquaintance with the school of Saumur (that is, Amyraut and his tutor John Cameron). They certainly were not all devotees of Moïse Amyraut.

Yet here we must look at two pieces of evidence which are usually adduced to argue for Amyraut's influence at the Assembly. First, a letter of Scottish delegate Robert Baillie on 24th October 1645 is quoted to show that Amyraut was being read and inwardly digested by the Westminster Divines:

---

[32] R. Baxter, *Certain Disputations Of Right to Sacraments and the True Nature of Visible Christianity* (London: William Du Gard for Thomas Johnson, 1657), Preface.

[33] B.G. Armstrong, *Calvinism and the Amyraut Heresy: Protestant Scholasticism and Humanism in Seventeenth Century France* (Madison: University of Wisconsin Press, 1969), 88-96.

[34] Armstrong, *Calvinism and the Amyraut Heresy*, 172-177.

[35] Armstrong, *Calvinism and the Amyraut Heresy*, 99 n.102.

[36] Contra H.C. Hanko, *The History of the Free Offer* (Grandville, Michigan: Theological School of the Protestant Reformed Churches, 1989), chapter 5.

[37] Mitchell & Struthers, lv.

> Unhappily Amyraut's Questions are brought in on
> our Assembly. Many more loves these fancies here than
> I did expect. It falls out ill that Spanheim's book is so
> long a-coming out, while Amyraut's treatise goes in
> the Assembly from hand to hand.[38]

Baillie laments the fact that Frederick Spanheim, who was known
to be composing a great work, 'destined to crush definitively
Saumur',[39] had not yet published his magnum opus.[40] More
pertinently, he laments the distribution of Amyraut's work during
the debate on the redemption of the elect only, thus proving to
some that Amyraut's influence was weighty. It is true that
Amyraut's new book *Dissertationes Theologicae Quatuor* addressing
the issues of universal and particular grace (as well as his doctrine
of the Trinity) rolled off the presses in 1645, the same year as this
particular debate at Westminster.[41] Yet other books which made
people aware of hypothetical universalism were also published
around this time—in English, and without propagating either
Arminian views or following the controversial Saumur *ordo
decretorum* (order of the decrees)—including one by John
Saltmarsh,[42] a troublesome London minister well known to
members of the Assembly.[43]

---

[38] D. Laing (ed.), *The Letters and Journals of Robert Baillie volume 2* (Edinburgh: Robert Ogle, 1841), 324.

[39] Laplanche, quoted in Armstrong, *Calvinism and the Amyraut Heresy*, 105.

[40] F. Spanheim, *Exercitationes de gratia universali* (Leyden, 1646) in three volumes (c. 2600 pages).

[41] Armstrong, *Calvinism and the Amyraut Heresy*, 103, 172.

[42] J. Saltmarsh, *The Fountaine of Free Grace Opened By Questions and Answers proving the foundation of faith to consist only in Gods free love in giving Christ to dye for the sins of all, and objections to the contrary answered by the Congregation of Christ in London, constituted by Baptisme upon the profession of faith, falsly called Anabaptists, wherein they vindicate themselves from the scandalous aspersions of holding free-will, and denying a free election by grace* (London, 1645), 1-24. An annotation on the Thomason copy reads 'Jan: 21 1644' with the 5 in the imprint date crossed out. This material is attributed to John Saltmarsh by Wing and DNB.

[43] C. Hill, *Liberty Against the Law* (London: Penguin, 1997), 217. W. Barker, *Puritan Profiles: 54 influential Puritans at the time when the Westminster Confession of Faith was written* (Fearn, Ross-shire, Scotland: Mentor, 1996), 159, 243.

More acceptable to members of the Assembly was *Treatise of the Covenant of Grace* by John Ball, whom Baxter later claimed was universalist on the point of redemption.[44] Whether or not Baxter's claim is accurate (which is not straightforward to determine),[45] Ball's book is certainly aware of a counter-Remonstrant, hypothetically universal doctrine without the Trinitarian or decretal distinctives of Amyraut.[46] Ball was published posthumously by Simeon Ashe in 1645 and carried a laudatory 'To the reader' from notable divines including Edward Reynolds, Anthony Burgess, and Edmond Calamy (sic). They confessed, however, that 'our manifold employments have not suffered us to peruse it, so exactly, as otherwise we should have done' so we should not infer from their willingness to give testimony to the author's piety and sound learning approbation of all he wrote. On the intent of the atonement, Calamy and Reynolds came out in the Assembly's debates on different sides, after all.[47] We may well ask, then, whether if these men were unable to read a book by a friend in English that they gave their own names to, how much more might they have struggled to find time for the scholarly Latin writings of a more distant Frenchman? Which might have influenced them more in years previously as they formed their opinions on the issue at hand is not so easily answered as some might think either.

The second piece of evidence usually adduced in favour of calling the 'loyal opposition' by the name of 'Amyraldians' is that Gillespie explicitly names Cameron and Amyraut in his first speech in the debate.[48] So, says Troxel, 'It seems odd [to] maintain the influence of English sources when in fact the Minutes

---

[44] Baxter, *Certain Disputations*, Preface.

[45] See the discussion in H. Boersma, *A Hot Pepper Corn: Richard Baxter's Doctrine of Justification in Its Seventeenth-Century Context of Controversy* (Vancouver: Regent College Publishing, 2004 [1993]), 206-209.

[46] See J. Ball, *Treatise of the Covenant of Grace* (London: G. Miller for Edward Brewster, 1645), 204-264, esp. 205-206 which are quoted in Mitchell & Struthers, lx.

[47] Contra Troxel, 'Amyraut 'at' the Assembly', 49 n.17.

[48] Van Dixhoorn, *Minutes*, 693.

themselves record Mr Gillespie mentioning Cameron and Amyraut by name amidst the very debate in which this issue is discussed.[49] Yet logically, of course, it does not follow that because one participant mentions certain theologians that other participants necessarily were in agreement with them or had even read them. Even if an equation was drawn between Calamy's position and the teachings of Amyraut (and it is not entirely clear from the Minutes that Gillespie was directly accusing Calamy of dependence), it is surely correct to ask whether such an equation is legitimate or would be accepted and acknowledged by Calamy himself. After all, raising the suspicion of guilt by association is an old tactic in theological debate.

It is interesting to note in this regard that Calamy's immediate response after Gillespie has cited the Salmurians is to protest that 'in the point of election I am for special election and for reprobation I am for *massa corrupta*.'[50] Thus he indicates that he believes, as Ussher did,[51] that the object of predestination and reprobation is the sinful mass [*massa corrupta*] of mankind, i.e. that he is an infralapsarian. This answers the point Gillespie was just making about the order of the decree in Amyraut, and shows that Calamy is in fact in perfect accord with the later *Formula Consensus Helvetica* (the formula *anti-Amyraldensis*) on this point: God elected some of fallen humanity but decreed to *'leave the rest in the corrupt mass'* (*alios vero in corrupta massa relinquere*).[52] Amyraut, on the other hand, taught that God elected some out of the mass of *redeemed* humanity, the work of Christ to redeem all preceding the

---

[49] Troxel, 'Amyraut 'at' the Assembly', 50 n.22. Warfield, *The Westminster Assembly*, 142.

[50] Van Dixhoorn, *Minutes*, 693.

[51] Ussher, *The Judgement of the late Archbishop*, 41-42 for *massa corrupta*.

[52] Emphasis mine. For the Consensus in English see A. A. Hodge, *Outlines of Theology* (Edinburgh: Banner of Truth, 1972 [1878]), 656-663 (657). For the Latin here quoted see P. Schaff, *The Creeds of Christendom volume 1: The History of Creeds* (Grand Rapids: Baker, 1996 [1876]), 478, 487.

decree to save some and pass over others.[53] Calamy therefore does not appear to be an Amyraldian, and distances himself from Amyraut at this point.

All this is not to say that Amyraut had no followers at the Assembly. Seaman does appear to go down the French route when he says God has 'so far reconciled himself to the world that he would have mercy on whom he would have mercy' and later that 'every man is *salvabilis* [saveable] and God, if he please, may choose him, Justify him, sanctify him.'[54] God's choice, Seaman appears to be saying, is made out of the mass of humanity made salvable by the work of Christ. He spoke of salvability not '*quoad homines* [with respect to people] but *quoad Deum* [with respect to God].'[55]

Ussher would have agreed with this, since he himself had written that '*by Christ's satisfaction* to his Father he made the Nature of Man a fit subject for mercy, I mean thereby, that the *former* impediment arising on God's part is taken away.'[56] Yet British hypothetical universalists such as Ussher, Davenant, and John Preston did not agree with the Amyraldian *ordo decretorum* (order of the decrees).[57] They thus differed fundamentally from Amyraldianism,[58] and even denied elements of Amyraldianism.[59] It is historically most accurate to conclude with Moore then, that, 'hypothetical universalism is best seen as a relatively independent, earlier development, distinct from Amyraldianism and 'the Saumur theology' and worthy of its own place in the history of

---

[53] Moore, *English Hypothetical Universalism*, 218; Thomas, *The Extent of the Atonement*, 189-191; A. A. Hodge, *Outlines of Theology*, 231; R. L. Dabney, *Systematic Theology* (Edinburgh: Banner of Truth, 1996 [1871]), 235-236, 519-520.

[54] Van Dixhoorn, *Minutes*, 693, 694.

[55] Van Dixhoorn, *Minutes*, 693

[56] Ussher, *The Judgement of the late Archbishop*, 30.

[57] Moore, *English Hypothetical Universalism*, 158, 161, 188. Contra Thomas, *The Extent of the Atonement*, 151.

[58] See Warfield, *The Westminster Assembly*, 144.

[59] Warfield, *The Westminster Assembly*, 139.

Christian doctrine.... If anything, its origins were neither Scottish (Cameron) nor French (Amyraut), but Irish (Ussher).[60]

Hypothetical universalism, or Calvinistic universalism, was certainly 'a highly complex phenomenon with no one definitive formulation or uniformity of explanation.'[61] But then, as we will see, the 'Calvinist' or particularist position was not defended in a uniform manner either, or with homogeneous exegetical tactics. If the reader will forgive me it would, therefore, be a calumny against Calamy to call him an Amyraldian. That is not to say he had no interest in or links to Saumur: his close friend and fellow Assembly member Samuel Bolton (whose funeral sermon Calamy was to preach)[62] translated and attached a key work by Cameron to his famous (1645) book on Christian freedom.[63] So it appears likely that Calamy was familiar with at least the broad outlines of the French doctrine. Reid says 'his reading was very extensive.'[64] Yet despite having Hugenot ancestry,[65] he himself seems to have been an English hypothetical universalist in the Davenant-Preston mould, and not a French Salmurian.

So far then we have seen that there were four points of view on the table in the Westminster debate, which was more complex

---

[60] Moore, *English Hypothetical Universalism*, 219.

[61] Moore, *English Hypothetical Universalism*, 225.

[62] E. Calamy, *The doctrine of the bodies fragility: with a divine project, discovering how to make these vile bodies of ours glorious by getting gracious souls. Represented in a sermon preached at Martins Ludgate at the funerall of that worthy and reverend minister of Jesus Christ, Dr Samuel Bolton, Master of Christ College in Cambridge, who died the 15 of Octob. 1654. and was buried the 19 day of the same month. / By that painfull and pious minister of Gods Word Mr Edmund Calamy, B.D.* (London: Printed for Joseph Moore, 1654).

[63] S. Bolton, *The true bounds of Christian freedome or a treatise wherein the rights of the law are vindicated, the liberties of grace maintained, and the severall late opinions against the law are examined and confuted. Whereunto is annexed a discourse of the learned Iohn Camerons, touching the threefold covenant of God with man, / faithfully translated, by Samuel Bolton minister of the word of God at Saviours-Southwark* (London: J.L. for Philemon Stephens, 1645), 353-401.

[64] J. Reid, *Memoirs of the Westminster Divines* (Edinburgh: Banner of Truth, 1982 [1811]), 167.

[65] Barker, *Puritan Profiles*, 208.

than some have given it credit for. First, the proposition to be debated itself most probably reflected a particularism reminiscent of William Perkins, the most influential exponent and epitome of late Elizabethan Calvinism, which was to be stoutly defended by Rutherford, Gillespie, and others. Second, given its prominence in the opening salvos of the debate, the Arminian doctrine and the controversy this had provoked up to the Synod of Dort was obviously a factor in the minds of those seeking to frame the *Confession*. Third, Calamy extolled the virtues of a third way, that of the hypothetical universalism espoused by Bishop Davenant and others at Dort. And fourth, there was also the foreign version of hypothetical universalism advocated by Amyraut, whose views were known and discussed in the floor debate at Westminster. This last position was similar to that of Calamy, but by no means identical, and provided another viewpoint in the somewhat fluid and variegated history of Reformed thought on the atonement.

2. Did God Intend to Save and/or to Secure an Offer of Conditional Salvation?

The second stage of the debate at the Westminster Assembly on particular redemption focused on the related issues of God's intent and the offer of the gospel. The proposition to be debated was narrowed part of the way through the first day's discussion: 'This proposition to be debated. That Christ did intend to Redeem the elect only.'[66] Why the proposition was changed is not stated, although on day three (24th October) Robert Harris says, 'The best way to answer an erroneous opinion is well to state the question' and this may have played some part in the thinking of those who altered the focus of the debate.[67] The new subtly different proposition placed the emphasis on God's intent, design, and purpose in sending Christ to die, a suitably 'eternal' perspective for a debate on 'God's eternal decree' of course. Yet the two perspectives (eternal and historical, divine and human) could

---

[66] Van Dixhoorn, *Minutes*, 694.

[67] Van Dixhoorn, *Minutes*, 700.

not be easily disentangled as the deputies quickly fell into a discussion of the universal offer of the gospel. Effectively, the question thereafter was did God intend to save his elect people, or to save them *and also* to offer a conditional salvation to anyone else who believes?

Calamy had said at the start that in sending Jesus to die God had a dual intent, 'absolute for the elect, conditional for the reprobate, in case they do believe'.[68] That second, conditional intent, was now examined. Calamy began by arguing from Scripture, and the debate would return several times to the exegesis of the texts he cited in favour of his position—John 3:16 and Mark 16:15 (the latter of which, we should note, is not considered to be authentic by modern critical scholarship).[69] Calamy argued that 'the world' which God is said to love in John 3:16 could not signify merely the elect 'because of that 'whosoever believes',[70] or as Richard Vines put it 'the words doe not else run well.'[71] This was an argument which 'universalists' often leaned heavily upon. William Perkins had exegeted the verse this way,[72] and later advocates of particular atonement would spend time and energy countering objections to this.[73] Indeed, after this debate, in the second edition of the so-called *Westminster Annotations*, the comments on 'love' in John 3:16 are dramatically expanded to show how 'Christ speaks not here of the common love of God where he

---

[68] Van Dixhoorn, *Minutes*, 692.

[69] B.M. Metzger, *A Textual Commentary on the Greek New Testament: Second Edition* (Stuttgart: Deutsche Bibelgesellschaft, 1994), 102-106. R. T. France, *The Gospel of Mark NIGTC* (Carlisle: Paternoster, 2002), 685-688.

[70] Van Dixhoorn, *Minutes*, 694.

[71] Van Dixhoorn, *Minutes*, 697.

[72] William Perkins, *An Exposition of the Symbole or Creed of the Apostles (1595)*, 474, 'By world, we must not understand every particular man in the world, but the Elect both among the Jewes and Gentiles.'

[73] E.g. J. Owen, *The Death of Death in the Death of Christ* in W. H. Goold (ed.), *The Works of John Owen: Volume 10* (Edinburgh: Banner of Truth, 1967 [1647]), 319-329.

wills the good of conservation to the creature... but of his special love' of the elect only.[74]

Calamy then turned to Mark 16:15-16, using it to link the universal proclamation of the gospel to universal redemption saying, 'if the covenant of grace be to be preached to all, then Christ redeemed, in some sense, all – both elect and reprobate... universal Redemption be the ground of the universal promulgation... else there is no verity in promulgation.' Stephen Marshall weighed in to the ensuing debate to reinforce the sense that for the Calvinist universalists, a key issue was 'that there can no *falsum subesse* to the offer of the gospel' that is, nothing false or deceptive behind it.[75] Ussher and the British delegation at Dort, who also cited Mark 16:15 as warrant for linking the universal offer with universal redemption,[76] were equally concerned with the 'verity' and sincerity of the offer.[77]

The exegesis of these verses was key to the remainder of the debate as recorded. It is interesting to note that although several deputies spoke up to disagree with Calamy's handling of John 3:16, they were not unanimous in their own interpretations. For instance, Gillespie questioned whether 'the world' must always in Scripture mean 'the whole world', and he could not understand how God could be said to love those he had reprobated. This was a common question well before this debate, having been discussed by Peter Lombard (c.1100-1160) and Thomas Aquinas (c. 1225-1274), for example, centuries before.[78] Calamy admitted,

---

[74] J. Downame (ed.), *Annotations Upon all the Books of the Old and New Testament* (1651). The first edition published in 1645 has, under John 3:16, only a cross-reference to 1 John 4:9 and the single word, 'mankind.' Wing lists this work, which was not an official publication of the Assembly itself and so better termed *The English Annotations*, under J. Downame, who may have been the editor or compiler.

[75] Van Dixhoorn, *Minutes*, 694, 695.

[76] *The Collegiat Suffrage*, 48-49.

[77] Ussher, *The Judgement of the late Archbishop*, 3, 24. *The Collegiat Suffrage*, 46.

[78] See P. Lombard, *The Sentences Book 3: On the Incarnation of the Word* trans. G. Silano (Toronto: Pontifical Institute of Mediaeval Studies, 2008), 134 (Distinction 32 Chapter 5) and T. Aquinas, *Summa Theologica* trans. *Fathers of the English Dominican Province, Volume 1* (New York: Benziger, 1948), 113-116 (Part 1 Question 20).

'that it signifies the elect sometimes' but he did not think it did here, and then he proceeded to make a distinction between God's special love for the elect and his general love for the reprobate.[79]

Lightfoot found a third way, saying 'I understand the word 'world' in a middle sense. It is only in opposition to the nation of the Jews.'[80] As Harris put it later, 'By 'world' there is meant the world of gentiles as appears in the whole chapter.' The next day, Rutherford made a case that 'love' in John 3:16 must be speaking of 'the special, particular love of God commensurable with election', since parallel passages spoke of such a love (e.g. John 15:13). He concluded from his study of 'love' in Scripture that there was 'not one scripture in all the New Testament where it can be expounded for the general.' Indeed, he adduced several texts (Ephesians 5:21, Galatians 2:20, Romans 5:8) which spoke of a 'restricted special love.'[81]

Regarding Mark 16, there was even more variety in the responses to Calamy. Gillespie stated that the command to believe there 'doth not hold out God's intentions' (note that key word 'intentions'), in the same way that his command to Abraham to sacrifice Isaac was also not a measure of what he intended to actually take place. Thus he utilised the distinction between God's will of decree and his will of command (or as he put it *voluntas/ voluntis decreti & mandati*).[82] Whatever the reason for them, he said, the 'general offers of the gospel are not grounded upon the secret decree' which was, after all, the subject of that part of the *Confession* under discussion.[83] Lightfoot saw another reason for a general offer to be made to the reprobate: 'For the universal offer, God intends as the salvation of the elect, so the inexcusableness of the wicked.' Mr Price questioned the logic of using Mark 16 at all declaring, 'it doth not follow that Christ did die intentionally for

---

[79] Van Dixhoorn, *Minutes*, 696.

[80] Van Dixhoorn, *Minutes*, 696.

[81] Van Dixhoorn, *Minutes*, 699.

[82] Van Dixhoorn, *Minutes*, 695.

[83] Van Dixhoorn, *Minutes*, 696.

the redemption of all.' And besides, 'to a congregation of Reprobates the reason of the promiscuous offer is because we do not know who is elect and reprobate.'[84]

Mr Harris summed up his concerns about the universalists' handling of the conditional language of Mark 16 and John 3 saying, 'I doubt whether there be any such thing at all as conditional decree.'[85] He was, like Reynolds on the first day, also puzzled by the idea of a condition being set in God's decree which the reprobate could not perform anyway and 'God never intends to give them'.[86] Assembly member Thomas Hill rejected hypothetical universalism just a short time later on the grounds that when we 'speak of any thing as to Salvation, there is a commensuration betwixt the three persons in the Trinity, and their workings.'[87] Perhaps all of these reasons or some combination of them would have been held by Calamy's other opponents in this debate. It certainly seems that there was a diverse and wide-ranging response on this point, but whether the concerns of Calamy, Vines, and others would be ignored completely in the final text of the *Confession* is something we must look at more closely in the next chapter.

Conclusion: Acknowledging Diversity

To summarise then, Reformed theology as presented by the Westminster divines was far from monochrome. There was consensus that questions about the limitations of the atonement were important and needed addressing, but there were at least a handful of recognisably different opinions. The exegetical arguments about intentionality and the offer of the gospel reveal

---

[84] Van Dixhoorn, *Minutes*, 697.

[85] Van Dixhoorn, *Minutes*, 701.

[86] Van Dixhoorn, *Minutes*, 692.

[87] Thomas Hill, *The Spring of Strengthening Grace* (London, 1648), 5. Cf. Van Dixhoorn, *Confessing*, 156 note 1. On the 'discordant Trinity' response to hypothetical universalism (employed by Gottschalk, Bavinck, Helm, and others), see Gatiss, *For Us and For our Salvation*, 12-13.

that there were also a variety of approaches to defending the more mainstream Reformed position against the minority position of the Calvinist hypothetical universalists in Britain. It appears then that there was a certain degree of flux in the debate at this formative stage of the seventeenth century and a diversity of recognisably Reformed views that were considered within the pale of orthodoxy. Reformation and post-Reformation theology is often distorted by modern arguments and slogans; and here especially, as John Fesko puts it, 'fine nuances that were once carefully argued are lost with the ham-fisted separation between five-point and four-point Calvinism.'[88] At the Westminster Assembly, however, on this as on other points, there were clearly some 'shades of opinion within a generic Calvinism.'[89]

---

[88] J. V. Fesko, *The Theology of the Westminster Standards: Historical Context and Theological Insights* (Wheaton, IL.: Crossway, 2014), 189.

[89] See Barker, *Puritan Profiles*, 176 for this phrase.

A Deceptive Clarity?
Particular Redemption in the
Westminster Standards

This chapter is a modified and expanded version of an article first published in Reformed Theological Review 69.3 (December 2010), 180-196.

In the previous chapter, I examined the deliberations of the Westminster Assembly concerning particular redemption, or as it is sometimes known, limited atonement.[1] We noted there the considerable debate amongst the divines on this controversial subject, with at least four different positions being considered by the delegates: Dutch Arminianism, French Amyraldianism, Calvinist hypothetical universalism with a British pedigree, and the more widespread and international mainstream Reformed consensus. Amongst the delegates there were clearly 'shades of opinion within a generic Calvinism.'[2] Yet there remains considerable debate amongst theologians and historians as to whether the finally approved text of the *Westminster Confession* leaves room for the hypothetical universalism espoused by some

---

[1] On the debates over what to call this doctrine, see my *For Us and For Our Salvation*, 14-16.

[2] See W. Barker, *Puritan Profiles*, 176.

prominent divines or not. Was there an intentional lack of precision in the approved text, a deceptive clarity which smoothed over the controverted points for the sake of tolerating some (albeit circumscribed) diversity?

Some seem to simply assert that the *Confession* has always been thought consistently particularistic and therefore it cannot possibly have left any room for the 'universalism' of people such as Calamy.[3] This debate has often taken place against the backdrop of calls for confessional revision in the Presbyterian churches, for whom the *Confession* acts as a subordinate doctrinal standard, and so a certain amount of background tension must often be assumed. We should also recognise that the historical debate has been conducted in a context where this doctrine has been the subject of particularly heated debate. John Macleod Campbell, for example, was tried for denying particularist doctrine in the Church of Scotland of the nineteenth century,[4] and he spearheaded opposition to limited atonement from *within* the Reformed camp.[5] Definite or limited atonement continues to be 'one of the most controversial teachings in Reformed soteriology'[6] rejected by neo-orthodox Barthians,[7] as well as many within the

---

[3] This seems to be the rather doctrinaire and ahistorical foundation of Sebastian Rehnman's 'A Particular Defence of Particularism' in *Journal of Reformed Theology* 6 (2012), 24-34 responding to Jonathan D. Moore, 'The Extent of the Atonement: English Hypothetical Universalism versus Particular Redemption' in Mark Jones and Michael Haykin (eds.), *Drawn into Controversie: Reformed Theological Diversity and Debates within Seventeenth-Century British Puritanism* (Gottingen: Vandenhoeck & Ruprecht, 2011), 124-161.

[4] G. M. Tuttle, *So Rich a Soil: John McLeod Campbell on Christian Atonement* (Edinburgh: Handsel Press, 1986).

[5] R. A. Blacketer, 'Definite Atonement in Historical Perspective', 305. J. McLeod Campbell, *The Nature of the Atonement and its Relation to Remission of Sins and Eternal Life third edition* (London: Macmillian, 1869 [1856]).

[6] R. A. Blacketer, 'Definite Atonement in Historical Perspective', 304.

[7] J. B. Torrance, 'The Incarnation and Limited Atonement' in *Scottish Bulletin of Evangelical Theology* 2 (1984).

Anglican Reformed tradition who follow David Broughton Knox and J. C. Ryle.[8]

Generally speaking there have been two sides to the debate over the Westminster Standards on this point. First, it has been argued or assumed by many that limited atonement clearly won the day.[9] Those in sympathy with the tradition of Turretin and the Helvetic Consensus such as Warfield, Cunningham, and A.A. Hodge supported this view with the aim of resisting what they saw as latitudinarian tendencies in their own day.[10] Their view was that hypothetical universalism, Amyraldianism, or 'post-redemptionism' is clearly ruled out by the *Confession*.[11] John Murray claims that the Minutes of the Assembly do not support the contention that an 'Amyraldian' doctrine is allowed.[12] Yet, *pace* Murray, the Minutes of the debate on their own neither support nor contradict such a contention. Neither, contra Warfield, can we say with confidence where 'the weight of the debate' lay because although what we have is 'the most fully reported of all the debates on this chapter',[13] we do not have a comprehensive record of each divine's contribution, and hardly any detail at all of what was said in the chamber October 24th-31st.[14] Still less can we

---

[8] See T. Payne (ed.), *D. Broughton Knox, Selected Works, Volume 1: The Doctrine of God* (Kingsford NSW: Matthias Media, 2000), 260-266 and J. C. Ryle, *Expository Thoughts on John: Volume 1* (Edinburgh: Banner of Truth, 1987 [1869]), 61-62.

[9] R. T. Kendall, *Calvin and English Calvinism to 1649* (Carlisle: Paternoster, 1997 [1979]), 184 n.2.

[10] On which see W. G. T. Shedd, *Calvinism: Pure and Mixed: A Defence of the Westminster Standards* (Edinburgh: Banner of Truth, 1986 [1893]), vii-xi.

[11] B.B. Warfield, *The Westminster Assembly and Its Work*, 142; *Calvin and Calvinism* (Grand Rapids: Baker, 2003 [1932]), 364. W. Cunningham, *Historical Theology: A review of the principal doctrinal discussions in the Christian church since the apostolic age, Volume 2* (Edinburgh: Banner of Truth, 1960 [1862]), 326-336. A. A. Hodge, *The Confession of Faith: A Handbook of Christian Doctrine Expounding the Westminster Confession* (London: Banner of Truth, 1961 [1869]), 73.

[12] J. Murray, *Collected Writings of John Murray Volume 4: Studies in Theology* (Edinburgh: Banner of Truth, 1982), 256.

[13] Warfield, *The Westminster Assembly*, 142, 138.

[14] Warfield, *The Westminster Assembly*, 142. See Van Dixhoorn, *Minutes*, 701-702.

deduce what must have happened in the framing of the *Westminster Confession* from some supposed law of historical inevitability, that there is 'increased precision in particularism' and lack of ambiguity as new creeds are formed in church history.[15]

Just to be clear, I myself am neither a Presbyterian nor a hypothetical universalist. Yet the Minutes of the debate do, however, alert us to the historical possibility at least that the learned and eloquent hypothetical universalists at Westminster may have been able to exert an influence on the finally adopted text. They may have worked to enable it to be interpreted in a manner not incompatible with their own position. Mitchell was certainly aware of the debate raging over confessional subscription when he and Struthers edited their edition of the Assembly's Minutes.[16] His cautious conclusion is that it was not impossible that the 'more liberal views' of Calamy and others were to an extent tolerated in the final text.[17] Charles Augustus Briggs, on the other hand, simply asserted without demonstration that, 'The *Westminster Confession*... did not decide any of these mooted questions... There is nothing here to which a New School Calvinist need object. It does not enter into the question in dispute... A statement to which these divines [Calamy et al.] agreed, made in view of such expressions of opinion, could not rule out these opinions... The chief English divines were in thorough sympathy with the School of Saumur. Therefore the *Westminster Confession* cannot be quoted against the so-called New School of Theology.'[18]

So let us now examine key parts of the *Confession* which have been cited in this interpretative quarrel to see how they may have been understood by advocates of the different views expressed at

---

[15] The very tendentious Whiggish argument of Rehnman, 'A Particular Defence of Particularism', 31-32.

[16] Mitchell & Struthers, xiii.

[17] Mitchell & Struthers, xx, lv-lxi.

[18] C. A. Briggs, *Theological Symbolics* (Edinburgh: T&T Clark, 1914), 374, 377, 378, 379. See also C. A. Briggs (ed.), *How shall we revise the Westminster Confession of Faith?: A bundle of papers.* (New York: Charles Scribner's Sons, 1890), 22.

the Assembly itself. We will discover that from a distance there is a deceptive clarity on the subject in the actual text, which hides a certain underlying ambivalence. While modern hypothetical universalists may find the *Confession* unpalatable, contemporary Calvinists who took this dissenting view may not have been quite so uncomfortable.

'Of God's Eternal Decree'

We begin, naturally, with WCF 3.6 which was the text under discussion in October 1645.[19] After asserting the redemption of the elect by Christ, the final clause reads, 'Neither are any other redeemed by Christ, effectually called, justified, adopted, sanctified, and saved, but the elect only.' In my view, Mitchell is probably most correct when he writes:

> Those who in modern times have pronounced most confidently that the more restricted view is exclusively intended, seem to me to have unconsciously construed or interpreted the words, 'neither are any other redeemed by Christ, effectually called, justified, adopted, sanctified, *and* saved, but the elect only,' as if they had run, 'neither are any other redeemed by Christ, or effectually called, or justified, adopted, sanctified, and saved, but the elect only.' But these two statements do not necessarily bear the same meaning. Calamy, Arrowsmith, and the others who agreed with them, may have felt

---

19 The text of WCF 3.6 reads: 'As God hath appointed the Elect unto glory; so hath he, by the eternal and most free purpose of his Will, fore-ordained all the means thereunto. Wherefore they who are elected, being fallen in Adam, are redeemed by Christ, are effectually called unto faith in Christ, by his Spirit working in due season, are justified, adopted, sanctified, and kept by his power through faith, unto salvation. Neither are any other redeemed by Christ, effectually called, justified, adopted, sanctified and saved; but the Elect only.' The *Confession of Faith*, and the *Larger Catechism* are both quoted throughout this article from the facsimile of the original 1648 edition published as *The Westminster Standards: An Original Facsimile* (Audubon, NJ: Old Paths Publications, 1997). With regards to WCF 3.6 I also had the privilege of examining (in August 2008) the original handwritten autograph held at Westminster College, Cambridge.

justified in accepting the former, though they might have scrupled to accept the latter.[20]

He is correct about the restrictive reading of the sentence since A. A. Hodge gives precisely that 'or... or... or' reading in his commentary on the *Confession*.[21] Later, he glosses it as 'Neither are any other redeemed by Christ...but the elect only', passing over a crucial part of the sentence.[22] At this point the *Confession* itself says, however, that only the elect are redeemed, called, justified, and saved. The hypothetical universalists would have been happy to agree with this concatenation since they believed the terms following 'redeemed by Christ' were part of the application of redemption, not the achievement of the atonement or the purchase of redemption itself.[23] They restricted the application of redemption to the elect as much as the particularists, and would be perfectly happy to affirm, with WCF 10.1 that effectual calling, for instance, is restricted to the elect.[24]

This can be seen in the debate: Rutherford countered Calamy's position by saying 'I deny this connexion because it holds as well in election and Justification as in redemption: if he believe he is as well elected and justified as redeemed.' Calamy replied, 'We do not speak of the application, for then it would bring it in' but Rutherford came back and said 'There is no difference betwixt redemption and justification in this[25] that is, redemption accomplished and redemption applied. If the *Confession* had said, 'neither are any other redeemed by Christ but the elect only' the evidence of this exchange suggests that Calamy would have disagreed. The final text, however, rolls redemption and application together and

---

[20] Mitchell & Struthers, lvii.

[21] A.A. Hodge, *The Confession of Faith*, 74.

[22] A.A. Hodge, *The Confession of Faith*, 154.

[23] Fesko, *The Theology of the Westminster Standards*, 201 agrees that WCF 3.6 'does not present a challenge to the hypothetical universalists.'

[24] The text of WCF 10.1 reads: 'All those whom God hath predestinated unto life, and those only, he is pleased in his appointed and accepted time, effectually to call...'

[25] Van Dixhoorn, *Minutes*, 695.

applies both to the elect only, which Calamy was not denying. Thus the *Confession* could be understood here to be asserting no more than when the Canons of Dort declare it was God's will that Christ should 'effectually redeem out of every people, tribe, nation, and language, all them, and them only, who from eternity were elected unto salvation.'[26]

There is a question over this interpretation. Cunningham avers that reading the list of terms in WCF 3.6 as if it was being asserted 'merely that the whole of them, taken in conjunction, cannot be predicated of any others' is 'a mere truism, serving no purpose.' This final sentence of WCF 3.6 'was manifestly intended to be peculiarly emphatic, and to contain a denial of an error reckoned important.' So, 'the *Confession*, therefore, must be regarded as teaching, that it is not true of any but the elect only, that they are redeemed by Christ, any more than it is true that any others are called, justified, or saved.'[27] This seems to me to strain the plain reading of the sentence's grammar, and to be a case of special pleading. Moreover, if the sentence were truly designed to be 'peculiarly emphatic' as a denial of hypothetical universalism then in the context of the debate on the floor of the Assembly it certainly could have been made much clearer.[28]

Looking at the proof texts which the Assembly attached to this sentence does not lend credence to the more restrictive view. It is important to remember that these verses (attached to the *Confession* at the request of Parliament on 20th January 1646)[29] refer not just to the Bible texts but were intended to also send users of the *Confession* back to the standard exegetical treatments of those texts. The first proof for this important sentence in WCF 3.6 is John 17:9. The 1645 *Westminster Annotations* on John 17:9, written by John Ley, had commented that Jesus interceded 'Not

---

26 *The Judgement Of The SYNODE Holden at DORT* (London: John Bill, 1619), 24 (Article 8).

27 Cunningham, *Historical Theology: Volume 2*, 328.

28 Contra Warfield, *The Westminster Assembly*, 143.

29 Mitchell & Struthers, 323.

for reprobates.'[30] This verse was alluded to in the debate by Henry Wilkinson who said 'You know they cannot be partakers of Redemption against whom Christ takes special exception. Christ prayed not for the world.'[31] He may have meant this as an argument against Calamy, but hypothetical universalists following Ussher said that it simply did not follow that 'He prayed not for the world, Therefore, He payed not for the world.'[32] They made the intercession of Christ a part of the application of redemption,[33] which was a different matter. So there is nothing here for someone like Calamy to take exception to, on their own terms. Romans 8:18-39 is again arguably about the application of predestination and cited to demonstrate the inevitability of the elect's perseverance, and does not help to decide the issue regarding our sentence's intended interpretation one way or the other.

John 6:64-65 is cited as a proof for effectual call, which is mentioned after redemption; again, for someone like Calamy this would be part of redemption applied rather than redemption accomplished. John 10:26 and the similar John 8:47 both 'prove' that only the elect of God will hear and believe in God's word, but they do not address the issue of whether Christ died for the non-elect who will not believe. 1 John 2:19 concerns the perseverance of those who are 'of us', no doubt understood here as the elect. It is not denied that the elect are redeemed: the previous sentence in WCF 3.6 asserts as much, and the proofs there (1 Thessalonians 5:9-10 and Titus 2:14) would seem to be adequate to make that point. But it is clear that the proofs do not imply the restrictive or 'non-collective' meaning for the final sentence of WCF 3.6 and would in fact be compatible with a contemporary hypothetical

---

[30] J. Downame (ed.), *Annotations Upon all the Books of the Old and New Testament (1645)* on John 17:9. For more on these annotations, see R. Muller & R. Ward, *Scripture and Worship: Biblical Interpretation and the Directory for Public Worship* (Phillipsburg: P&R, 2007), 4-11.

[31] Van Dixhoorn, *Minutes*, 695.

[32] Ussher, *The Judgement of the late Archbishop*, 13.

[33] Ussher, *The Judgement of the late Archbishop*, 13-14.

universalist reading of it. Whether such a reading of those Scriptures is legitimate is, of course, a different issue.

Chad Van Dixhoorn asserts that 'Paragraphs 6 and 7, when read together, clarify that even subtle forms of seventeenth-century hypothetical universalism are excluded in chapter 3 considered as a whole.'[34] Yet I am not convinced that the assertions in WCF 3.6 or 3.7, even when read together (which naturally they ought to be) in any way negate the hypothetical universalist position as held by someone such as Calamy or Davenant. They did not deny that God 'passed by' the non-elect and ordained them 'to dishonour and wrath for their sin' (WCF 3.7). What they denied is that God sent Jesus to die without *any* reference to them. The British delegation's submission to the Synod of Dort, for example, had made it clear that although they thought there was a certain conditional intent in the atonement, 'the decree of Election is definite, not conditional.'[35] They indeed affirmed that God freely predestines some to damnation for their sin, just as WCF 3.7 does.[36]

So the precise way that this part of the *Confession* is phrased could be asserted by both Calvinist hypothetical universalists and the more mainstream Reformed particularists. It does not appear definitively to take sides on the questions at issue between them.

'Of Christ the Mediator'

The issue of particular redemption surfaces again in chapter 8 of the *Confession*, and in *Larger Catechism* Q. 59. WCF 8.5 asserts that the Lord Jesus 'purchased, not only reconciliation, but an everlasting inheritance in the Kingdom of Heaven, for all those

---

[34] Chad Van Dixhoorn, *Confessing the Faith: A Reader's Guide to the Westminster Confession of Faith* (Edinburgh: Banner of Truth, 2014), 56 note 1.

[35] Milton, *British Delegation*, 229.

[36] Milton, *British Delegation*, 238-243.

whom the Father hath given unto him.'[37] Section viii goes on to
say that, 'To all those for whom Christ hath purchased
Redemption, he doth certainly, and effectually apply, and
communicate the same.'[38] This is often cited as attempting to link
redemption accomplished with redemption applied in such a way
as to make them coterminous — *everyone* for whom Christ died,
everyone for whom he has purchased redemption, has redemption
applied to them. As Murray says, commenting on WCF 8.8,
'impetration and application are coextensive... This excludes any
form of universal atonement.'[39] It does, on the face of it, do just
that. Yet, again, we find that seventeenth-century 'Calvinist
universalists', such as Ussher, were happy to affirm this same truth,
by making some fine distinctions. Ussher wrote that,

> *Impetration...* I hold to be a fruit, not of his
> Satisfaction, but Intercession... it is a great folly to
> imagine that he hath impetrated *Reconciliation* and
> Remission of sins for that world [for which he
> prayed not, John 17:9]. I agree therefore... That
> *application* and *impetration*, in this latter we have in
> hand, are *of equal extent*; and, That forgiveness of sins
> is not by our Saviour impetrated for any unto whom
> the merit of his death is not *applied* in particular.[40]

Richard Baxter, another seventeenth-century hypothetical
universalist (convinced by reading Prolocutor Twisse, he

---

[37] The full text reads: 'The Lord Jesus, by his perfect obedience, and sacrifice of himself,
which he, through the eternal Spirit, once offered up unto God, hath fully satisfied the
Justice of his Father; and purchased, not only reconciliation, but an everlasting
inheritance in the Kingdom of Heaven, for all those whom the Father hath given unto
him.'

[38] The full text reads: 'To all those for whom Christ hath purchased Redemption, he
doth certainly, and effectually apply, and communicate the same, making intercession
for them, and revealing unto them, in, and by the Word, the mysteries of salvation,
effectually persuading them by his Spirit to believe, and obey, and governing their
hearts by his Word and Spirit, overcoming all their enemies by his Almighty Power
and Wisdom, in such manner, and ways, as are most consonant to his wonderful and
unsearchable dispensation.'

[39] Murray, *Collected Writings of John Murray Volume 4*, 256.

[40] Ussher, *The Judgement of the late Archbishop*, 19-20.

claimed),[41] would hold something similar a few years later.[42] If Baxter is right about John Ball's universalism,[43] then we should also note that Ball too affirmed coextensive impetation (the obtaining of salvation by Christ) and application, writing of 'the acquisition of righteousness by the death of Christ' that 'for whomsoever it is acquired, to them it is applied.'[44] Ussher could hold to this coextensive purchase and application idea only by separating two aspects of Christ's high priestly work – his satisfaction (for all) from his intercession (for the elect), and speaking of the latter alone as impetation.

WCF 8.8 makes reference to Christ's intercession, citing Romans 8:34 in support, as well as 1 John 2:1-2 which was the very text used by the Remonstrants in support of their version of universal atonement.[45] Here, Christ's intercession for his people is certainly one aspect of redemption applied, not purchased/impetrated to use the usual distinction. This makes it difficult for the hypothetical universalist like Ussher who identifies impetation with intercession to agree with WCF 8.8 in its more natural and usual sense. It may not have been the way they would have preferred to phrase things, but it was possible to harmonise such a statement with their universalism (albeit, perhaps, with some intricate mental gymnastics).

---

[41] R. Baxter, *Certain Disputations*, Preface. I am not convinced that Twisse and Baxter are at exactly one on the subject, but my point here is that Baxter thought they were. Twisse's thoughts can be found in his *The Doctrine of the Synod of Dort and Arles* (1631), 16, where he says that Christ was sent and intended 'to make a propitiation for the sinnes of the whole world, so farre as thereby to procure both pardon of sinne and salvation of soule to all that doe believe,' but also that 'he dyed not for all, that is, he dyed not to obtaine the grace of faith and repentance for all, but only for God's elect.'

[42] Mitchell & Struthers, lviii.

[43] Baxter, *Certain Disputations*, Preface. See the discussion in H. Boersma, *A Hot Pepper Corn*, 206-209.

[44] See J. Ball, *Treatise of the Covenant of Grace* (London: G. Miller for Edward Brewster, 1645), 255.

[45] P. Schaff, *The Creeds of Christendom volume 3: The Evangelical Protestant Creeds* (Grand Rapids: Baker, 1996 [1876]), 546.

The proofs on the first sentence of WCF 8.8 are John 6:37, 39 and 10:15-16: Christ lays down his life for the sheep, who subsequently hear his voice, come to him, and are raised up. To my mind the most natural explanation of those verses in their contexts and this section of the *Confession* is in accord with particular redemption. But it is not completely clear that a *sophisticated* Calvinist hypothetical universalist would not also be able to affirm the truths enshrined here; some in the seventeenth century itself clearly did, even if their interpretation was, as Warfield puts it, 'more subtle than satisfactory.'[46] Perhaps the fluctuations of Assembly life and politics enabled the particularists to have their way more on some days and on some sections of the *Confession* than on others. It was, after all, a human assembly, and should not be endued with divine attributes such as perfect coherence and consistency.

'Of God's Covenant with Man'

Finally, it is instructive to note that the hotly disputed texts in the Assembly's debate on God's Eternal Decree are both cited later as proofs for WCF 7.3 on the covenant of grace:

> Man, by his Fall, having made himself incapable of Life by that Covenant, the Lord was pleased to make a Second[e], commonly called the Covenant of Grace; Wherein he freely offereth unto sinners Life and Salvation by Jesus Christ; requiring of them Faith in Him, that they may be saved[f], and promising to give unto all those that are ordained unto Life, his holy Spirit, to make them willing, and able to believe.[g]

John 3:16 and Mark 16:15-16 are both cited with regard to the offer of salvation to sinners at note *f* (after the word 'saved') along with Romans 10:6, 9 and Galatians 3:11. Hanko asserts that in this clause 'the idea of the offer as used by the school of Amyraut and as promoted by the Davenant men was not intended by the

---

[46] Warfield, *The Westminster Assembly*, 144.

Westminster divines,'[47] but he does not note the explicit use here of the proof texts so beloved of 'the Davenant men'. English hypothetical universalists and their more particular brethren could agree, of course, that whoever believes is saved. They both affirmed that the gospel could be presented as *if thou shalt confess with thy mouth the Lord Jesus, and shalt believe in thine heart that God hath raised him from the dead, thou shalt be saved* (Romans 10:9).[48]

The particularists would have wanted to add the final clause about God granting the elect the ability to believe.[49] Calamy and others would have been delighted to ensure mention of both effectual salvation and a general gospel offer, 'the truth they were mainly anxious to conserve.'[50] Moreover, when debating WCF 3.6 Marshall had insisted, in response to Gillespie's argument that man is bound to believe, that 'there is not only a *mandatum* [mandate or commission] but a promise.'[51] This too (despite Warfield's put down)[52] is explicitly enshrined in WCF 7.3 with the language of both 'requiring' and 'promising'. Delicate distinctions have been made, and this point of debate (which is about the covenant, as Burgess pointed out to Marshall) has been rightly addressed not in the text of WCF 3.6 on God's eternal decree, but in WCF 7.3 on the covenant where it more properly belongs.

Schaff is incorrect to say that WCF 7.3 'is in substance the theory of the school of Saumur.'[53] Chapter 7 of the *Confession*, for

---

[47] H.C. Hanko, *The History of the Free Offer*, chapter 5.

[48] The Bible is quoted throughout this chapter from the Authorized Version (KJV), since that was the version in most common use at the time of the Assembly. The translators of that version had, incidentally, also used the Jerusalem Chamber of Westminster Abbey, the venue for the Westminster Assembly's debate on this issue.

[49] *Larger Catechism* Q. 59 (15).

[50] Mitchell & Struthers, lviii.

[51] Van Dixhoorn, *Minutes*, 696.

[52] Warfield, *The Westminster Assembly*, 142.

[53] P. Schaff, *The Creeds of Christendom volume 1: The History of Creeds* (Grand Rapids: Baker, 1996 [1876]), 773.

instance, presents a standard Reformed bi-covenantal approach to Scripture (covenant of works, covenant of grace) whereas Saumur was famous for Cameron's unique threefold covenant view.[54] This gained both circulation and currency in England when Assembly member Samuel Bolton attached 'Certain Theses or Positions of the Learned John Cameron, Concerning the three-fold Covenant of God with Man' to his work on Christian freedom, published in 1645.[55] In addition, Amyraut taught 'that man has the natural ability so that he can respond to the offer of grace but that he will not inasmuch as he is morally corrupt.'[56] So it is at least debatable whether he could have affirmed the final clause of WCF 7.3 (or *Larger Catechism* Q. 67) with its insistence on spiritual assistance being necessary to make us both willing and able to believe.

There is no room for a conditional decree in WCF 2.2 (which states that nothing is contingent to God) or indeed in chapter 3. So WCF 7.3 is highly unlikely to be a 'compromise between conditional universalism taught in the first clause, and particular election taught in the second' as some have claimed.[57] Rather it is an affirmation of both particular election and universal offer in their proper places and relations. Chapter 3 was the place to confess truths about election and divine intentionality; Chapter 7 was the place to confess the complementary truth of the gospel offer and to mention the promise of the Spirit who applies

---

[54] G.M. Thomas, *The Extent of the Atonement: A Dilemma for Reformed Theology from Calvin to the Consensus* (Carlisle: Paternoster, 1997), 167-171. J. Cameron, *De Triplici Dei cum Homine Foedere* (Heidelberg, 1608). Amyraut held to essentially the same threefold view as Cameron, publishing his own *Theses Theologicae de Tribus Foederibus Divinis* in 1664.

[55] S. Bolton, *The true bounds of Christian freedome or a treatise wherein the rights of the law are vindicated, the liberties of grace maintained, and the severall late opinions against the law are examined and confuted. Whereunto is annexed a discourse of the learned Iohn Camerons, touching the threefold covenant of God with man, faithfully translated, by Samuel Bolton minister of the word of God at Saviours-Southwark* (London: J.L. for Philemon Stephens, 1645), 353-401.

[56] B. G. Armstrong, *Calvinism and the Amyraut Heresy: Protestant Scholasticism and Humanism in Seventeenth Century France* (Madison: University of Wisconsin Press, 1969), 94. Schaff, *The Creeds of Christendom volume 1*, 481.

[57] Schaff, *The Creeds of Christendom volume 1*, 772-773.

election through faith. One has reference to God's eternal perspective, the other to his temporal dealings with humanity. 'These [two] classes of truths, when drawn face to face,' says Dabney, 'often seem paradoxical,' but 'there is no real collision' since 'God's sovereignty is no revealed rule for our action.'[58]

'Of the Lord's Supper'

Chapter 29 of the *Confession* states that the Lord's Supper is a 'Commemoration of that one offering up of himself, by himself, upon the Cross, once for all: and, a spiritual Oblation of all possible praise unto God, for the same: So that, the Popish Sacrifice of the Mass (as they call it) is most abominably injurious to Christ's one, only Sacrifice, the alone Propitiation for all the sins of his elect' (WCF 29.2). It is certainly in complete harmony with definite atonement to say that the cross is the only propitiation for the sins of the elect (the context being a desire to rule out any other propitiatory sacrifice), and that it is the propitiation for all their sins (not just some). This was probably the intention behind Article 31 of the Church of England also, which is closely parallel to WCF 29 (but lacks the tighter focus on 'his elect').[59]

We should certainly note, however, that the *Confession* does not say the cross is the propitiation for the sins of the elect *only*. In that sense, hypothetical universalists of various kinds would potentially be able to affirm this statement, though they may not have chosen to phrase it in precisely this way. They may also

---

[58] R.L. Dabney, *Systematic Theology* (Edinburgh: Banner of Truth, 1996 [1871]), 527.

[59] The Article states, 'The Offering of Christ once made in that perfect redemption, propitiation, and satisfaction, for all the sins of the whole world, both original and actual; and there is none other satisfaction for sin, but that alone. Wherefore the sacrifices of Masses, in the which it was commonly said, that the Priest did offer Christ for the quick and the dead, to have remission of pain or guilt, were blasphemous fables, and dangerous deceits.' It should be noted that this is an affirmation of the sufficiency of the cross against a Roman Catholic view of the Lord's Supper, so the first half of the Article cannot be twisted to claim that the Articles teach hypothetical universalism. See my *For Us and For Our Salvation*, 99-111 on definite atonement in the Anglican formularies.

quibble that the final clause does not accurately reflect 1 John 2:2 since it puts 'elect' where 1 John has 'whole world.' Yet suggestively the *Confession* does not at this point cite 1 John 2:2 as its proof at all, preferring Hebrews 10:14 where the cross is said to have perfected 'them that are sanctified.' The other proofs at this point (Hebrews 10:11, 12, 18) focus on the unrepeatable nature of Christ's sacrifice, which is what is meant by saying his offering was made 'once for all' (i.e. once-and-for-all). This section of chapter 29 is not, therefore, a compromise attempting to say that the atonement was 'for all' and also for the elect, nor is it a contradiction of WCF 3.6 (as some alleged in the seventeenth century).[60]

'Are the Elect Only Effectually Called?'

One last word should be spared for the *Larger Catechism* debate of May 1647. Mitchell avers that, 'when the *Larger Catechism* was being prepared, another effort was made by the representatives of the Davenant school to get their opinions distinctly sanctioned and positively expressed in that formulary.'[61] The committee suggested:

> Q. What common favours redound from Christ to all mankind?
>
> A. Besides much forbearance and many supplies for this life, which all mankind receive from Christ as Lord of all, they by him are made capable of having salvation tendered to them by the gospel, and are under such dispensations of Providence and operations of the Spirit as lead to repentance.[62]

---

[60] See John Owen's letter to Peter Du Moulin on the equivalent clause in the Savoy Confession (XXX.ii) in P. Toon (ed.), *The Correspondence of John Owen (1616-1683) with an account of his life and work* (Cambridge: James Clarke and Co., 1970), 165-166.

[61] Mitchell & Struthers, lix.

[62] Mitchell & Struthers, 369.

'Capable of having salvation tendered to them' sounds like the language Calamy used at the start of the WCF 3.6 debate when he said Christ 'did pay a price for all... that all men should be *salvabiles* [saveable]... Christ in giving himself did intend to put all men in a state of salvation in case they do believe.' Lazarus Seaman used similar language when he affirmed that, 'All in the first Adam were made liable to damnation, so all are liable to salvation in the second Adam.'[63] The Assembly seemed unhappy with this, and the question was recommitted and 'the Commissioners from the Church of Scotland are desired to be present.'[64] The influence and skill of the Scots Rutherford and Gillespie was no doubt required by the particularists in the committee room against these ideas.[65] A compromise was attempted whereby it was said 'the gospel where it cometh doth tender salvation by Christ to all',[66] but the final text of *Larger Catechism* Q.68 speaks only of the elect and others who are 'outwardly called.'[67] The 'Davenant men' failed to get their opinions distinctly sanctioned here; but they did, it seems, force the Assembly to express itself carefully and in such a way that they could assent to.

Conclusions: The Limits of Diversity

Michael Dewar insists that 'it cannot be urged that the 'Dordracenists' and the Westminster Fathers were other than

---

[63] Van Dixhoorn, *Minutes*, 692, 694.

[64] Mitchell & Struthers, 369.

[65] Rutherford later argued at length against Davenant's view in his book *The Covenant of Life Opened* (1654), 181-192.

[66] Mitchell & Struthers, 393.

[67] The full text reads: 'Q. Are the Elect onely effectually called? A. All the Elect, and they only, are effectually called; although others may be, and often are, outwardly called by the ministery of the Word, and have some common opperations of the Spirit, who, for their wilfull neglect and contempt of the grace offerd to them, being justly left in their unbelief, doe never truly come to Jesus Christ.'

polemical in their intentions, and divisive in their results.'[68] With regard to Arminianism and Roman Catholicism that may well be true—their views were ruled offside. Yet in relation to Calvinist hypothetical universalism of the British variety, the picture does not appear to me to be quite so stark. Commenting on chapter 8 of the *Confession*, Richard Baxter is emphatic that it is not against his universalist view (which he grandiosely claims was that of 'half the Divines in England'), and goes on to say, 'I have spoken with an eminent Divine, yet living, that was of the Assembly, who assured me that they purposely avoided determining that Controversy, and some of them professed themselves for the middle way of Universal Redemption.'[69]

This harmonises with the view of Richard Muller who claims that the *Westminster Confession* was designed to be inclusive of those hypothetical universalist views which were 'consciously framed to stand within the confessionalism of the Canons of Dort.'[70] As Muller says, 'The *Westminster Confession* was in fact written with this diversity in view, encompassing confessionally the variant Reformed views on the nature of the limitation of Christ's satisfaction to the elect, just as it was written to be inclusive of the infra- and the supralapsarian views on predestination.'[71]

Troxel is technically correct to say that 'the *Westminster Confession of Faith* does not teach or endorse the Hypothetical Universalism of Moyse Amyraut.'[72] Yet there were a number of 'middle ways', not all of which were, as we have seen, so obviously

---

[68] M.Dewar, 'The Synods of Dort, the Westminster Assembly and the French Reformed Church 1618-1643' in *Churchman* 104.1 (1990), 38.

[69] Baxter, *Certain Disputations*, Preface.

[70] R.A. Muller, 'John Cameron and Covenant Theology' in *Mid-America Journal of Theology 17* (2006), 36-37.

[71] R.A. Muller, *Post-Reformation Reformed Dogmatics Volume 1* (Grand Rapids: Baker, 2003), 76-77. David L. Allen, *The Extent of the Atonement: A Historical and Critical Review* (Nashville: B&H Academic, 2016), 250 says he concurs with my view and that of Muller on this point.

[72] A.C. Troxel, 'Amyraut 'at' the Assembly: The Westminster Confession of Faith and the Extent of the Atonement' in *Presbyterion* 22/1 (1996), 55.

excluded. Perhaps this has been overlooked because our view of seventeenth-century hypothetical universalism has been too monochrome and 'Amyraldian', not sufficiently sensitive to the variation which existed at the time. This may well be the fault of Richard Baxter, who found the merger of British hypothetical universalism and Amyraldianism a convenient oversimplification, since it gave the impression of 'a united and coherent testimony to the correctnesss of his own version of 'the middle way.'[73]

It could also be that modern versions of Calvinist universalism are not as sophisticated as the carefully framed Calvinist universalism of a more scholastic age. The most natural reading of parts of the *Confession* could appear to us today to be straightforwardly particularist. Yet seventeenth-century 'universalists' were able to affirm such things by making fine distinctions, even if the language finally adopted did not, as they might have hoped, entirely reflect their own preferences. As Moore comments, this lends credence to the thesis that it was 'the universal redemptionists who availed themselves most of scholastic distinctions, whereas it was the strict particular redemptionists who upheld an Augustinian simplicity in their soteriology.'[74]

Examined in its historical context, the *Confession* is perhaps less precise on this issue than some would have liked it to be. Whether this came about because of the explicit intent and design of the Assembly as a whole or simply because of the exigencies and fluctuations of ecclesiastical politics it is difficult to say. We cannot conclude with certainty that the Assembly *qua* the Assembly was aiming to be tolerant of diversity at this point, though it is clear that Reformed scholars generally at the time did not consider it an issue of such primary importance that they condemned Amyraldian opponents as 'heretics' (particularists like

---

[73] J.D. Moore, *English Hypothetical Universalism*, 219.

[74] Moore, *English Hypothetical Universalism*, 222 n.19.

John Owen even appreciating much of the work of 'the illustrious Amyrald').[75]

There is, nevertheless, the potential for intra-Reformed unity in the end-product of the deliberations at Westminster. Gerald Cragg, commenting on this period in the development of Reformed theology, boldly asserts that 'within the dominant theological school there were innumerable shades of opinion, and the various sects could fight bitterly enough among themselves, in spite of the Calvinism common to them all. The triumph of their creed was so complete that they could afford the luxury of disagreement. Thus, at the very moment when the citadel of Calvinism seemed to be impregnable, fissures began to disfigure its walls. The unanimity was deceptive because it was superficial.'[76] Yet the deceptive clarity of the *Westminster Confession* appears to my mind to be anything but superficial. It is, rather, careful and studious. Writing at a time when his denomination was considering confessional revision and whether to allow a large group of Arminians and hypothetical universalists into the fold, even B.B. Warfield heartily and eirenically allowed those he (inaccurately) called Amyraldians 'a right of existence' under the *Confession*. He thought, however, that 'the letter of the symbol scarcely justifies it'.[77]

We ought always to confess candidly where our views may be eccentric or in a minority against the larger tradition. Yet it remains to be seen whether Reformed Christians in our days, on either side of this debate, will be prepared like Warfield to concede a level of diversity and toleration here.

---

[75] Cameron's work is cited approvingly by Owen in *Works*, 16:303, and noted in 2:369; 8:500, 526, 529; 10:303; 16:289, 362, 364; 18:67, 69; 20:89, 151, 153; 23:181. In 10:507 he speaks positively of 'Cameron and Voetius, those two thunderbolts of theological war'; and in 10:488–489 he includes Cameron in a list of 'very learned theologians' along with 'the professors at Saumur.'

[76] G.R. Cragg, *From Puritanism to the Age of Reason: A Study of Changes in Religious Thought Within the Church of England 1660-1700* (Cambridge: CUP, 1966), 17.

[77] Warfield, *The Westminster Assembly*, 144 n.94 from an article first published in 1901.

From Life's First Cry:
John Owen on Infant Baptism
and Infant Salvation

This chapter is a significantly enlarged version of the 2008 St Antholin's Lecture, published in Lee Gatiss (ed.), Preachers, Pastors, and Ambassadors: Puritan Wisdom for Today's Church (Latimer Trust, 2011). I wish to thank Pascal Denault and Crawford Gribben especially for stimulating interaction on these issues.

With the great Assembly of puritan divines sitting in Westminster, a sermon was preached each morning in Westminster Abbey. One such sermon from 1644 by Mr Stephen Marshall, minister of Finchingfield in Essex, sparked something of a controversy when another minister chose to publish a long and weighty response to it. The sermon, itself somewhat longer than usual, was part of a series on the Ten Commandments, the Lord's Prayer, the Creed, and the Sacraments and took as its subject the doctrine of infant baptism. Marshall outlined the basic historical, theological, and biblical case for the practice.[1] Mr John Tombes, who was fast gaining a reputation as one who was

---

[1] S. Marshall, *A Sermon of the Baptizing of Infants* (London, 1644). On Marshall's reputation and influence as a preacher, see W. Barker, *Puritan Profiles*, 120-127.

against infant baptism, read Marshall's printed sermon and decided it must be answered.

Tombes had already been turned down for a prestigious preaching post by a committee on which the influential Marshall sat, because of his views on this subject.[2] As 'the archetypal Anglican Antipaedobaptist'[3] he was particularly concerned to justify his own position in a church and nation which had long accepted the practice of baptising the children of believers. Tombes' response was about three times the length of Marshall's sermon, and was bound along with some of his other polemical writing on the subject, the first of many such published works to come from his pen over the next few years.[4] Marshall replied to Tombes's response, and soon others weighed in too. Thus began a long and spirited exchange of views amongst the English puritans of the mid-seventeenth century concerning the place and privileges of children in the church.

This debate over infant baptism certainly made waves in Oxford, where John Owen, 'Prince of Puritans' was Dean of Christ Church (1651-1660) and Vice-Chancellor (1652-58).[5] At the annual academic convocation in 1652, for example, Henry Savage delivered a dissertation specifically against John Tombes's views. Moreover, in 1654, Tombes was appointed as a 'Trier', charged with the examination and approval of ministers. This was a high profile role, and would naturally have drawn attention to Tombes and his distinctive theological convictions from the universities where new clergy were being trained by men such as

---

[2] The post was *Preacher for the Honourable Societies of the Temples*, in London.

[3] M.T. Renihan, *Antipaedobaptism in the Thought of John Tombes: An untold story from Puritan England* (Auburn, MA: B&R Press, 2001), 47.

[4] J. Tombes, *An Examen of the Sermon of Mr Stephen Marshal about Infant Baptisme* (London, 1645). In total he wrote at least 14 books touching on the issue of baptism according to Renihan, *Antipaedobaptism*, 66. His paper on the issue presented to the Westminster Assembly probably accounts for Marshall's verbosity in outlining the case for infant baptism in his sermon; as Renihan, 142 comments, 'Polemicising with Tombes brought about tedious work for all parties involved'!

[5] For more on Owen's life and times, see Lee Gatiss, *John Owen: The Genius of English Puritanism* (London: Lost Coin, 2016).

Owen (also a Trier).[6] It is into this rhetorical and theological context that we can place Owen's own work on infant baptism, which is (unfortunately) undated.[7] Whether it originates from the 1640s, perhaps as a position paper sent to the Westminster Assembly,[8] from the 1650s when the debate was evidently current in Oxford, or from the post-Restoration period when Richard Baxter also continued to wield his prolific pen against Tombes,[9] we cannot say with certainty. Yet Owen's only work devoted solely to the sacrament of baptism (or the auditor's write-up of his presentation) is a short treatise of about 2400 words simply called *Of Infant Baptism*, and is a classic example of puritan theological exegesis and polemical argumentation.[10]

The doctrine of infant baptism, especially its denial by Anabaptists, was a major catalyst for the development of covenant theology in the sixteenth and seventeenth centuries, a movement

---

[6] See Renihan, *Antipaedobaptism*, 44-45.

[7] The text in *The Works of John Owen* (Johnstone and Hunter, 1850-1853), volume 16 is reprinted from an edition of his 'Sermons and Tracts' only published posthumously in 1721 and perhaps never intended for publication at all. The next treatise in the *Works*, 'A vindication of two passages in Irenæus against the exceptions of Mr Tombs' (pages 263-265 of Volume 16), is a direct reply to Tombes's *Antipaedobaptism Part 3*, section 89, pages 760-762 which was published in 1657. If this 'vindication' was originally appended to *Of Infant Baptism*, as seems possible judging from the final point made there about 'particular testimonies may be pleaded and *vindicated* if need be' (emphasis mine), then it is not entirely unlikely that he completed both around 1657-1658.

[8] Tombes had sent a short *Exercitation* on the subject to a committee of the Assembly. Owen himself was not a member of the Westminster Assembly, but may possibly have been asked by members for his opinion.

[9] Tombes moved to a chapel-at-ease in Bewdley, where he would not be required to baptise anyone, in 1649 (Renihan, *Antipaedobaptism*, 52 footnote 44). According to *Reliquiae Baxterianae* (London: Matthew Sylvester, 1696), Part I, 96, Tombes vigorously pursued Baxter, his near neighbour, for a public debate which finally took place in January 1649/50. Baxter's first work dedicated to the issue was *Plain Scripture Proof of Infants Church-Membership and Baptism being the arguments prepared for... the publick Dispute with Mr Tombes at Bewdley* (1650).

[10] There is no hint of any evidence to suggest this treatise does not originate with Owen, though it could possibly be a write-up by someone else of an Owen sermon/presentation. Sir John Hartopp did take detailed and full notes on Owen's sermons, for example. Toon, *The Correspondence of John Owen*, 157-158 has a letter Owen wrote to Lady Hartopp upon the death of her baby daughter (probably Anne, who died in 1674), which may indicate a personal interest in the subject under discussion here.

in which Owen was very much involved. Yet it was not merely a scholastic exercise that led the greatest mind amongst the puritans to consider the related subjects of infant baptism and infant salvation. Owen and his first wife had eleven children together, only one of whom survived past infancy.[11] Sadly, such immense tragedy was not unusual or exceptional for his time,[12] which meant that the puritans generally gave more thought than perhaps we do today to issues of infant salvation. They did not always have the luxury of time to consider whether to baptise their children or not.

We turn our attention then to the pithy and tightly woven argument which Owen makes for infant baptism. He has four sections to his argument, but in true puritan fashion the fourth section has eight major sub-points and several sub-points have sub-sub-points! So I will try to clarify how it all fits together as we proceed. My first point deals with Owen's first three sections, lines of argument I-III.

1. What is the Question?

Owen begins in the style of an Oxford disputation by defining very carefully the question to be debated. He clears the ground for his more positive arguments by denying three things. First, he says, the issue is not 'whether professing believers... not baptised in infancy, ought to be baptised.' This, he states, is an

---

[11] Two of his sons died in a plague in 1655, just before the date I have suggested Owen wrote *Of Infant Baptism*, according to P. Toon, *God's Statesman: The Life and Work of John Owen* (Exeter: Paternoster, 1971), 63. His daughter Mary had died in July 1647 aged only three weeks (Toon, 38 footnote 3).

[12] For example, A.G. Matthews, *Calamy Revised* (Oxford: Clarendon Press, 1988 [1934]), 13-14 records that Samuel Annesley had 24 children, only three of which survived him. One of these was Susanna, the mother of John and Charles Wesley (and 16 others!). D.A. Thompson, *Baptism, Church and Society in Modern Britain* (Milton Keynes: Paternoster, 2005), 1 narrates something of the story of the seventeenth-century Revd Isaac Archer who lost eight of his nine children in infancy, and as many as three out of ten children in puritan New England did not reach their first birthday according to C.A. Brekus, 'Children of Wrath, Children of Grace: Jonathan Edwards and the Puritan Culture of Child Rearing' in M.J. Bunge (ed.), *The Child in Christian Thought* (Cambridge: Eerdmans, 2001), 316.

uncontroversial truth, confessed by all Christians. Presumably the wording of the Great Commission in Matthew 28:18-20 was clear enough in its insistence that disciples of Jesus ought to be baptised, even if in actual fact that is not universally the case. There are some Christians, converted and nurtured through the Salvation Army for example, who have never been baptised, and there are always others who have 'not gotten around to it yet'. Whilst it is gloriously true that baptism is not strictly necessary for salvation, it is clearly abnormal in New Testament terms to neglect baptism altogether.[13] After all, there are many things which are 'not strictly necessary for salvation' but which are either beneficial to growth in faith, or matters of simple obedience to God's word (e.g. Bible reading, prayer, the Lord's Supper).

Second, Owen continues, neither is the debate about whether faith and repentance should precede baptism in such disciples. It obviously should, and Owen would insist on pastors taking great care over this, so as not to baptise adult converts without being sure their profession of faith is genuine. He claims to be more assiduous and careful about this than most antipaedobaptists, for whom admission to baptism was something to be extremely scrupulous about. By clarifying that this is not the main issue, he rules out any simplistic appeal to verses (such as Acts 8:12) which speak of repentance or faith coming before baptism as if they settled the issue of baptizing infants. To pile up quotations, from either the Bible or great theologians of the past, showing that faith did or should precede baptism *in adults* is not pertinent to the question of infant baptism, since it is perfectly consistent with the paedobaptist position. Owen possibly has Tombes in his sights here since he made much of a list of several verses in which either

---

[13] See *Westminster Confession* 28.5.

John the Baptiser or the Apostles baptised adults after a profession of faith and/or repentance.[14]

Third, Owen denies that all infants should be baptised. In other words, he and his fellow paedobaptists do not wish to argue that every child born into the world without exception ought to be baptised. Some children, he says, ought not to be baptised, i.e. those 'whose parents are strangers from the covenant.' This is the first mention in the argument of that important concept of 'the covenant', to which we will return again as Owen develops his case. It is sufficient to note at this stage that Owen was not in favour of indiscriminate baptism nor would he have approved of a policy of baptising the children of anyone who happens to live in the parish (whether they are committed to Christ and his covenant people or not). As we will see later, Owen was of the view that some of those born outside the covenant who died in infancy were actually elect and saved; yet that did not mean they should be baptised (since God alone knows those who are his) or that any child could be baptised simply in the hope that they might be one of the elect. Baptism was, then, part of the outward administration of the covenant, a sign to be given only to those

---

[14] See *An Examen of the Sermon of Mr Stephen Marshal*, 153. For a modern example of this kind of argument, see R. H. Stein, 'Baptism in Luke-Acts' in T. R. Schreiner & S. D. Wright (eds.), *Believer's Baptism: Sign of the New Covenant in Christ* (Nashville: B&H Academic, 2006), 35-66. Since the context of Luke-Acts must be the whole of Scripture (breathed out by the same divine author), to consider a doctrinal question settled by appeal to narrative examples in only a section of the whole would be premature, even if the examples were directly relevant to the issue at hand. Whilst this kind of 'biblical theology' description of what a particular corpus of biblical material says can be useful, unless we move from 'what does Luke-Acts say' to a consideration of how that coheres with the rest of the Bible and how it is relevant to the systematic question being asked, it is ultimately misleading and cannot be normative. The rest of the Schreiner-Wright volume does attempt this. However, it is to be feared that many would simply conclude that 'if in Luke-Acts baptism is for adults who have heard the gospel and professed faith, then infant baptism cannot be right.' It is that hermeneutical fallacy which Owen is here addressing.

whose profession of saving faith and repentance was judged sincere, and to their children.[15]

So, Owen has cleared away three false definitions of the question he has chosen to discuss, in order to focus the dispute more precisely. The issue for him is not whether believers who weren't baptised in infancy should be baptised—they should. It is not whether faith and repentance should come before baptism in such converts—it should. And it is not whether all infants are to be baptised indiscriminately—they should not. Therefore he concludes that 'the question is only concerning the children or infant seed of professing believers who are themselves baptized.' And the question is, should *they* be baptised?

It is not pedantic or 'scholastic' to narrow the question down in the way Owen did. Clarity is vital in such debates, especially where passions can often run high. It is also important not to forget at the beginning of his argument that Owen believes in adult 'believer's baptism' (or credobaptism) as much as any antipaedobaptist.[16] Indeed, as a keen supporter of missions to the un-reached people groups of Great Britain and Ireland who worked and prayed for the propagation of the gospel, he would have taken great joy in the baptism of such new converts.[17] This is a healthy reminder that a firm belief in infant baptism need not

---

[15] See *A Declaration of the Faith and Order Owned and practised in the Congregational Churches in England, Agreed upon and consented unto By their Elders and Messengers in Their Meeting at the Savoy, October 12, 1658* (London, 1658) section 29.4. This is identical to *Westminster Confession* 28.4 except that it strengthens the limitations on who can be baptised: believers and their children, 'and those only' (the last three words being added at the Savoy). Owen was instrumental in drawing up this 'Savoy Declaration', which is a lightly edited version of the *Westminster Confession*, and so the revisions made are significant when considering Owen's own views, especially if my view (above, footnote 7) of the date of *On Infant Baptism* is correct.

[16] As I have pointed out in my article, 'The Anglican Doctrine of Baptism' in *Foundations 63* (2012), 65, Anglicans are enthusiastic credobaptists. The Church of England baptises three times as many adults on profession of faith each year as the Baptist Union of Great Britain, demonstrating that a paedobaptist denomination can also in a sense be a credobaptist one. So where I use the term 'antipaedobaptist' (Tombes's designation of choice in the title of his magnum opus) this is not meant as a slur, but merely as a convenient designation in this context.

[17] The theme of Owen's heart for gospel propagation is brought out in Toon, *God's Statesman* e.g. 41, 80.

involve neglecting the evangelisation of the nation, or indeed replacing such a vision with the potentially more parochial concern of breeding the next generation.

Many Christians now and in Owen's day were baptised as babies but came to a living faith only later in life. It is perhaps natural for such people to question the validity of what could appear from their position of new-found vibrancy to have been merely an empty ritual. Yet just because a practice may have been abused in the past does not mean there is no right and proper, biblically-mandated use for it. For Owen to make it clear from the start that non-covenantal, indiscriminate baptism is not what paedobaptism is meant to be about could be incredibly helpful in preventing such people from (if I may put it like this) throwing out the baby of the biblical doctrine with the dirty font water of nominal faith. We may be rightly sceptical about the policy of certain churches because they seem to have failed in their duty to preach the gospel clearly and nurture faith in those they initiate into baptism. Yet this should make us passionate not to abolish infant baptism but to see it reformed according to a more biblical pattern, administered and followed up correctly. That, I believe, was Owen's concern in the face of radical antipaedobaptism in his day, when much that had been merely 'traditional' was reassessed and abandoned.

We must now turn to the substantive part of his argument to see if he was able to put the doctrine of infant baptism on a sufficiently secure foundation to make its retention viable. We are dealing now, then, with the eight major sub-points of section IV in his short treatise on baptism.

2. Why Not Baptise Infants?

Owen's first major point in effect throws back a question to those who would deny infant baptism. Where, he asks, does Scripture forbid such a thing? Which Bible text says that the children of believers should not be baptised? Opponents of infant baptism 'can produce no testimony of Scripture wherein their negation is formally or in terms included, nor any one asserting what is inconsistent with the affirmative.' That is, there is no verse forbidding infant baptism and no verse inconsistent with infant baptism. We have already noted above that some non-paedobaptists would point to a pattern in Acts where baptism follows the reception of preaching and a profession of faith. Tombes, for example, has a list of such verses, from which he logically concludes 'in which places, profession of repentance and faith is still made the antecedent to baptism: but this does not agree to infants, therefore they are not to be baptised.'[18] Yet Owen replies in a withering manner that, 'it is weak beneath consideration to suppose that the requiring of the baptism of believers is inconsistent with that of their seed.' That is, if one is going to oppose this practice, then one needs to produce clear arguments from Scripture which address it and oppose it directly. To assert that believers must be baptised is not a logical argument against baptising their children as well, since the two things are by no means mutually exclusive.

Owen's second major point is a similarly aggressive rhetorical thrust against what he perceives as the structural flaws in the antipaedobaptist case. Not only are there no verses against infant baptism, his opponents also have no examples in Scripture or in early church history where the children of believers were not given 'the same sign and seal of the covenant' as their parents. There were no examples of circumcised fathers with uncircumcised sons or baptised parents with un-baptised children —if they were being brought up in the knowledge of God, then they received the same sign as their parents.[19] There was no counterexample in Scripture or 'the approved practice of the

---

18 Tombes, *Examen*, 153 cf. Renihan, *Antipaedobaptism*, 132-135. As with all quotations made out of seventeenth-century sources in this chapter, I have updated the spelling and punctuation. American readers will be delighted to learn that 'to baptise' and its cognates was often spelled with a 'z' in seventeenth-century English.

19 We might note Exodus 4:24-26 where Moses had not circumcised his son or Joshua 5:2-9 where the entire wilderness generation had not been circumcised either. The Lord was clearly not pleased about the lack of the covenant sign upon the covenant children, and this was soon corrected.

primitive church.'[20] There was significant debate about the historical evidence from the early church,[21] but Owen's point is undeniable regarding the lack of evidence in Scripture. There were, Owen implies, serious and significant silences when it came to assessing the evidence for the non-paedobaptist case.

Owen was of course not alone in pointing to such gaps in the opposition's argument. Stephen Marshall had done the same thing in his Westminster Abbey sermon which sparked off the initial publishing war with Anglican antipaedobaptist John Tombes. Like Owen, Marshall points out that nowhere in the New Testament is there a command 'that the children of believers when they are grown, should be instructed and baptised, though instructed by their parents... nor any example where ever that was done.' But he confessed that non-paedobaptists had their own spin regarding arguments from silence when they pointed out that 'there is no command, no express institution, or clear example in all the New Testament of baptising of infants.' To this he freely admitted, and yet he denied the legitimacy of the logical leap then made: to say 'that Christians are not tied to observe that which is not expressly and in so many words set down in the New Testament' was 'not true divinity'. Why not? Because there were several areas in which Christians did not require a specific word in the New Testament to bind them: there was no express law against polygamy, for example, and no reiteration of the forbidden degrees of marriage (as in Leviticus 18).[22] Did that mean that Christians could take multiple wives or have sexual intercourse

[20] By which Owen means the early church of the first few centuries after Christ. See Renihan, *Antipaedobaptism*, 145 where Tombes casts doubt on infant baptism in the early church saying, 'it is a wonder to me, that if it were so manifest as you speak, you should find nothing in Eusebius for it, nor in Ignatius, nor in Clemens Alexandrinus, or in Athanasius, not in Epiphanius'. Silences in historical remains could be taken either way it seems.

[21] One contemporary defence of a paedobaptist reading of the historical texts was Robert Ram's *Paedo-Baptisme or, The Baptising of Infants Justified* (London, 1645). The debate continued in the classic exchange between J. Jeremias, *Infant Baptism in the First Four Centuries* (London: SCM, 1960) and K. Aland, *Did the Early Church Baptize Infants?* (London: SCM, 1961).

[22] Though Marshall acknowledges Paul's horror regarding the specific incestuous relationship in 1 Corinthians 5.

with their siblings? Surely not! There was no express command or example in the New Testament to justify women receiving the Lord's Supper either, but that did not mean they were not fit to partake of that sacrament. Should the children of believers be denied access to the other sacrament on the same grounds?[23]

Arguments from silence cannot be compelling on their own. They must be part of a larger case, as indeed they are for both Owen and Marshall. But it is significant that Owen begins here with a challenge to non-paedobaptists. It is common experience in many conservative evangelical circles today to find that the burden of proof on this issue is simply assumed to lie with paedobaptists. It is they who must justify what is sometimes considered to be their pragmatic continuance of a Roman Catholic practice, as if the case for not baptising infants was so patently obvious from Scripture as to not require justification.[24] Owen reminds us that there is a burden of proof on both sides of the divide here, and a heavy burden at that for antipaedobaptists. It is not an issue which can be easily and straightforwardly settled by brandishing a few proof texts; it is more like trying to piece together a complex jigsaw in which some of the key pieces seem to be missing, and there is legitimate debate over how the gaps might be filled in a manner most in keeping with their surroundings.

So first, Owen challenges those against infant baptism to be more rigorous in their methodology and to admit the weaknesses in their case. Some of the pieces they would no doubt like to see

---

[23] Marshall, *A Sermon of the Baptizing of Infants*, 34-35.

[24] For a provocative exposure of and answer to this sort of thinking see P. J. Leithart's, 'The Sociology of Infant Baptism' in his *The Baptized Body* (Moscow, ID: Canon Press, 2007), 113-136 where he concludes (pages 135-136) that 'Baptist theology and baptismal practice seem reasonable and natural only because our definitions of 'reasonable and natural' are thoroughly infected with the modern notion that consent is the alpha and omega of social, moral, and religious life.' Indeed, early Anabaptists were committed theologically to 'free will' according to K. G. Miller, 'Complex Innocence, Obligatory Nurturance, and Parental Vigilence: 'The Child' in the Work of Menno Simons' in Bunge, *The Child in Christian Thought*, 207 and D. C. Steinmetz, *Luther in Context* (Bloomington: Indiana University Press, 1986), 59 (on Hubmaier). More recently the case against paedobaptism has been argued differently, sometimes with more Reformed views of theological anthropology.

are missing. Then once it is clear that this debate is not simply over the interpretation of a few isolated verses but over how the Bible as a whole is structured and put together it should be easier to proceed with a certain level of charity and the patience born of humility. Inference and implication will have to play an important part in any answer to the question of infant baptism. So Owen will challenge us in subsequent arguments to recover confidence in a Reformed hermeneutic that sees the Bible as the one unfolding story of God's unchanging plan of salvation, a hermeneutic which provides the big picture into which infant baptism fits harmoniously, comfortably, and securely.

3. Making Things Worse for Children

Owen's third major argument in his treatise on baptism concerns the revocation of spiritual privileges given by God. The essence of his argument here is that if the non-paedobaptists are right, God has made things worse for the children of believers now that Christ has come. What he says is this: 'A spiritual privilege once granted by God unto any cannot be changed, disannulled, or abrogated, without an especial divine revocation of it, or the substitution of a greater privilege and mercy in the room of it.'

The spiritual privilege he refers to is that in Genesis 17 God granted the infant seed of believing Abraham a right to participate in the covenant, including its initial seal. The covenant was cut with Abraham and his children, and as part of it Abraham and his male children were all to receive the covenant sign.[25] To deny the children of believers that right to the initial seal of the covenant (though the sign may have been changed) cannot be appropriate unless God has expressly changed his instructions. As Marshall said in his sermon, speaking of the first disciples as they

---

[25] Owen does not make the rather obvious paedobaptist point here that Abraham (a 'believer' since at least Genesis 15:6) was definitely not told to wait until his children shared his faith before he circumcised them. Whilst it is true that it is those who believe who are sons of Abraham (Galatians 3:7) this cannot function as an argument against infant baptism since it evidently did not function as an argument against infant circumcision.

went about baptising and teaching, 'it behoved the Lord to give them a caution for the leaving out of infants in this new administration, that they might know his mind, if that he intends to have them left out—which that ever he did in word or deed, cannot be found in the Scriptures.'[26] Besides, God would only do that, Owen says, if he was replacing the privilege those children enjoyed with something greater for them, which antipaedobaptists do not think he has. Therefore, now that Christ has come, the children of believers are apparently in a worse situation spiritually than they were before, if the antipaedobaptists are correct.[27]

Owen traces out several implications of adopting this view. First, if the privilege given to the children of believers in Genesis 17 is now to be revoked, then the lordship of Christ over the church is being overruled. For he himself has not spoken to remove the right of children to receive the seal of the covenant, as Owen has already established: the New Testament says nothing about children now being excluded from the outward sign of covenant membership. So then, 'To abolish or take away any grant of privilege made by him to the church, without his own express revocation of it, is to deny his sovereign authority.'

Second, if a spiritual privilege given by God to his people is revoked then we should expect a greater privilege to have been granted in its place.[28] Otherwise it appears contrary to his goodness, love, and care for the church, which Owen does not wish to see impugned. It is one thing to remove, for example, the Jerusalem Temple and its glories but God clearly substituted in its place 'a more glorious spiritual temple and worship' in Christ.

---

[26] Marshall, *A Sermon of the Baptizing of Infants*, 39.

[27] Antipaedobaptist Robert Barrow, *A Briefe Answer to A Discourse Lately Written by one P.B... Wherein is Declared... That the Baptizing of Infants hath no authority from the Scriptures* (London: 1642), 13 declares simply that 'although infants were of the church before Christ yet the Lord hath manifestly declared, that they should not be so now', basing his argument on Galatians 4:22-31.

[28] Owen is not speaking here about the granting of spiritual gifts to individuals, which he may or may not decide to take away from time to time, as he wills.

John Tombes had at least two answers to this sort of argument. First, he said that some individuals in the former dispensation did have greater privileges than those in the new; for example, 'no man besides Abraham is called the father of the Faithful; no woman besides one, The mother of Christ'.[29] This does not quite answer Owen here, since he clearly has in mind privileges of the covenant people in general, rather than individual privileges and blessings as part of salvation history.

Tombes's best answer to this type of argument was to throw back at paedobaptists what he saw as an inconsistency: if things cannot be worse for children under the new covenant then why not include infants in the Lord's Supper, since they were part of the Passover? He pointed to this inconsistency on many occasions.[30] Needless to say this aroused strong opposition from Marshall and other puritans,[31] who were not in favour of paedocommunion, partly on the grounds that whether children participated in the Passover or not was a contentious point, and partly on the grounds that 1 Corinthians 11:28-29 seemed to them to lay down that participants should be capable of examining themselves spiritually and discerning the body, which infants could not.[32] Both the *Book of Common Prayer* and the *Westminster Directory of Public Worship* found no place for infants in the Lord's Supper, although it is now permitted and widely practiced in the Church of England and some Presbyterian

---

[29] Renihan, *Antipaedobaptism*, 125.

[30] See Renihan, *Antipaedobaptism*, 123-124. A. H. Strong used this same argument in the nineteenth century and was answered by B. B. Warfield in 'The Polemics of Infant Baptism' in *Studies in Theology, The Works of Benjamin B. Warfield: Volume 9* (Grand Rapids: Baker, reprinted 2003), 401-402.

[31] Marshall, *A Sermon of the Baptizing of Infants*, 51-52.

[32] Calvin had addressed the issue this way in *Institutes* 4.16.30. Some might argue on the basis of 1 Corinthians 10:1-5 that Paul envisages infants as being involved in both sacraments because they were involved in the Old Testament events Paul compares them to — baptism into Moses at the Red Sea, and partaking of the spiritual food of manna and water from the rock in the desert. I am grateful to Martin Foord for this insight.

churches, something which divides conservative evangelicals.[33] It may be that Jewett (no paedobaptist!) was right to say that, 'the argument from the covenant for infant baptism, when managed with adroitness, has about it an aura of plausibility; but the more convincingly it is pressed, the more embarrassed is the defense [*sic*] of believer communion.'[34]

Sadly, Owen does not address this tangential but significant question in his short treatise. He is, however, very concerned that if God were to make things worse for covenant children, to take away a spiritual privilege once solemnly granted, it would be particularly contrary to 'his constant course of proceeding with it [the church] from the foundation of the world, wherein he went on in the enlargement and increase of its privileges until the coming of Christ.' In other words, having a right to the seal of the covenant is a spiritual privilege, and things have always been improving and getting better for the church in terms of its spiritual privileges. There has been a progression in redemptive history. God's people were better off after Abraham than before; they were more blessed after Sinai, then with the replacement of the tabernacle for the more permanent Temple and its worship. The spiritual privileges of God's people were constantly being enlarged—with the grant of kingship, the sending of the prophets, and then with the coming of Christ and the Spirit. Owen's argument, then, is this: if this is how God works, why with the great and final revelation of his Son would he remove and revoke

---

[33] For discussion amongst conservative evangelical Anglicans on this issue, see R. Beckwith and A. Daunton-Fear, *The Water and the Wine: A Contribution to the Debate on Children and Holy Communion* (London: Latimer Trust, 2005) for an argument against paedocommunion, and M. Mason, 'Covenant Children and Covenant Meals: Biblical Evidence for Infant Communion' in *Churchman* 121/2 (2007), 127-138 for an argument in favour.

[34] P.K. Jewett, *Infant Baptism and the Covenant of Grace* (Grand Rapids: Eerdmans, 1978), 207.

completely such an immense spiritual privilege as believers' children had previously enjoyed?[35]

To suppose that this is actually what God has done (which was the non-paedobaptist position) seemed to Owen to take away from the glory and honour of Christ and the gospel, the great culmination of all God's dealings with his people. He states that it would be contrary 'to all his promises, the honour of Christ, and a multitude of express testimonies of Scripture.' He does not at this stage cite which promises and Scriptures he has in mind, but Stephen Marshall's sermon cites Hebrews 8:6 and 2 Corinthians 3:10 amongst others as showing that the privileges of believers under the new covenant were greater, not less, than those under the old. He also points out that in Christ there is neither male nor female (Galatians 3:28)—so girls as well as boys may now be baptised, a clear enlargement of the privilege.[36] Tombes agreed that privileges had been enlarged, but only in regard to the inclusion of gentiles and the increased clarity of revelation in the new era.[37]

Later in his argument, however, Owen will refer to several Old Testament texts which mention believers and their children as

---

[35] We might mention here the sometimes controversial question of how much the Old Testament saints knew about God. Even just a glance at volume 1 of his *Works* shows that Owen is very clear on this. Speaking of the Old Testament and God revealing himself to Moses in Exodus 33:18-23 he says: 'This is all that God would grant, viz., such external representations of himself, in the proclamation of his name, and created appearances of his glory, as we have of a man whose back parts only we behold as he passeth by us. But as to the being of God, and his subsistence in the Trinity of persons, we have no direct intuition into them, much less comprehension of them [that is, in the Old Testament].' See *Christologia: On the Person of Christ* in Owen, *Works*, 1:67. Again, it is true of Old Testament saints that, 'Neither they nor the angels knew clearly either the sufferings of Christ or the glory that should ensue.' *Works*, 1:263. And yet, 'The meanest believer may now find out more of the work of Christ in the types of the Old Testament, than any prophets or wise men could have done of old.' (page 101). This is because, '*when the Son of God 'appeared in the flesh*,' and in the discharge of his office, — God himself, as unto his being, and manner of existence in three distinct persons, with all the glorious properties of the divine nature, was illustriously manifested unto them that did believe' — *Meditations and Discourses on the Glory of Christ* in *Works*, 1:298 emphasis mine.

[36] See Marshall, *A Sermon of the Baptizing of Infants*, 30.

[37] Tombes, *Antipaedobaptism*: Part 3, 704-705.

together part of the future new order.[38] These texts certainly do not indicate that God will be going back on the inclusion of children within the covenant arrangement as soon as the messiah comes. So God has not left 'the seed of believers, whilst in their infant state, in the same condition with those of pagans and infidels… contrary to God's covenant' as Owen accuses non-paedobaptists of believing. Quite the contrary, God's promises assure believers about the continuing status and importance of their children in God's plan.[39]

There is a powerful pastoral argument here which all those tasked with the spiritual education of children would do well to ponder. Should we think of them as 'pagans and infidels' requiring evangelisation, which Owen points out is the logical conclusion of seeing believers' children as outside the covenant?[40] It is of course agreed by people on both sides of the debate that 'we as Christians should give ourselves to teaching the gospel to our children and praying for them privately and publicly' and that 'children of believing parents do not need baptism to be taught the Ten Commandments, the Lord's Prayer, and the gospel in all its fullness.' Paedobaptists and non-paedobaptists can both pray 'that none of our children ever know any lengthy period of conscious rebellion against God'.[41] Yet the antipaedobaptist position requires a fundamentally different attitude be adopted towards such children.

For instance, Mark Dever insists that Christians should 'not treat your children as if you presume they are elect' and 'parents

---

[38] He refers to Isaiah 22:24, 44:3, 61:9, and 65:23. We might also add the 'everlasting' covenant prophecies such as Isaiah 59:20-21, Jeremiah 32:38-40, or Ezekiel 37:25.

[39] See also the comments on Hebrews 4:15 in Owen, *Works*, 21:417-418 which are on these same lines.

[40] Peter Leithart, *The Baptised Body*, 115, speaks in a similar way to Owen about the Baptist view of children: 'The nurture of their early years may indeed involve Christian training – instruction in the Bible, teaching the child to pray, involvement in the church, and so forth – but it is not seen as the nurture of a Christian child… it is nurture of a pagan or unbelieving or neutral child.'

[41] Mark Dever, 'Baptism in the Context of the Local Church' in *Believer's Baptism*, 333, 350, and 348 footnote 28.

should not presume to be certain of their children's faith.'[42] So must they be taught that passages such as Ephesians 1:1-14 are inapplicable to them personally, since they are only allowed to look in at the blessings of the predestined Christian objectively, from the outside? And would it not be inconsistent for children presumed to be un-elect and without faith to be permitted to sing hymns (such as 'In Christ Alone') which put into their mouths confident assertions about their eternal security? Other Reformed Baptists would agree that it is presumptuous to nurture our children as if they could be disciples of Christ without a conversion experience or at least mature intellectual capacity.[43] So it seems that although they *may* be converted before they are permitted to drive a car, we must not speak to our children in a way that implies we think they have been, but should instead wait and see how they turn out later. "'Time will tell' is the point of many of Christ's parables," says Dever.[44] It is also the point of many of Christ's parables that the truth about things is only revealed on Judgment Day, but does this mean that we should wait until someone has lived a whole life of credible discipleship before we baptise them, on their deathbed, because only then can we be sure?

On the other hand, passages such as Ephesians 6:1-4 do seem to call on Christian parents to treat their children as *Christians*. As the great Puritan, William Perkins said, 'the children of believers are born holy and Christian.'[45] From their earliest years they are not just to be 'taught about God' but nurtured within the

---

[42] Dever, 'Baptism in the Context of the Local Church', 343 footnote 17 (sub-point 17), 349.

[43] See e.g. D. Gundersen, *Your Child's Profession of Faith* (Amityville, NY: Calvary Press, 1994). For a critical paedobaptist review of this, see R. Lusk, *Paedofaith: A Primer on the Mystery of Infant Salvation and a Handbook for Covenant Parents* (Monroe, LA: Athanasius Press, 2005), 154-158.

[44] 'Baptism in the Context of the Local Church', 333.

[45] See Bray (ed.), *Galatians-Ephesians*, 74. Ditto Kaspar Olevianus on the previous page, who writes that 'Christian parents can comfort themselves by saying that their children are not Gentile sinners but natural Christians by birth... Baptism does not make a pagan Christian but rather seals a promise that already belongs to the child.'

covenant and disciplined according to it (verse 4). In verses 1-3 children are even commanded to obey their parents 'in the Lord' (*en kurio*) and are given a promise to be apprehended by faith. Interestingly, they are not commanded here to repent and believe 'just like mummy and daddy did', but to grow in the family faith as they are nurtured in obedience to it. Presumably if Paul can apply the command and promise of the fifth commandment to the children of believers in Ephesus then some other appropriate scriptural (covenantal) promises, threats, comforts, and assurances might also be held out to them to receive and accept by faith.

In Ephesians 6, Paul chose to emphasise the positive side of the fifth commandment rather than speaking about the sanction children could face if they broke it under the old covenant (e.g. Deuteronomy 21:18-21). Such positive motivations can work exceptionally well, so that we do not need to indulge in 'frightening poor innocent children with talk of hell fire and eternal damnation' as some might, in order to somehow provoke a conversion experience.[46] As Lewis Schenck rightly says, 'It was unfortunate that the Great Awakening made an emotional experience, involving terror, misery, and depression, the only approach to God.'[47] Some may never have such an experience, but grow up knowing and loving Jesus from their earliest days. At some point they will be born again, but it may be an unnoticed, un-dramatic event. Would it be right to presume such children are unregenerate and un-elect?

Moreover, a child's faith may not have the cognitive sophistication of an adult's, but that does not mean they are incapable of relying on and trusting Christ until they have passed

---

[46] The great American preacher Jonathan Edwards was accused of this, with some justification it seems, according to Brekus, 'Children of Wrath, Children of Grace', 321 (see also pages 313-320 on his sermons to children). See the careful remarks of T. A. Sizemore, *Of Such is the Kingdom: Nurturing Children in the Light of Scripture* (Fearn, Ross-Shire: Christian Focus, 2000), 67 on Edwards and his context.

[47] L.B. Schenck, *The Presbyterian Doctrine of Children in the Covenant: An Historical Study of the Significance of Infant Baptism in the Presbyterian Church* (Phillipsburg, NJ: P&R, [1940] 2003), 71.

through puberty.[48] Nor does it suggest that all we can do is teach them 'law' (to be nice, obedient sinners) until they are old enough to 'grasp the gospel properly' and be saved. Speaking of infants, Jesus said that '*of such* is the kingdom of heaven' (Matthew 19:14). He did not just mean that people who are *like* children in some way are saved (a point made elsewhere in Matthew 18:3).[49] He meant that infants themselves would make up a part of his kingdom.[50] This text doesn't mention infant baptism, of course, but the gestures and expressions of our Lord here are a strong indirect argument in favour of it.[51] Yet as Owen argues it, to see the children of believers as 'young servants of the king'[52] is compatible and consistent only with the paedobaptist position. Since they have that immense privilege, however, the church has a duty towards children: to pray for them, to instruct them 'according unto their capacities', to advise parents on their

---

[48] Jewett, *Infant Baptism and the Covenant of Grace*, 168 is right to say that 'few have found the courage to rest the weight of their case on so tenuous a foundation' as the idea that very young babies have 'a kind of inchoate faith germinating like a seed in the soul'. Some like Lusk, *Paedofaith* would build a great deal on the idea of 'baby faith' (from Psalm 22:9-10 for example), and it is true that Luther, Calvin, and Turretin spoke about a kind of faith in infants. But the case for infant baptism does not need to include or rest upon this, as P. C. Marcel, *The Biblical Doctrine of Infant Baptism: Sacrament of the Covenant of Grace* trans. P.E. Hughes (London: James Clarke, 1953), 209-218 clearly shows.

[49] The word is τοιούτων (*toiouton*, 'of such', or 'to such' ESV) in the Greek of Matthew 19:14, Mark 10:14 and Luke 18:16. Bearing in mind how this adjective is used elsewhere in the Gospels (e.g. Matthew 9:8; Mark 4:33, 6:2, 7:13; Luke 9:9; John 4:23), it simply cannot mean 'those like this' while excluding the children themselves. See also Calvin's comments on Matthew 19:14 in *Commentary on a Harmony of the Evangelists, Calvin's Commentaries Volume XVI* (Grand Rapids: Baker, 1993), 390-391 (volume 2) and the comments of Spurgeon (a Baptist) quoted in Sizemore, *Of Such is the Kingdom*, 136.

[50] Charles Hodge, *Systematic Theology: Volume 1* (Hendrickson, reprinted 1999), 27 says, 'Of such He tells us is the kingdom of heaven, as though heaven was, in great measure, composed of the souls of redeemed infants'. See also the similar thoughts of J.C. Ryle, *Expository Thoughts on Luke: Volume 2* (Edinburgh: Banner of Truth, 1986), 268 on Luke 18:16.

[51] As J.C. Ryle says in *Expository Thoughts on Mark* (Edinburgh: Banner of Truth, 1985), 203.

[52] R.C. Sproul, 'In Jesus' Name, Amen' in G. Strawbridge (ed.), *The Case for Covenantal Infant Baptism* (Phillipsburg, NJ: P&R, 2003), 310.

upbringing, to visit and encourage them, and to prepare them to come into 'full communion' with the church. Owen therefore advised that not only should parents be taught about their duties and responsibilities towards their children, but each church should have a teacher set aside especially for their instruction.[53]

Was Owen Becoming a Baptist?

Finally, under this heading, it is important to consider some recent claims that Owen's covenant theology either was, or tended towards, or moved towards being anti-paedobaptistic. Carl Trueman hints at some kind of disjunction between Owen's covenant theology and his paedobaptism, though he notes that it never seemed to cause Owen any great heartache or lead him to modify his doctrine and practice.[54] Pascal Denault's book, *The Distinctiveness of Baptist Covenant Theology*, however, goes much further. It contains a section headed 'John Owen the Baptist.'[55] Denault is aware that Owen was always a paedobaptist, but he quotes a seventeenth-century Baptist, contemporary with Owen, averring that Owen's covenant theology 'leaves no room for Infant Baptism but excludes it beyond all possibility of reconciliation.'[56] Moreover, he claims Owen flat-out contradicts himself: his 'Of infant baptism and dipping' contradicts what he wrote in his Hebrews commentary; the former was written while he was a Presbyterian, Denault claims, while the latter, 'mature and definitive thinking of Owen' shows how he had changed his thinking once he became a Congregationalist. In conclusion, 'Owen's commentary on chapter 8 of the Book of Hebrews leaves

---

[53] Owen, *Works*, 16:22-24.

[54] Trueman, *John Owen: Reformed Catholic, Renaissance Man*, 79.

[55] Pascal Denault, *The Distinctiveness of Baptist Covenant Theology: A Comparison between Seventeenth-Century Particular Baptist and Paedobaptist Federalism* (Birmingham, AL: Solid Ground Christian Books, 2013), 18.

[56] Denault, *Distinctiveness*, 20, quoting Edward Hutchinson, *A Treatise concerning the Covenant and Baptism* (1676), 34-35.

no doubt as to the consistency of his federalism with that of the credobaptists.'[57]

Hence, Owen's heavily covenantal exposition of Hebrews 8:6 is reprinted in *Recovering a Covenantal Heritage: Essays in Baptist Covenant Theology*, along with a chapter devoted to Owen's covenant theology by Thomas Hicks.[58] This co-opting or conscripting of Owen into the antipaedobaptist fold alongside chapters on Tombes and the Baptist *Confessions* and Baptistic exegesis of key texts is a little jarring, especially since there is no mention of baptism itself in either chapter. We are told, however, that seventeenth-century Baptists agreed with Owen on the differences between the covenants and hence that 'Owen's thesis reflects the view of the Baptist theologians behind the 2LCF [*Second London Confession of Faith*].'[59]

Owen's covenant theology certainly was not the same as the Baptist theologians of the seventeenth century. His covenant theology did not 'perfectly fit' theirs. The very simple fact is that Owen always considered infant baptism to be an absolute requirement of his covenant theology. His construal of federalism, albeit different from mainstream Reformed thought on some issues,[60] supported, promoted, and demanded infant baptism—a practice he never deviated from throughout his entire ministry and was defending in covenantal terms until his dying breath.

I have no doubt that his understanding of baptism deepened throughout the course of his ministry, and perhaps he thought of

---

[57] Denault, *Distinctiveness*, 23.

[58] Thomas Hicks, 'John Owen on the Mosaic Covenant' in Richard C. Barcellos, *Recovering a Covenantal Heritage: Essays in Baptist Covenant Theology* (Palmdale, CA: RBAP, 2014), 175-192 and the reprint of Owen in the same volume, pages 257-324.

[59] Barcellos, *Recovering a Covenantal Heritage*, 11-12.

[60] As I demonstrate in *Adoring the Fulness of the Scriptures in John Owen's Commentary on Hebrews* (Cambridge PhD thesis, 2013), 136-195, Owen's covenant theology does mature and change, and owes a debt to both Lutheran and Salmurian currents of thought, though this by no means aids the Baptistic attempt to co-opt him since Lutherans and theologians such as Cameron and Amyraut were all, as far as I am aware, paedobaptists.

it in different ways at different stages of his own development. He may have emphasised different aspects of it in different contexts. It is also perfectly possible that he might be inconsistent, of course. Crawford Gribben has tried to expose some changes in Owen's thoughts on baptism, although it seems to me that all he does is over-read some allusive asides.[61] But I fail to see any paradigm shift away from infant baptism. His 'tract' on the subject, as I said above (footnote 7), does most probably pre-date the first volume of his Hebrews commentary, but it is not from his very early Presbyterian phase. Moreover, throughout the Hebrews commentary (published in four volumes between 1668-1684) Owen makes the exact same theological moves as in the tract. For example, he says that:

- Believers' children are God's people and should not be 'excluded from the initial ordinance of the covenant' since no-one loses out by the coming of Christ;[62]

- Infant baptism is one of the 'greatest' and 'choicest rights and privileges' of the gospel covenant, and 'children have a right to the initial seal of the covenant';[63]

- It is indeed 'derogatory to the glory of Christ and honour of the gospel' to suppose that the church is now deprived of this signal

[61] C. Gribben, *John Owen and English Puritanism: Experiences of Defeat* (Oxford: Oxford University Press, 2016), 63 makes too much of one of the answers in Owen's 'Lesser Catechism' (*Works*, 1:469) about baptism making one a child of God: this is an allusion to the language of the *Prayer Book* catechism and is about solemnly sealing the covenant; neither does it remove the need for faith in our adoption, which is acknowledged a few questions beforehand by Owen. The *Westminster Directory* not only says children are 'federally holy before baptism', as Gribben rightly says (and claims Owen was diverging from), but also speaks of them being 'now baptised and solemnly entered into the household of faith'— both can be true and acknowledged together by Reformed theology, so there is no need to say Owen abandons anything. Again, on page 120, I think Gribben over-reads a line in a sermon to make it seem like Owen was changing his mind about the inclusion of children, when that was far from his purpose there.

[62] Owen, *Works*, 21:328 on Hebrews 4:9 (first published in 1674).

[63] Owen, *Works*, 21:329 on Hebrews 4:9.

favour and spiritual privilege of 'the application of the initial seal of the covenant unto the seed of believers';[64]

- Infants are in the covenant, were baptised in apostolical times, and should be now;[65]

- Parents bless their children by 'communicating unto them the privilege of the initial seal of the covenant, as a sign, token, and pledge of their being blessed of the Lord' and by 'careful instructing of them in the mercies and duties of the covenant';[66]

- Giving the 'initial seal of the covenant' to our kids has always been God's way, 'never by him revoked';[67]

- 'And whatever is pretended by some unto the contrary, it is a most eminent divine privilege, to have the seal of the covenant in baptism communicated unto the children of believers in their infancy; and a means it hath been to preserve many from fatal apostasies.'[68]

These are fairly vigorous contributions to the debate with Baptists. It seems very clear to me that not only was Owen an unwavering advocate for the practice but — very specifically and explicitly — his covenant theology, as seen throughout his most 'mature and definitive' work at the end of his career, supported, promoted, and demanded infant baptism. That was what he called his 'constant and uninterrupted practice' and it seems always to have been based on covenantal arguments.[69]

Some Baptists agreed with some aspects of Owen's covenant theology, namely his rejection of the *Westminster Confession's* understanding of the Mosaic covenant as an administration of the

---

[64] Owen, *Works*, 21:418 on Hebrews 4:15.

[65] Owen, *Works*, 22:58 on Hebrews 6:2 (first published in 1680).

[66] Owen, *Works*, 22:317-318 on Hebrews 7:1-3 (cf. 22:392 on Hebrews 7:9-10).

[67] Owen, *Works*, 22:433 on Hebrews 7:12.

[68] Owen, *Works*, 24:145 on Hebrews 11:24-26 (first published in 1684 just after Owen died).

[69] Owen, *Works*, 13:259 (1657).

covenant of grace. There is no evidential basis for more grandiose claims. It may be necessary to reject that scheme in order to become a Baptist, but in and of itself it is not necessarily a step in that direction. To get to Kentucky, I may have to go to Heathrow airport; but if you see me at Heathrow, you would be wrong to conclude that I *must* be on my way to Kentucky (I may be travelling to Philadelphia, or Poland, or Wittenberg, or just picking someone else up from Terminal 4). In the same way, simply to distance oneself from one aspect of the *Westminster Confession* is not to become a Baptist, even if that may be a necessary step on that road. Nor is it fatally undermining to paedobaptism. Owen certainly did not think so. In any case, *contra* Thomas Hicks, there were far more than two or three covenant theology options; one of the big issues in this recent confusion is a failure to build a more comprehensive and careful taxonomy of seventeenth-century covenant theologies. Edmund Calamy, preaching on the subject of the covenants in 1647, outlined five alternative covenant schema, each held by men he had heard or read. There were probably many more by the end of the century.[70]

4. Infant Regeneration and Salvation

Returning to Owen's argument in his short tract: someone may ask, 'Granted that children may be regenerate (God does not work in adults alone), does that necessarily mean they ought to be baptised?' As a Baptist, for instance, Mark Dever states that 'refusal to baptize is not intended as a statement asserting that the child is not regenerate but simply as a reluctance publicly to affirm that which has not yet been maturely evidenced.'[71] The context is more about young children who profess belief than infants who have just been born, but the point is the same: how 'mature' is 'maturely evidenced'—two years, five years, or fifty years?

---

[70] E. Calamy, *Two Solemne Covenants Made between God and Man: viz. the Covenant of Workes, and the Covenant of Grace (1647)*, 1–2. F. Roberts, *Mysterium et Medulla Bibliorum. The Mysterie and Marrow of the Bible: viz. God's Covenants with Man (1657)*, 738f divides the different views he knew about into four.

[71] 'Baptism in the Context of the Local Church', 350.

Obviously this line of argument contains something of a Baptistic presupposition that baptism is about affirming the candidate's faith, whereas Reformed paedobaptists like Owen would be happier to say that it was primarily about the promise and covenant of God.[72] Yet even if such an argument could be made without this presupposition, Owen will not accept the core idea that someone can be regenerate and yet denied a right to baptism. The two things go together—'They that have the thing signified have a right unto the sign of it'. This is the core of Owen's fourth and fifth points in section IV.

The text which undergirds Owen's argument here is Acts 10:47. There we find the apostle Peter and his believing Jewish colleagues amazed at the grace of God shown to the gentiles gathered at Cornelius's house. When they received the Holy Spirit, Peter asked, *Can anyone withhold water for baptizing these people, who have received the Holy Spirit just as we have?* Owen takes this as a principle, that those who are partakers in the thing signified have a right to the outward sign of it. How can they be denied the lesser if they already possess the greater? Later he cites Acts 2:38-39 as also demonstrating this same principle, and says, 'That unto whom the covenant or promise doth belong, to them belongs the administration of the initial seal of it.' Interestingly, the Ethiopian Eunuch in Acts 8:36 asks, 'What prevents me from being baptised?' which also appears to be consistent with this way of thinking: he believed the good news brought to him by Philip and wondered if there was any reason why he should not therefore receive the sign of baptism. Philip's consequent baptising of him would seem to demonstrate early agreement with this principle.[73]

---

[72] Miller, 'Complex Innocence', 201 avers that 'For Simons, baptism represents the believer's faith, while for Luther and Calvin baptism represents God's promise, a contrast Simons may not fully grasp or appreciate.' Not all Baptists would agree with Menno Simons or Mark Dever of course.

[73] It should be noted that whereas some Baptist exegesis of Acts assumes that the pattern of 'faith then baptism' seen there must normative for today, Dever and others must argue that the equally prevalent pattern of immediate baptism after conversion 'need not be the normative practice today' ('Baptism in the Context of the Local Church' 334 footnote 11).

Owen then considers the application of this principle to children. He states that the children of believers are all capable of the grace signified in baptism. That is, they are not angels or animals incapable of regeneration but have the potential to be born again. They also have *potentia credendi*, the potential to believe, though as with adults the transformation of this into an actual disposition of faith must be a gracious gift of God (see Philippians 1:29; 2 Peter 1:1, 3; Ephesians 2:8). God is free to give this to whoever he chooses; a mature intellectual capacity is never made a pre-condition for his gift. Infant salvation, therefore, does not entail a denial of salvation by faith alone—unless faith is thought to be a 'work' which only adults are capable of performing, rather than a gift granted by God to his elect (see Acts 13:48).

Owen then moves into what might today be considered much more controversial territory when he says that some of those children 'are certainly partakers of [that grace], namely, such as die in their infancy... therefore they may and ought to be baptised'. Owen assumes that the children of believers who die in infancy are partakers of the grace signified in baptism—that is, regeneration, new birth—just as much as those who profess faith as adults are. And he concludes that since that is the case, they ought to be baptised. He is not arguing for the post-mortem baptism of dead children. This is not his solution to the debate over the meaning of 'baptism for the dead' in 1 Corinthians 15:29! He is arguing that since believers' children are capable of the grace signified (as evidenced in the salvation of those who die in infancy) they ought to be permitted the sign.[74]

How can Owen base so much on infant regeneration and salvation? It helps to understand that this was not a widely disputed point in his day. Broadly speaking, most Reformed

---

[74] J.C. Ryle, *Expository Thoughts on Mark* (Edinburgh: Banner of Truth, 1985), 204 argues in the same vein in comments on Mark 10:16, saying, 'It is allowed on all sides that infants may be elect and chosen of God unto salvation, — may be washed in Christ's blood, born again of the Spirit, have grace, be justified, sanctified, and enter heaven. If these things be so, it is hard to see why they may not receive the outward sign of baptism'.

theologians around Owen's time agreed that the infants of believers, dying in infancy, were saved.[75] As Lewis Schenck says, 'The Reformed church has always believed, on the basis of God's immutable promise, that all children of believers dying in infancy were saved... because the promise was 'unto us and our children.'[76] Kuyper adds an important qualifier here when he says that Calvinists 'have never usurped the right to pronounce on the presence or absence of spiritual life in infants. They only stated how God would have us consider such infants, and this consideration based on the divine word made it imperative to look upon their infant children as elect and saved, and to treat them accordingly.'[77]

There were, however, some differences of opinion in the Reformed tradition regarding the children of unbelievers. Some, such as Zwingli, Bishop John Hooper, and Augustus Montague Toplady saw death in infancy as a sign of God's election, whoever the child's parents were. Others rejected the idea that any infant dying outside the covenant was saved. Many, such as the great puritan Bible commentator Matthew Henry, were merely agnostic about those born to unbelievers. Yet when it came to the children of believers there was a great consensus that (as the Synod of Dort puts it), 'godly parents ought not to doubt of the election and salvation of their children whom God calls out of this life in their infancy.'[78] Owen's own view is that since God is perfectly free to elect anyone there may well be some infants born and dying outside the covenant who are nevertheless saved: he had 'no doubt

---

[75] B.B. Warfield, 'The Development of the Doctrine of Infant Salvation' in *Studies in Theology, The Works of Benjamin B. Warfield: Volume 9*, 429-438.

[76] Schenck, *The Presbyterian Doctrine of Children in the Covenant*, 118. See Calvin, *Institutes*, 4.16.17-19.

[77] Quoted in Schenck, *The Presbyterian Doctrine*, 18. See also the views of Richard Baxter, which accord with this, in *The Nonconformist Advocate* (1679), 53 (Part 2).

[78] Article 1.17 in *The Judgement Of The Synode Holden at Dort* (London: John Bill, 1619). The 1662 *Book of Common Prayer* declares that, 'It is certain by God's Word, that children which are baptised, dying before they commit actual sin, are undoubtedly saved.' See L. Gatiss, *The Tragedy of 1662: The Ejection and Persecution of the Puritans* (London: Latimer Trust, 2007), 22-23 for some puritan objections to this.

but that God taketh many unto him in Christ whose parents never knew, or had been despisers of, the gospel.'[79] Crawford Gribben suggests that this conclusion of Owen's was 'unsatisfactory' and 'betrayed assumptions that Owen may not have been able to align with other elements of his thinking, and may suggest that he was publishing a doctrine he had not sufficiently considered.'[80] While it may be true that one early aside about baptism removing 'inherent lust' is not followed through elsewhere in his work,[81] his view on the salvation of dying children (even those born to non-Christians) fits perfectly acceptably within the Reformed mainstream.

On this subject Owen seems to be building on an essentially undisputed truth and trying to establish another 'by good and necessary consequence' (as *Westminster Confession* 1.6 says).[82] Marshall had also done something similar in his sermon.[83] Such an appeal was possible because even many non-paedobaptists believed firmly in the salvation of those who die in infancy. The view of sixteenth-century Anabaptist leader Menno Simons may in fact have been closest to Zwingli's position,[84] as was that of nineteenth-century Baptist Charles Haddon Spurgeon, who said:

---

[79] *Display of Arminianism* (1642) in Owen, *Works*, 10:81. I can find no basis for saying that Owen believes that all who die in infancy are elect as is claimed in T. L. Tiessen, *Who Can Be Saved? Reassessing Salvation in Christ and World Religions* (Leicester: IVP, 2004), 210 (citing A. H. Strong), though this is one of the more insignificant of the inadequacies in Tiessen's analysis. I am deeply unconvinced by the analogy he draws between saved infants and unevangelized adults, and unimpressed by the atomistic exegesis he uses to defend it and undermine alternatives.

[80] Gribben, *John Owen and English Puritanism*, 51. Gribben himself goes on to link Owen's early statement on baptismal efficacy with the work of Cornelius Burgess, who was a leading contributor to the Westminster Assembly and by no means an ill-informed or incoherent fringe figure in Reformed Puritanism. His criticism on the following page seems to rely on an assumption that pagan adults and elect children are to be treated in exactly the same way.

[81] See *Works*, 10:80.

[82] On this, see the very useful Ryan M. McGraw, *By Good and Necessary Consequence* (Grand Rapids: Reformation Heritage Books, 2012).

[83] Marshall, *A Sermon of the Baptizing of Infants*, 45.

[84] See Miller, 'Complex Innocence', 203.

> I have never, at any time in my life, said, believed, or
> imagined that any infant, under any circumstances,
> would be cast into hell. I have always believed in the
> salvation of all infants... I do not believe that, on this
> earth, there is a single professing Christian holding
> the damnation of infants; or, if there be, he must be
> insane; or utterly ignorant of Christianity.[85]

He also preached that 'If we had a God, whose name was Moloch,
if God were an arbitrary tyrant, without benevolence or grace, we
could suppose some infants being cast into hell; but our God, who
heareth the young ravens when they cry, certainly will find no
delight in the shrieks and cries of infants cast away from his
presence.'[86] This may not be entirely consistent; Marshall points
out that if (on antipaedobaptist assumptions) faith *must* precede
baptism for children as well as adults because Scripture says faith
is essential for salvation, then that precludes infants from being
saved not just from being baptised.[87] John Tombes, it should be
said, was much less certain about infant salvation. Although he
says that 'salvation belongs to some infants' and 'there is ground
for a strong hope of the salvation of infants of Christian believers
so dying' (even a 'strong probability'), his overall conclusion is that
'there is no certainty concerning the salvation of this or that
particular infant of a believer dying, nor is there a sure ground for
faith concerning it, nor is the hope of it certain, and we are to
suspend our judgement concerning it.'[88]

Owen does not here elaborate on all the details of the doctrine
of infant salvation itself. Owen would no doubt approve of the
insistence by Nash, Webb, Warfield, and others that confidence in
infant salvation is only coherent if one has a Calvinist (monergistic)

---

[85] In I.H. Murray (ed.), *Letters of Charles Haddon Spurgeon,* (Edinburgh: Banner of Truth, 1992), 150 (Letter 1869).

[86] Sermon number 411 'Infant Salvation' (available at http://www.spurgeon.org/sermons/0411.htm).

[87] Marshall, *A Sermon*, 45. Marcel, *The Biblical Doctrine of Infant Baptism*, 213-214 makes the same point.

[88] Tombes, *Antipaedobaptism*: Part 3, 562, 557, 560, 555.

soteriology, and is not strictly possible in a consistently Arminian or semi-Pelagian theology.[89] It is important to note that he does not affirm that infants are 'innocent' or worthy of salvation: he is quite clear that they are born in sin (Psalm 51:5), spiritually dead, and facing God's curse (Ephesians 2:1-3). So, he says, the only way they can be saved is if they are regenerated, born again (John 3:3).[90] He might have pointed to 2 Samuel 12:22-23 for an example of an infant being saved,[91] or Luke 1:15 for an example of an infant (even an embryo) being filled with the Spirit.[92] This is far from proving the salvation or regeneration of every infant of course; yet it does demonstrate that a mature capacity to understand the gospel is not strictly necessary, biblically speaking, for infants to be regenerate or saved. So we cannot infer that they are automatically damned on the basis of original sin or because they are unable to access the means of grace.[93] It is important to stress that we are here discussing infants who die in infancy, not all infants. Some infants grow up to reject the gospel, and no one would say they were saved simply by virtue of having once been infants!

---

[89] For more on this, see R. H. Nash, *When a Baby Dies: Answers to Comfort Grieving Parents* (Grand Rapids: Zondervan, 1999) and R. A. Webb, *The Theology of Infant Salvation* (Harrisonburg, Virginia: Sprinkle Publications, [1907] 2003).

[90] As a contrast to this, and to attempts to root infant salvation in election, see the view of W. H. Griffith Thomas in A. H. Hamilton, 'The Doctrine of Infant Salvation: Part 2' in BSac 101/404 (October 1944), 472-473, who bases it upon a supposed universality in the atonement. The same link can be found in a seventeenth century funeral sermon for an infant by Samuel Acton, *Dying Infants Sav'd by Grace, Proved* (London: 1699), 9. See Warfield's answer to this contention in 'The Doctrine of Infant Salvation', 439.

[91] Owen alludes to this text in his letter to Lady Hartopp, on the death of her daughter in *Works*, 1:cxvi-cxvii. He is equally clear that the child's enjoyment of blessedness is a result of God's grace alone, shown in his covenant promises. Tombes denies this exegesis of the text in *Antipaedobaptism*: Part 3, 558.

[92] Cf. Luke 1:41, 66. Some have also seen 2 Kings 4:8-37, Job 3:16-17, Ecclesiastes 6:3-6 and Jeremiah 31:15-17 (cf. Matthew 2:18) as important texts to consider here.

[93] *Westminster Confession* 10.3 (Savoy 10.3) says that 'Elect infants, dying in infancy, are regenerated, and saved by Christ, through the Spirit, who worketh when, and where, and how he pleaseth: so also are all other elect persons who are incapable of being outwardly called by the ministry of the Word.'

Owen's conclusion here is that 'regeneration is the grace whereof baptism is a sign or token. Wherever this is, there baptism ought to be administered.... infants who die in their infancy have the grace of regeneration, and consequently as good a right unto baptism as believers themselves.'

In his fifth point, Owen makes the case that if God explicitly does not want someone to be baptised then they are eternally damned, since the sign and the grace must go together. This is why impenitent sinners are not to be baptised, because not having the reality they have no right to the sign. But he goes on to say that if the sign is denied to believers' infants then that implies (by the same logic) that God is denying them the reality of salvation too—'and then all the children of believing parents dying in infancy must, without hope, be eternally damned'. He does not wish to contemplate such a consequence. It is certainly not that for Owen baptism is absolutely essential for salvation, but rather that if God desires the sign of salvation to be withheld it must be because he withholds salvation itself from such infants.[94]

What shall we make of Owen's attempt to use infant regeneration/salvation as part of his case for infant baptism? As a recognition that baptism and the language of regeneration often go together in Scripture (e.g. Galatians 3:26-27, Romans 6:3-4), it could be helpful. As an argument for the baptism of anyone who is regenerate, it has obvious strengths. As an argument for the baptism of those infants of believers who are about to die it has some coherence, if one grants the idea that such infants are saved. However, if Owen is arguing for more (i.e. that all believers' children should be baptised), there seems to be a gap in his logic here, a missing step. Such an argument may be represented like this:

---

[94] Owen says elsewhere that elect infants are saved even if they die before being baptised. See *A Discourse of Spiritual Gifts*, in Owen, *Works*, 4:432. W. Hubbock, *An Apologie of Infants in a Sermon: Proving by the revealed will of God that children prevented by death of their baptisme, by Gods election, may be saved* (London: 1595), 9 takes issue especially with the Roman Catholic view that infants dying before baptism are damned.

1. Believers' infants are capable of being regenerated (of which baptism is the sign).

2. Some of them definitely are regenerated (i.e. those who die in infancy).

3. Therefore believers' infants should be baptised.

Step 3 does not seem to be a legitimate conclusion, given his premises. What is being left unsaid here? Is he suggesting, as some do, that we presume all believers' infants are in some sense regenerate and therefore have a right to be baptised?[95] Many other Reformed theologians (including Ursinus, Voetius, and Witsius) used an argument from the regeneration of covenant children who die in infancy in their polemics with Anabaptists.[96] If that's what Owen believed, he leaves the 'presumed regeneration' step in the argument unstated. Or is he merely talking about the capacity to be regenerate? If so, he has left himself open to the suggestion that on his logic anyone who is *capable* of being regenerated should be baptised. And does that not include the children of unbelievers, since he himself held that some of them are undoubtedly elect and so will be regenerated at some point? Yet he has already stated that such should not be baptised.

Has he therefore proved too much with this argument? The solution here does not appear to be straightforward or clearly spelled out in the condensed line of reasoning Owen presents. I do not think he is merely trying to establish that we should baptise all believers' children *in case* they die and prove thereby to have had a right to baptism (because, dying in infancy, they are saved). The evidence Owen brings can, however, be successfully deployed against his opponents' presuppositions in this way: if some children are saved they must be regenerated, and if

---

[95] See Schenck, *The Presbyterian Doctrine*, xiv, 11. For an overview of Reformed debates over presumptive regeneration and whether it can be used as a basis for infant baptism, see R.J. Mouw, 'Baptism and the Salvific Status of Children: An Examination of Some Intra-Reformed Debates' in CTJ 41 (2006), 242-251.

[96] See G. Vos, *Redemptive History and Biblical Interpretation* (Phillipsburg, NJ: P&R, 1980), 264.

regenerated then they have a theological right to be baptised; and if at least *some* children have a legitimate right to be baptised, then antipaedobaptists are wrong to say that no child should be baptised.[97]

Certainly to read Owen this way fits his polemical context and makes good logical sense of his otherwise difficult argument. On this reading, it does present a substantial counter to a familiar non-paedobaptist assertion, building on a commonly agreed premise that would be hard (theologically and pastorally) to deny. Yet however we evaluate the success or otherwise of this particular line of reasoning, clearly this argument involving the undeveloped assumption of infant salvation is not sufficient to establish the validity of infant baptism on its own.

5. Children and Parents Go Together

The principle that the sign (the external rite) and the grace (the spiritual reality) of baptism go together may be on firmer ground in Owen's sixth sub-point. Here he contends that children are by nature part of the same covenant as their parents, and are said by Scripture to be associated in it with them.[98] If true, this would be a strong argument that the sign of the covenant ought to be administered to them, since they already possess the covenant relationship which it seals. This perspective conceives of 'the thing signified' by baptism as at least partly a covenant relationship which can be objectively verified rather than an inner spiritual reality (such as regeneration) which cannot. Hence Owen argues from creation and from Romans 5:14 and 1 Corinthians 7:14 that children are dealt with by God in terms of the same covenant as their parents and 'those who, by God's appointment, and by virtue of the law of their creation, are, and must of necessity be, included in the covenant of their parents, have the same right with them unto the privileges of that covenant.' Owen had made this connection and argument for infant baptism since his earliest

---

[97] I am grateful to Gert van den Brink for pointing me to this solution.

[98] See also his comments on Hebrews 9:18-22 in *Works*, 23:354.

published work.[99] It was a connection that went back to the earliest days of the Reformation.

This argument is more in keeping with the general thrust of Owen's approach in previous points about the covenant. It argues on the basis of objective covenantal categories rather than from presumed or inferred subjective spiritual realities in the child itself, and is thus able to be focused on a promise of God which is where the Reformed doctrine is always strong. Stephen Marshall had used a similar line of defence, saying 'Thus it is by the laws of almost all nations... children follow the covenant-condition of their parents.'[100] Whether 1 Corinthians 7:14 could be used to prove the 'federal holiness' of the children of believers was of course hotly disputed. Marshall defended against several objections but Tombes summarised the usual rejoinder when he pointed out that on Marshall's exegesis of the passage an unbelieving spouse could legitimately be said to be part of the covenant and therefore be baptised, just as much as the children of such a union, since both were said to be 'holy.'[101]

Marshall and Tombes argued over whether 1 Corinthians 7:14 was referring to matrimonial/civil legitimacy or federal holiness/status.[102] Either way, however, Owen is not using the verse to say children are holy and therefore should be baptised, as some would.[103] He is merely using it as an example of how children are accounted to be in the same covenantal state as their parents. Whether the status being referred to is civil or spiritual, the verse does clearly show that the children share that legal standing with their parents, which is all Owen is asking it to prove. If children

---

[99] See *Works*, 10:81 (from 1643).

[100] Marshall, *A Sermon of the Baptizing of Infants*, 15.

[101] Tombes, *An Examen*, 79. Marshall in turn responded with further exegesis in *A Defence of Infant-Baptism* (London, 1646), 145-164.

[102] W. Hubbock, *An Apologie of Infants*, 22 referred to the view Tombes espoused as a Jesuit argument.

[103] *A Directory For The Publique Worship of God* (London, 1645) otherwise known as the *Westminster Directory*, states (page 21) that those baptised 'are Christians, and fœderally holy before baptism, and therefore are they baptised.'

share the same legal standing within the covenant as their parents then they have a right to the sign and seal of that covenant. This is how Thomas Cranmer had argued for infant baptism against the Anabaptists of his day too:

> Finally, their cruel ungodliness extends to baptism, which they do not want to be administered to infants, though for no reason whatsoever. For the children of Christians do not belong any less to God and the church than the children of the Hebrews once did, and since circumcision was given to them in infancy so also baptism ought to be imparted to our children, since they are participants in the same divine promise and covenant [*foederis*], and have been accepted by Christ with the greatest human kindness.[104]

For all its strengths, this argument must also account somehow for the strand of biblical evidence which does see baptism specifically as a sign of regeneration/new life and not merely a covenant relationship e.g. Romans 6:3-4 and Colossians 2:11-12. The Anglican answer is to say that 'Baptism is not only a sign of profession, and mark of difference, whereby Christian men are discerned from others that be not christened, but it is also a sign of Regeneration or New-Birth, whereby, as by an instrument, they that receive Baptism rightly are grafted into the Church' (Article 27). The right reception or efficacious appropriation of baptism may occur in or some time after the sign itself is applied. It is of course the response of faith, which enjoys the benefits granted by the legal 'instrument' of baptism. The *Westminster Confession*, the *Savoy Declaration*, and the Church of England all agree that, 'The efficacy of baptism is not tied to that moment of time wherein it is administered.'[105] Indeed, as the famous Gorham Judgment delivered by the supreme tribunal of the Church of England in

---

[104] Gerald Bray (ed.), *Tudor Church Reform: The Henrician Canons of 1535 and the Reformatio Legum Ecclesiasticarum* (Woodbridge, Suffolk: Boydell Press, 2000), 204-205. See also Bray (ed.), *Galatians-Ephesians*, 73-74 (Olevianus and Perkins).

[105] *Westminster Confession* 28.6 (*Savoy* 29.6)

1850 made clear, 'the grace of regeneration does not so necessarily accompany the act of baptism that regeneration invariably takes place in baptism; that the grace may be granted before, in, or after baptism; that baptism is an effectual sign of grace by which God works invisibly in us, but only in such as worthily receive it—in them alone it has a wholesome effect; and that without reference to the qualification of the recipient it is not in itself an effectual sign of grace; that infants baptized and dying before actual sin are undoubtedly saved, but that in no case is baptism unconditional.'[106]

Owen would agree elsewhere that baptism is linked to the new life spoken of in Romans 6, and is clear that without eventual faith all the privileges and benefits of baptism are lost (as we have seen above).[107] 'Of this regeneration baptism is the symbol, the sign, the expression, and representation' says Owen in *The True Nature of a Gospel Church* (published posthumously in 1689), and hence, 'unto those who are in a due manner partakers of it, it giveth all the external rights and privileges which belong unto them that are regenerate, until they come unto such seasons wherein the personal performance of those duties whereon the continuation of the estate of visible regeneration doth depend is required of them. Herein if they fail, they lose all privilege and benefit by their baptism.'[108] Yet he always had the same objective understanding of how to view baptised people, writing in 1647, 'That it was the manner of the saints, and the apostles themselves, to esteem of all baptized, initiated persons, ingrafted into the church, as sanctified persons; so that, speaking of backsliders, he could not make mention of them any otherwise than as they were commonly esteemed to be, and at that time, in the judgment of charity, were to be considered. Whether they were true believers or no... they could not be otherwise described.'[109] In his *Greater Catechism* he said baptism belongs 'Unto all to whom the promise

---

[106] See J.R.W. Stott, 'The Evangelical Doctrine of Baptism' in *Churchman* 112/1 (1998), 54.

[107] e.g. *A Discourse Concerning the Holy Spirit* in Owen, *Works*, 3:560-561.

[108] Owen, *Works*, 16:12.

[109] Owen, *Works*, 10:367.

of the covenant is made; that is, to believers, and to their seed', thus (again) showing his consistent commitment to this objective covenantal basis for infant baptism, from the 1640s until his death.[110]

Again we see then that the case for infant baptism has to be made by way of inference, consequence, and careful deduction. It cannot be decided simply by way of decisive proof-texting. Owen, however, is on clearer ground when he returns to arguments concerned with the covenant, and his logic here is less confusing than in the previous point.

6. Final Arguments

Owen's seventh argument in his short treatise on baptism revolves again around the covenant which God made with Abraham, to be God to him and to his offspring. Elsewhere he argues that whenever God declares that he will be God to someone (*I will be your God…*) this is covenant language, by which God engages himself to work on their behalf and for their good.[111] So if God promises to be God to the children of believers, he is taking them into covenant with himself. This is what he explicitly said to Abraham in Genesis 17:7, declares Owen, and Christ has fulfilled that very same covenant: he came to 'confirm the promises given to the patriarchs' (Romans 15:8), and to be 'the messenger of the covenant' (Malachi 3:1).[112] So, he argues, if God is no longer a God unto believers and their offspring, if believers' children are no longer to be part of the covenant, then Christ has not faithfully confirmed the truth of God in his promise to Abraham. We can no longer trust God to keep his promises! To get around this, Tombes wanted to deny that the covenant of which Christ was

---

[110] Owen, *Works*, 1:491.

[111] Owen, *Works*, 19:84. The context is a discussion of the *pactum salutis* or covenant of redemption, whereby the Father and the Son covenanted together in eternity concerning our salvation. I am grateful to the late Professor Willem van Asselt for first pointing me to Owen's exegetical argument here.

[112] Owen also cites Luke 1:72-73 as showing that Christ's coming was explicitly related to God remembering 'his holy covenant, the oath he swore to our father Abraham'.

the messenger was the same as the Abrahamic covenant; that was 'not a pure Gospel-covenant' but 'mixed' he claimed, with some spiritual, some temporal and some material promises.[113] Owen, however, replies that, 'Let it be named what covenant he was the messenger of, if not of this. Occasional additions of temporal promises do not in the least alter the nature of the covenant.'

According to Owen, Christ has fulfilled 'the covenant with Abraham, enlarged and explained by following promises.' Not only did the original promise include Abraham's children but Owen goes on to list other verses where it is said that 'the promises made unto the fathers were, that their infant seed, their buds and offspring, should have an equal share in the covenant with them' (Isaiah 22:24, 44:3, 61:9, 65:23). So again, to deny that children of believing parents had the same right and interest in the covenant as their parents was 'plainly to deny the fidelity of Christ in the discharge of his office.' If children are not to be accounted a part of the same covenant as their believing parents then Jesus has not done what he promised he would do, and God cannot be trusted. This again is a variant on the covenant arguments that Owen has already presented, but proven from different texts. Importantly, he makes it clear that children were included in God's plans way before the 'old covenant' of Sinai ('the covenant in its legal administration'). Their inclusion predates the now abolished Mosaic law but was part of the more comprehensive and overarching covenant promise to Abraham which endures in Christ.

We are ready now to hear his summary of the case:

> In brief, a participation of the seal of the covenant is a spiritual blessing. This the seed of believers was once solemnly invested in by God himself. This privilege he hath nowhere revoked, though he hath changed the outward sign; nor hath he granted unto our children any privilege or mercy in lieu of it now under the gospel, when all grace and privileges are

---

[113] Renihan, *Antipaedobaptism*, 72.

enlarged to the utmost. His covenant promises concerning them, which are multiplied, were confirmed by Christ as a true messenger and minister; he gives the grace of baptism unto many of them, especially those that die in their infancy, owns children to belong unto his kingdom, esteems them disciples, appoints households to be baptized without exception. And who shall now rise up, and withhold water from them?

Owen adds here the argument often made from the household baptisms in Acts,[114] as part of the overall picture being developed. Like Warfield, he does realise that 'infant baptism should not be founded solely on these passages alone',[115] yet they do provide potential evidence at least that where there were children present (other baptisms in Acts were of solitary individuals or groups of adults) they were included in the administration of the seal of the covenant for 'the culture of that day assumed that children were usually part of the family... the preference is for, not against, the inclusion of family members. It had been that way since the time of Noah (Genesis 7:1), Abraham (Genesis 17:12-13), Joshua (Joshua 24:15), and David (2 Samuel 12:10).'[116] As David Peterson comments, drawing attention to the parallel in Jewish proselyte baptism, 'it would be remarkable if no babies were included in any of the four household baptisms mentioned by Luke.'[117]

Owen's eighth and last point is to say that more could be said, and arguments from church history could usefully be employed at

---

[114] Acts 16:15, 16:32-33, 18:8. See also Acts 11:14 and 1 Corinthians 1:16. Marshall also enlists the household baptisms in a minor role in his *Sermon of the Baptizing of Infants*, 40. It is interesting that Paul performed two household baptisms in Philippi and later wrote to them that 'What you have learned and received and heard and seen in me—practice these things' (Philippians 4:9).

[115] Warfield, 'The Polemics of Infant Baptism', 397. Stein, 'Baptism in Luke-Acts', 62 warns against building too much on them.

[116] J.M. Watt, 'The *Oikos* Formula' in Strawbridge, *The Case for Covenantal Infant Baptism*, 84.

[117] David G. Peterson, *The Acts of the Apostles* (Grand Rapids: Eerdmans, 2009), 461.

this stage of the argument. Indeed, he goes on to engage in just such an argument (against Mr Tombes) on the very next page. It may well be significant that since his brief opening remarks about the silences of church history, he has only put forward biblical and doctrinal evidence, choosing to consign further arguments over church history to the end of the case (and not really developing them to any great extent). It is possible that this could be construed as something of a rebuke or correction to Tombes, Marshall, and others who indulged in extensive historical arguments at the beginning of their works on the subject, prior to biblical exegesis. Whether such a rebuke is intended here, it is certainly safe to say that for Owen we should begin with the Bible and build our doctrine from there. Church history and custom is important but should never be primary when it comes to determining our present practice.

Conclusion: A Solid and Consistent Argument

In his short treatise which we have been examining, Owen presents a rationale for covenantal infant baptism.[118] He defines the question carefully, and sets about proving his case with biblical and theological arguments designed to interact with and counter the attack made on the practice by antipaedobaptists such as John Tombes.[119] He has his eye throughout on the glory and honour of Christ which he perceives to be under threat if the children of believers are not given the sign of the covenant which Christ has confirmed. He seeks to defend not just a doctrine but the loving care God has for the church, which he felt was not always adequately appreciated. He argues by way of inference and consequence, sometimes less successfully, but always with a view

---

[118] For more on the covenantal nature of baptism in an English context, see Lee Gatiss, 'The Anglican Doctrine of Baptism', especially pages 86-88. Owen was, of course, a good Anglican (in a doctrinal sense). See 'Anglicanism and John Owen' in *Crux* 52.1 (2016), 44-53.

[119] As Renihan, *Antipaedobaptism*, 223 says, 'All of the major works on baptism in the middle thirty years of the seventeenth century were written to interact with Tombes.' He was 'the sharpening agent for the Covenantal Paedobaptistic view' (page 210). Cf. pages 11-12.

to the practical implications not just for baptism but for other areas of theology and practice as well.

Significantly, he does not seem to have Roman Catholic errors particularly in mind as he develops this short treatise. Nor does he so anathematise non-paedobaptists that differences over this doctrine become a bar to toleration in and of themselves.[120] In 1645 he wrote that, 'It is hard to say whether the error of the Papists, requiring baptism of absolute, indispensable necessity to the salvation of every infant, or that of the Anabaptists, debarring them from it altogether, be the most uncharitable.'[121] Yet his respect for the Baptist preacher John Bunyan is well known,[122] and he did not, like some Presbyterians, want to criminalise Baptists.[123] In 1657, he compared them to the Donatists, but said it would be be difficult to label them schismatics for their errant doctrine of baptism alone.[124] And while he refused in 1669 to defend their opinions and practices, saying 'You know our judgment and practice to be contrary unto theirs... wherein (God assisting) we shall continue to the end', he did write to the

[120] For Owen's views on toleration see *Of Toleration: and the Duty of the Magistrate about Religion* in *Works* 8:163-206 about which R. G. Lloyd, *John Owen: Commonwealth Puritan* (Pontypridd: Modern Welsh Publications, 1972), 62-63 comments, 'it was the first work on toleration ever to be published in England while the author's own party was in power.'

[121] Owen, *Works*, 1:491 (this footnote is in the original publication). Here he also indicates that he thought the best mode of administering baptism was by sprinkling. In *Works*, 16:267 he writes against the necessity of 'dipping.'

[122] See Toon, *God's Statesman*, 161-162. See also Bunyan's *Differences in Judgement about Water-Baptism no Bar to Communion* (London, 1673) in which he took an eirenic position towards paedobaptists in contrast to other 'Baptists' such as Kiffin, Paul, and Danvers. Bunyan claimed Owen endorsed his arguments, though we have no preface by Owen to prove that; see Gribben, *John Owen*, 250.

[123] See 'An Ordinance for the punishing of Blasphemies and Heresies', in C. H. Firth and R. S. Rait (eds.), *Acts and Ordinances of the Interregnum, 1642-1660* (London, 1911), 1133-1136 which would have criminalised those who taught that 'the baptizing of Infants is unlawfull, or such Baptism is void, and that such persons ought to be re-baptized again, and in pursuance thereof shall baptize any person formerly baptized.'

[124] Owen, *Works*, 13:184. He says Baptists do the same thing as the Donatists, though not for exactly the same reasons. They may tend towards the schismatic while Owen, he says, remains a child of the church of England.

Governor of Massachusetts that it wasn't 'indispensably necessary' to be quite so rigorous in physically punishing the Baptists there.[125] Given all that I have presented above, there is no evidence whatsoever that his theological distaste for antipaedobaptism was lessened by the years or by personal familiarity with Baptists or by *any* alleged 'developments' in his own theology; though he was tolerant of some of them in a way he was not tolerant of Socinians and others.[126]

It is interesting that Owen does not rest his argument for infant baptism on paedofaith or on a particular reading of the new covenant described in Jeremiah 31. He does not build it upon a single text such as Colossians 2:11-12 as some might.[127] What Owen is concerned with, however, is expounding the doctrine of infant baptism in a way that pays attention to the whole unified sweep of biblical revelation from creation to consummation, in order to demonstrate that Jesus does indeed secure and command the destiny of his children, from life's first cry until their final breath.

---

[125] Toon, *The Correspondence of John Owen*, 145-146 (a letter from Owen and other Independent ministers).

[126] Gribben, *John Owen and English Puritanism*, 140 and elsewhere speaks of milestones in Owen's career whereby he came to find 'ways of working alongside Baptists.' For Owen's greater dislike of Socinians, see Lee Gatiss, 'Socinianism and John Owen' in *The Southern Baptist Journal of Theology* 20.4 (Winter 2016). The article can also be found at http://equip.sbts.edu/wp-content/uploads/2017/03/SBJT-20.4-Gatiss-Socinianism-2016.pdf

[127] *Westminster Confession* 28.1 speaks of baptism as admission into the visible church, and it is perhaps also noteworthy that Owen does not use that language in the posthumously published baptism treatise (cf. its omission from the *Savoy Declaration* 29:1). He does however say in Owen, *Works*, 15:95 that we are baptised not into particular churches but 'unto the catholic church visible.' So that if the specific church where we were baptised goes awry, our baptism is not thereby invalidated.

Strangely Warmed: John Wesley's Arminian Campaigns

This is an enlarged and modified version of the 2014 St Antholin Lecture, first published by Latimer Trust. I wish to especially to thank Ermine Desmond, my Cornish Calvinist friend Steve Walton, and my Arminian friends, Tom McCall and Fred Sanders, for their interaction on some of this material.

As we have seen, the Reformed faith is no arid intellectual curiosity, but was meant to be preached and lived with passion and conviction. One man who epitomises that is George Whitefield (1714-1770). Whitefield has been rightly celebrated as one of the primary causes, humanly-speaking, of the Evangelical Revival of the eighteenth century. His most recent biographer lauds him as America's spiritual founding father.[1] His name has been kept alive by evangelical Baptists and evangelical Presbyterians, especially in North America.[2] Yet he has been

---

[1] Thomas Kidd, *George Whitefield: America's Spiritual Founding Father* (Yale: Yale University Press, 2014).

[2] For example, the Banner of Truth published his journals and a (surprisingly) small selection of his sermons. And Whitefield's greatest biographer is the Canadian Baptist, Arnold Dallimore.

strangely neglected in large measure by English Anglicans, despite being a thoroughgoing Church of England man.[3]

This relative neglect of Whitefield may not be surprising, however, when we consider that early on, the eighteenth-century evangelists were often barred from Anglican pulpits. One of those places seems to have been St Helen's, Bishopsgate, which today has something of a reputation as a flagship evangelical church. More than once when I was on the staff there I was told the story of how graceless and dead St Helen's must have been in those heady days of the revival. Why? Well, John Wesley came to preach at St Helen's one Tuesday lunchtime in May 1738, and afterwards he wrote in his diary that someone said to him, 'Sir you must preach here no more.'[4]

Obviously the doctrines of grace and salvation were despised and misunderstood in eighteenth-century Bishopsgate! Yet I was always intrigued by this, so I did a bit of research. I read George Whitefield's journals and I found that he had preached at St Helen's as well, one Sunday afternoon in August 1736, and had been received far more favourably. In one of his journal entries he says that as he ascended the stairs to the pulpit he felt they sneered at him on account of his youth but, 'they soon grew serious and exceedingly attentive.' It ended well, for Whitefield: 'After I came down, [they] showed me great tokens of respect, blessed me as I passed along, and made great inquiry who I was.'[5]

What was going on? Why, if Whitefield was received so well, was Wesley not also embraced at this clearly evangelical church? I suspected it was an evangelical church because I discovered that in

---

[3] See Lee Gatiss, 'George Whitefield — the Anglican Evangelist' in *The Southern Baptist Journal of Theology* 18.2 (2014), 71-81.

[4] Journal entry for Tuesday 9th May 1738 in T. Jackson (ed.), *The Works of John Wesley* (Grand Rapids: Baker, 2007), 1:93. The Sunday before he had been told something similar by those at nearby St. Lawrence's and St. Katherine Cree, having been 'enabled to speak strong words at both.'

[5] G. Whitefield, *George Whitefield's Journals: A new edition containing fuller material than any hitherto published* (Edinburgh: Banner of Truth, 1960), 77. He also narrates how dazed he was by the size of the church and the congregation at first, but was calmed by 'considering in whose name I was about to speak.'

1662, the minister (Arthur Barham) had been ejected by the Act of Uniformity;[6] one of his successors (Thomas Horton) had published sermons full of God's election, Christ's penal substitution, particular atonement, the imputation of the active obedience of Christ, irresistible grace, the importance of promiscuous gospel preaching to all, and the necessity of the new birth;[7] and an eighteenth-century Lecturer at the church (Erasmus Middleton) was a famous Calvinistic Methodist, a graduate of Kingswood School, who edited *The Gospel Magazine* after Augustus Toplady. So what was I missing about John Wesley and the Evangelical Revival? The problem, I later found, is that the controversy started by Wesley in his strangely heated opposition to Reformed Anglican doctrine, has been systematically hushed up and played down by historians and hagiographers alike.[8] So much so, that opposition to Wesley is even now taken by some with little knowledge of Wesley's actual teaching to be straightforward opposition to the gospel itself.

I was less surprised, however, at the strong reactions against Mr Wesley when I tracked down the printed version of his sermon on Romans 8:32, which is the text he preached on at St Helen's in May 1738. It is a sermon he used on many occasions. From start to finish it is a sustained, emotive, combative, highly prejudiced and somewhat patronizing rant against Reformed doctrine, Calvinism. He went on and on about how believing in predestination was bad for your spiritual health and that it destroyed all zeal for good works, especially the good work of evangelism. No-one will evangelize if they believe in predestination, he asserted.

Predestination, Wesley pronounced, was 'a doctrine full of blasphemy.' He complained bitterly against 'the horrible blasphemies

---

[6] See my *The Tragedy of 1662*, (London: Latimer Trust, 2007), 30, 39, 43-48 on Arthur Barham, the Presbyterian Vicar of St. Helen's, ejected in 1662.

[7] See Thomas Horton (Rector from 1666), *Forty-six Sermons upon the Whole Eighth Chapter of the Epistle of the Apostle Paul to the Romans* (London, 1674), 9-14, 50, 501-503.

[8] See my survey of the histories by Bebbington, Gibson, Ryle, Balleine, and Noll in *The True Profession of the Gospel: Augustus Toplady and Reclaiming our Reformed Foundations* (London: Latimer Trust, 2010), 33-35.

contained in this horrible doctrine.'[9] To those who might disagree with his convictions he said, 'You represent God as worse than the devil; more false, more cruel, more unjust... no scripture can prove predestination... I abhor the doctrine of predestination.' He then went on to portray those who believe in the Reformed doctrine of predestination as worse than the baby-sacrificing worshippers of the false god Moloch. And this is not just a brief, off-the-cuff aside—this is the tenor of the whole sermon, and the reason it was published.[10]

I have to say that doing a bit of historical research certainly changed my mind about where St Helen's stood in the eighteenth century. My sympathies are clearly with the discerning minister or churchwarden who sought to protect the church from hearing such divisive and melodramatic things again. If I'd been there as Wesley preached, I think I too would have said, 'Sir you must preach here no more.'

Julia Wedgwood's nineteenth-century biography of Wesley makes the rather insightful comment that Wesley's sermon against predestination has 'in it something of that provoking glibness with which young or half-cultivated people settle in a few sentences questions that have exercised the deepest minds ever since the dawn of speculation... Indeed, it is evident on reading this sermon that, of all the deep works which had been written on the subject, Wesley had never read one.'[11] Yet he pronounced so

---

[9] Calvin had termed predestination *decretum horribile* (*Institutes*, 3.23.7), and Wesley is playing on how that sounds in English. But this semantic anachronism fails to acknowledge that in Latin the word *horribilis* does not have the sense of 'disgusting, odious, loathsome.' It is more akin to 'awesome, fearful' and can even have a good sense, 'astonishing, tremendous, amazing.' Calvin was awestruck by predestination, not repulsed, saying in his French translation, '*Je confesse que ce décret nous doit épouvanter*' — it is frightening. Cf. *Institutes* 3.20.17 where he speaks of *horribilis Dei majestas*, which does not mean he finds God horrid.

[10] See *The Works of John Wesley*, 7:380-383. See the startling accusations in his hymn 'Universal Redemption' about such people too: 'Whoe'er admits; my soul disowns, The image of a torturing God, Well-pleased with human shrieks and groans, A fiend, a Molock gorged with blood! Good God! that any child of Thine, So horribly should think of Thee! Lo! all my hopes I here resign, If all may not find grace with me.'

[11] J. Wedgwood, *John Wesley and the Evangelical Reaction of the Eighteenth Century* (London: Macmillan, 1870), 226-227.

forcefully on these weighty issues. This sermon was printed and reprinted many times in the following years, despite the howls of protest from Whitefield and others who pleaded with Wesley not to publish it at all.

Now, it has been suggested to me that Wesley just didn't understand grace when he preached like this in 1738. His heart had yet to be 'strangely warmed' by the gospel when he had his so-called 'Aldersgate experience', at St Botolph's, Aldersgate near St Paul's Cathedral in the City of London. It is true that the St Helen's sermon was on May 9th, and the reported warming of Wesley's heart was not to happen until May 24th. However, he disliked predestination, just as his mother did, from very early on.[12] Iain Murray rightly notes that 'Wesley's opposition to Calvinism stiffened rather than weakened.'[13] His heart was always strangely warmed against it.

Wesley was, always would be, and always had been an Arminian. Arminians were fiercely opposed to things such as unconditional predestination which they regarded as Calvinist nonsense. So Wesley printed this sermon and several other polemical works time and time again. Not just in 1738, but in 1739 and 1740 as well, when the Revival was in full swing. He published about a dozen explicitly anti-Calvinist, anti-predestination works just in the few months after Whitefield's return to England following a mission to America. It was a deliberate ploy to mock, caricature, and oppose Reformed theology, and especially 'the hellish doctrine' of predestination:

> O Horrible decree,
> Worthy of whence it came!
> Forgive their hellish blasphemy
> Who charge it on the Lamb.[14]

---

[12] See M. Wellings, 'Susannah Wesley, 1669-1742,' in A. Atherstone (ed.), *The Heart of Faith: Following Christ in the Church of England* (Cambridge: Lutterworth, 2008), 64-65.

[13] I.H. Murray, *Wesley and Men Who Followed* (Edinburgh: Banner of Truth, 2003), 68.

[14] From Wesley's hymn, 'The Horrible Decree' published in 1741.

Hymns were just one more weapon in his war against this doctrine.[15] Wesley's line was that 'God told me to preach and print this.' He had cast lots and received very clear guidance, he said, to 'preach and print' against predestination. The truth is though, it was all part of a rather sad and sordid power-play against Whitefield, who had left the rather imperious Wesley to look after the nascent evangelical movement while he went to preach in America. While Whitefield was out of the way, Wesley used his position to gather followers, pressurise booksellers to stock his Arminian tracts,[16] and form his own movement instead.

His distinctive rallying calls were his stance against predestination and his teaching on perfectionism. Arnold Dallimore's biography of Whitefield tells the full story in all its crude and shocking detail, of how Wesley tried to stamp his own mark and authority on the revival, and put himself at its head.[17] One of the things he did during this period was preach incessantly on the classic texts at issue between Calvinists and Arminians, such as 1 Timothy 2:3-6, John 1:29, and 1 John 2:2.[18] He was warmed to the fight, and would not let it lie.

---

[15] See J.R. Tyson, *Assist Me to Proclaim: The Life and Hymns of Charles Wesley* (Grand Rapids: Eerdmans, 2007), 99-116 on how the Wesleys' hymns opposed 'the poison of Calvin'. As a rejoinder, see George Thomson, Rector of St Gennys, Cornwall (1732-1782), who was a friend of Wesley's until he wrote, 'Believers would ye gladly know, why some the gospel net confine, whilst over others clear they go; the reason is the will divine. Seek ye to know why some can melt, beneath thy word, and some are stone; the cause why 'tis, and 'tis not felt, lies in Jehovah's breast alone... Then n'er let us his will dispute, nor foolishly his ways arraign, before their God let men be mute, 'tis fit and right that he should reign.' See G.C.B. Davies, *The Early Cornish Evangelicals* (London: SPCK, 1951), 48-49.

[16] See Wesley's letter to James Hutton in A. Dallimore, *George Whitefield: The Life and Times of the Great Evangelist of the 18th Century Revival. Volume 1* (Edinburgh: Banner of Truth, 1970), 314.

[17] See Dallimore, *George Whitefield*, 306-319 and volume 2, 18-41.

[18] See *The Works of John Wesley*, 1:188-193 (April -May 1739).

George Whitefield's Reply

Whitefield was extremely reluctant to enter the lists against Wesley on this subject. Yet eventually, when Wesley had turned up the heat too far, he felt constrained to offer a reply in a public letter to Wesley.[19] It was clear, courteous, and effective. What's more it was very restrained and mildly put in comparison with Wesley's bitter invective, especially when that is read in the context of Wesley's shenanigans in attempting to hijack and take over Whitefield's movement while he was abroad. One of the things he criticises Wesley for is ignoring the actual text he was meant to be preaching on:

> Had any one a mind to prove the doctrine of *election*, as well as of *final perseverance*, he could hardly wish for a text more fit for his purpose, than that which you have chosen to disprove it. One that does not know you would suspect you yourself was [sic] sensible of this: for after the first paragraph, I scarce know whether you have mentioned it so much as once, through your whole sermon.[20]

Whitefield refers to several books which he thinks helpful and unanswerable on the points in question. Clearly he *had* read some deep works written on the subject, and encourages Wesley more than once to go and do likewise. Whitefield even sent Wesley copies of books which he thought he might find helpful in answering his objections. Whitefield was standing on the shoulders of giants in the Puritan and Reformed tradition.

Wesley, who obviously identified Whitefield with the wider Reformed tradition, wrote that no Baptist or Presbyterian writer he had read knew anything of the liberties of Christ. His father

---

[19] Dallimore, *George Whitefield* 2:551-569 and George Whitefield's *Journals*, 563-588. See also several earlier private letters in Dallimore, *George Whitefield*, 1:571-581.

[20] Dallimore, *George Whitefield* 2:555; emphasis original. See Lee Gatiss, *For Us and For Our Salvation*, 24-27 on the use of Romans 8:32 in arguments about predestination and limited atonement from Augustine and Gottschalk to the Roman Catholic Catechism.

had once been imprisoned for speaking so furiously against the Dissenters, and John Wesley evidently shared his opinion of nonconformists. Whitefield counters this by arguing that Wesley's sermon associated him with a different tradition: Your idea of 'universal redemption is a notion sadly adapted to keep the soul in its lethargic sleepy condition, and therefore so many natural men admire and applaud it,' he wrote. 'Infidels of all kinds are on your side of the question. Deists, Arians, Socinians, arraign God's sovereignty, and stand up for universal redemption.' He then cites Article 17 to show that 'our godly reformers did not think election destroyed holiness.' He even questions Wesley's loyalty to the Church of England saying, 'I cannot but blame you for censuring the clergy of our church for not keeping to their articles, when you yourself by your principles, positively deny the 9th, 10th, and 17th.'[21]

Whitefield's response places him very firmly in what we can call the Reformed tradition of the Church of England. So he says, for instance:

> But, blessed be God, our Lord knew for whom he died. There was an eternal compact between the Father and the Son. A certain number was then given him, as the purchase and reward of his obedience and death. For these he prayed, John xvii, and not for the world. For these, and these only, he is now interceding, and with their salvation he will be fully satisfied.[22]

One can see why the hymnwriter Toplady says that Whitefield was not only a great evangelist but also 'a most excellent systematic divine.'[23] This is careful, covenantal, Calvinist divinity, preached with passion and fervour. In the rest of his reply to Wesley, Whitefield shows several times why he thinks such

---

[21] Dallimore, *George Whitefield* 2:559-569.

[22] Ibid., 568.

[23] A.M. Toplady, *The Complete Works of Augustus Toplady* (Harrisburg, Virginia: Sprinkle Publications, 1987), 494.

doctrines are a very good thing in terms of encouraging a godly life and spurring us on to evangelism—rather than being a bad thing as Wesley had alleged. Predestination, rather than something to be abhorred, was Whitefield's daily comfort and support, he said. This is warm piety allied to solid theology, all served up in a firm but friendly tone.

In one of his sermons Whitefield talks about those who dislike this sort of Reformed theology. 'They that are not led to see this, I wish them better heads; though, I believe, numbers that are against it have got better hearts: the Lord help us to bear with one another where there is an honest heart.'[24] But Wesley hated all this. Wesley's great grandfather was a well-known Puritan, John White. And Wesley's grandfather, Samuel Annesley, was a Puritan, nonconformist minister. He had a little meeting room in St Helen's Place, right next door to St Helen's, Bishopsgate. But Wesley's parents quickly abandoned their evangelical and puritan roots. His father was a Church of England clergyman, and John Wesley called himself a High Churchman born of High Church parents.[25] He was brought up to despise the Reformed faith and his puritan heritage.

Now, let us be clear on all this. Wesley may well have believed in all the objective facts of salvation such as substitutionary atonement and the bodily resurrection of Christ. But he wasn't just mistaken about 'small' or 'difficult' things like predestination; he was also confused about Christian perfection, which he taught as being attainable in this life, and he even wobbled on the doctrine of justification by faith alone. So if we go forward to Wesley's Methodist Conference in 1770, we find Wesley had been losing patience with the Evangelical Calvinists. He chose this moment, the year when George Whitefield died, to return to the Arminian distinctives, but particularly to justification and its relationship to holiness with which he had been wrestling. The Minutes of the Conference were, Jim Packer says, 'so drafted as to

[24] Lee Gatiss (ed.), *The Sermons of George Whitefield* (Wheaton, IL: Crossway, 2012), 2:447 (Sermon 61).

[25] John Telford (ed.), *The Letters of John Wesley: Volume 5* (London, 1931), 156.

appear to teach, Roman-style, that a man's works are the ground of his acceptance with God.' For example, as well as rebuking the Methodists for leaning 'too much towards Calvinism' (a poisonous plague which was worse than all the devices of Satan), Wesley told them this:

> [E]very believer, till he comes to glory, works *for*, as well as *from*, life… We have received it as a maxim that 'a man is to do nothing in order to justification.' Nothing can be more false… Is not this salvation by works? Not by the *merit* of works, but by works as a *condition*… we are every hour and every moment pleasing or displeasing to God, 'according to our works'.[26]

Read that again, slowly: we do good works *for* eternal life, not just spurred on by a new birth; it is false to say that we contribute nothing to our justification (i.e. it is not by faith alone); good works are a condition of our salvation. Wesley is not simply saying here that God has prepared good works for us to walk in (Ephesians 2:10).[27]

These sorts of assertion are rightly shocking to those taught to value our Reformation heritage. So, writes Iain Murray, 'If Wesley's theology was confused, why some might ask, should we value his memory today? The answer is that it is not in his theology that his real legacy lies. Christian leaders are raised up for different purposes. The eighteenth century evangelicals were primarily men of action, and in that role, John Wesley did and said much which was to the lasting benefit of many thousands.'[28] That may be true,

---

[26] J.I. Packer, 'Arminianisms,' in *Honouring the People of God: Collected Shorter Works of J. I. Packer Volume 4* (Carlisle: Paternoster, 1999), 301. For the text of the Minutes see e.g. F. Cook, *Selina Countess of Huntingdon: Her Pivotal Role in the 18th Century Evangelical Awakening* (Edinburgh: Banner of Truth, 2001), 278-279.

[27] As Tom Schreiner rightly says. after examining some of Wesley's conflicting statements about the imputation of Christ's righteousness, 'It seems that Wesley isn't always consistent, and he is also confusing, for in some instances he appears to merge justification and sanctification.' Thomas Schreiner, *Faith Alone: The Doctrine of Justification* (Grand Rapids: Zondervan, 2015), 93.

[28] I.H. Murray, *Wesley and Men Who Followed* (Edinburgh: Banner of Truth, 2003), 79.

in a way. But we may also want to go on and ask whether celebrity men of action can really be so easily excused a little dodgy theology on basic issues of salvation.

George Whitefield on the other hand, though he was rather prone to some dramatic excesses in his early years, was a much more admirable figure I think. He himself admitted that he spoke in a style 'too apostolical' in his early days, and as difficult as it might have been for a celebrity preacher, he publicly repented of it.[29] Some say Whitefield was merely an entertainer or dramatist, with little interest in theology.[30] But this is palpable nonsense! His Reformed theology gave his message and preaching a depth and stability that Wesley lacked. While Wesley's influence would spread far and wide across the globe, much of Whitefield's lasting legacy remained within the Church of England, and the evangelical movement. Most of the conforming evangelicals and those in the Countess of Huntingdon's Connexion were Reformed in theology like Whitefield.

Wesley's Continuing Campaigns

Now, it would be bad enough if Wesley and Whitefield fell out— the two great names in the Evangelical Revival—and at the height of all the awakening activity. But what if Wesley continued to press his case for Arminianism even further? What else would happen? Let's look further at Wesley's controversial campaigns, to put his spat with Whitefield into some kind of context. They are sometimes known as the Calvinist controversies. But that label was obviously invented to make Calvinism look as if *it* was the troublemaker. Others at the time did not see it that way: they saw that the problem was Wesley's Arminianism and his campaigns to promote it. It was he who, in Whitefield's words, threw in the bone of contention.

---

[29] See *The Works of the Reverend George Whitefield: Volume 2* (1771), 144. See also George Whitefield's *Journals*, 462 note 1 on retractions from his journals concerning his overly hasty, 'rash and uncharitable,' assessment of some American theologians.

[30] E.g. H.S. Stout, *The Divine Dramatist: George Whitefield and the Rise of Modern Evangelicalism* (Grand Rapids: Eerdmans, 1991).

The first Arminian controversy was that cold war between Wesley and Whitefield in the 1740s. In the 1750s and 1760s, James Hervey for the Reformed was attacked by John Fletcher and others for the Arminians.[31] This was round two. Round three, however, would see Wesley go up against the most able of all those on the Calvinist side of the debate: Augustus Montague Toplady. He is most famous as a hymn writer. He wrote *A Debtor to Mercy Alone* and the startling and oft-quoted lines from *Rock of Ages*, 'Nothing in my hand I bring, simply to thy cross I cling.' But he was also a preacher, a historian, and a controversialist of great talent.

Toplady linked Arminian theology to Pelagius, the arch-heretic who had opposed Augustine in the fourth century. Some might find this offensive perhaps, but Wesley was in fact happy to identify with Pelagius as (apparently) one of the righteous remnant in church history, a true Christian, a holy man, who had been unfairly stigmatized by the nasty abusive Augustine (who wasn't worth listening to). All Pelagius was trying to say, averred Wesley, was that a Christian can go on to perfection and fulfil the law of Christ.[32] Although it is very unusual in the whole of church history for anyone to voluntarily identify themselves and some part of their theology with Pelagius, Wesley deliberately and consciously phrases his exposition of Pelagius' doctrine on this point to sound just like his own.[33] Whether Wesley really *is* best characterised as a Pelagian is not really my point. He puts himself in the place of Pelagius here with a sympathetic tone and posture, not just by summarising his doctrine in the way he does, but by

---

[31] See J. Hervey, *Aspasio Vindicated in Eleven Letters from Mr Hervey to the Rev. John Wesley* (London, 1764) for an example of the literature from this second phase of the Arminian controversies.

[32] *The Works of John Wesley*, 6:328-329. Augustine may have 'bespattered' poor old Pelagius, but 'his word is not worth a rush' says Mr Wesley. Why? 'And here is the secret: St Augustine was angry at Pelagius: hence he slandered and abused him, (as his manner was).'

[33] See my further comments on Wesley's doctrine of original sin in *The True Profession of the Gospel*, 63, 105-107 particularly the ideas that no-one is damned for original sin, and that it no longer functions so as to render us unable to respond to God for salvation.

painting his opponents in the same way he paints Augustine (i.e. they all hate me and are nasty, horrible people etc.). As Wesley wrote in 1761, 'Who was Pelagius? By all I can pick up from ancient authors, I guess he was both a wise and a holy man.'[34]

Toplady also linked Arminianism to Rome. Indeed, he said, 'Arminianism is the forerunner which prepares the way for Rome, and, if not discarded in time, will one day open the door to it.'[35] J. C. Ryle seems to consider Toplady's identification of Arminians with Pelagians and Papists a scandalous outrage.[36] In fact, Ryle has done more than anyone to destroy Toplady's reputation because of this, in his popular book on the Christian leaders of the eighteenth century. Yet these were, of course, not unusual connections to make in the sixteenth, seventeenth, or eighteenth centuries. Whitefield (whom Ryle loves) and many others also drew attention to the theological links. Whitefield preached that Arminianism is the religion of 'the natural man', that we are all Papists or Arminians at heart, that 'Arminian principles' are 'antichristian principles' inspired and taught by Satan, and 'the back door to Popery'.[37] I am not defending this language as such, only pointing out that Toplady was not the originator or sole user of it. Indeed, it had been standard practice in the Puritan debates against Laudianism and the Remonstrants.[38]

---

[34] *Letter CCVI. To Mr Alexander Coates. July 7, 1761* in *The Works of the Rev. John Welsey* (Fourth Edition; London: John Mason, 1841), 224. Ironically, considering his thoughts about the 'horrible decree' of predestination, he advises Mr Coates, 'Avoid all those strong, rhetorical exclamations, 'O horrid! O dreadful! and the like'.'

[35] Toplady, *Complete Works*, 661-662.

[36] J.C. Ryle, *Christian Leaders of the Eighteenth Century* (Edinburgh: Banner of Truth, 1978 [1885]), 380.

[37] See Gatiss, *The Sermons of George Whitefield*, 1:219, 262, 266, 273, 387.

[38] Books were published in the seventeenth century with names like *A parallel: of new-old Pelgiarminian error and Pelagius redivivus: or Pelagius raked out of the ashes by Arminius and his schollers* (these both by Daniel Featley in 1626). John Owen's first publication in 1642 was called *A Display of Arminianism: Being a Discovery of the Old Pelagian Idol, Free Will, with the New Goddess Contingency, Advancing Themselves into the Throne of the God of Heaven, to the Prejudice of his Grace.*

It was also not unusual when elsewhere Toplady linked the rise of immorality in the country with the rise of Arminianism in the Church, especially under the Merry Monarch, Charles II. 'Let the clergy learn to despise the sinful pleasures, maxims, pursuits, and doctrines of the world; and the world will, from that moment, cease to despise the clergy,' Toplady wrote to the Bench of Bishops. 'Your lordships observe with pain the glaring and almost universal decay of moral virtue—this has been a growing calamity, ever since the restoration of the Stuart line in the person of Charles II. With that prince, Arminianism returned as a flood; and licentiousness of manners was co-extensive with it.'[39] Was that outrageous? Well, if it was, we could also point out that several leading Arminian Methodists including Wesley accused Calvinists of all manner of evils, alleging they were unchristian, heretical, Islamic, fatalistic, cold and emotionless sloths whose principles proved they must be uninterested in evangelism, and such like. So accusing *them* of a tendency to Pelagianism (an identification Wesley appeared happily to accept) hardly seems comparable on the insult scale.

The Zanchi Tract War

Toplady and Wesley came to blows in print between 1769 and 1772, in what I call the Zanchi Tract War.

In November 1769, Toplady published a translation of a work on predestination by Jerome Zanchius (1516-1590) which he entitled *The Doctrine of Absolute Predestination Stated and Asserted*. This had been influential in his own spiritual development while he was a student and he had originally translated it in 1760, when he was 19. After some prompting from his Baptist friend John Gill and others he overcame his diffidence and decided the time was now right to publish this translation.

Zanchi's book leans heavily on Luther's reply to Erasmus on the bondage of the will which we looked at in chapter 1, as well as on Augustine. It covers election, reprobation, particular

---

[39] Toplady, *Complete Works*, 278.

redemption, and various objections to those doctrines, concluding with a section promoting promiscuous gospel preaching to all and public teaching on predestination for the saints. The ultimate reason for focusing on this doctrine, he said, was that 'scarce any other distinguishing doctrine of the gospel can be preached in its purity and consistency without this of predestination.'[40]

A few months later, John Wesley wrote to his Methodist colleague Walter Sellon. He had already asked Sellon to write something against John Owen's work on limited atonement or particular redemption, disliking that doctrine intensely. He tasked Sellon with writing against Toplady as well, 'in order to stop the mouth of that vain boaster.' Evidently Wesley felt threatened by the arrival of the much younger Toplady on the scene.[41] It was Wesley himself, however, who made the most public response to the translation of Zanchi. He put out an abridgement of Toplady's work with the same title and published under Toplady's own name (but for his own profit).[42]

Three observations ought to be made on this abridgement. First, it does capture something of the general flow of Zanchius' argument and retain a few of the choicest quotations; as revision notes for an exam on Zanchius' philosophy this material might have some use. Second, however, Wesley removes entirely the biblical aspect of Zanchi's presentation. For example, in Toplady's translation there are around 350 quotations and citations from Scripture, around which the whole argument is built. In Wesley's abridgement there is just one biblical allusion (*Esau have I hated*) and that without giving the reference (Malachi 1:3 and Romans 9:13). This leaves an entirely different taste in the mouth and castrates the persuasive potential of the work for Christian readers.

---

[40] Toplady, *Complete Works*, 704.

[41] *The Works of John Wesley*, 13:44-45. In *The Letters of John Wesley: Volume 5*, 167 this letter also contains Wesley's description of Toplady as a 'lively coxcomb' (a conceited, showy person).

[42] 'The Doctrine of Absolute Predestination Stated and Asserted by the Reverend Mr A___ T___,' in *The Works of John Wesley*, 14:190-198.

Finally, and most alarmingly, Wesley himself added a whole paragraph to the book, which was all his own work. It was calculated to paint both predestination and Augustus Toplady in as bad a light as possible.

> The sum of all is this: One in twenty (suppose) of mankind are elected; nineteen in twenty are reprobated. The elect shall be saved, do what they will: The reprobate shall be damned, do what they can. Reader, believe this, or be damned. Witness my hand, A___ T___.[43]

Naturally, Toplady felt somewhat aggrieved by this gross misrepresentation. He replied to Wesley, pointing out that 'In almost any other case, a similar forgery would transmit the criminal to Virginia or Maryland, if not to Tyburn... If such an opponent can be deemed an honest man,' he continues, 'where shall we find a knave?'[44] There were harsh laws at the time against forgery, which did indeed (in an unrelated case) lead to the execution at Tyburn of one of Mr Wesley's acquaintances in 1777. But Toplady thought it better to refute Wesley's falsehoods than take him to court for his plagiaristic libel.

As far as this infamous final paragraph was concerned, for example, the numbers were wrong (and presumptuous!) and certainly not mine, said the younger man. In Toplady's opinion, 'The kingdom of glory will both be more largely and more variously peopled than bigots of all denominations are either able to think, or willing to allow.'[45] Wesley's summary of what he had written was also scurrilous, with entirely false implications. The elect are not saved 'do what they will' but 'chosen as much to holiness as to heaven.'[46]

---

[43] ibid., 191.

[44] Toplady, *Complete Works*, 721. Being sent to the American plantations for hard labour was a severe punishment; Tyburn was a central London venue for hangings.

[45] ibid., 726.

[46] ibid., 735.

Equally importantly, Toplady neither claimed nor thought that Arminians were all going to hell.[47] He never said one had to be a Calvinist to be saved. That, of course, would have been a strange thing for him to assert, given that he was an Arminian himself for several years after his conversion and does not subsequently re-date his conversion to the year he became a Calvinist. He thought many Arminians were 'pious, moderate, respectable men,' adding, 'Of these I myself know more than a few: and have the happiness to enjoy as much of their esteem, as they deservedly possess of mine.' He can even be very positive about some other prominent Arminians, calling them eminent and worthy, 'great ornaments to our church,' and not to be mentioned without honour, even while he disagrees fervently with their Arminianism.[48]

Wesley replied to Toplady's reply, and so on. It was a tract war. One commentator says that 'Toplady treated Wesley with the manners and decorum of a gentleman and the analytical objectivity of a scientist.'[49] He may have been slightly warmer than that. But what was he up against? At one point, Wesley compares the Calvinist God to a man who has his enemy's nine year old daughter raped so he can then strangle her to death because she has been 'deflowered'.[50] Toplady rightly thought this impious (to say the least), and some evangelicals refused to allow Wesley to preach in their churches because of this. Toplady complained against 'a man who is so liberally lamentable in his outcries against the doctrine of predestination, and carries to such

---

[47] J.C. Ryle, *Christian Leaders*, 380 seems uncritically to buy Wesley's misrepresentation when he claims that Toplady 'appears to think it impossible that an Arminian can be saved.' Ironically, given Ryle's rather superior censure of Toplady, this completely overlooks all Toplady's positive statements to the contrary (just as Ryle also overlooks all Wesley's violently negative language about Calvinists).

[48] See Toplady, *Complete Works*, 275, 389, 614-615, 730, 732.

[49] G.M. Ella, *Augustus Montague Toplady: A Debtor to Mercy Alone* (Eggleston, Durham: Go Publications, 2000), 34.

[50] *The Works of John Wesley*, 10:373. This may be an allusion to the note in Suetonius's life of the Roman emperor, Tiberius (Suet. Tib. 61.5): '*immaturae puellae, quia more tradito nefas esset uirgines strangulari, uitiatae prius a carnifice, dein strangulatae*' ('Since, according to an ancient tradition, it was sinful to strangle virgins, the young girls were first deflowered by the executioner, before being strangled').

horrid length his invectives against the purposes and providence of God.'[51]

It is no surprise that some Evangelicals refused to allow Wesley to use their churches. Toplady's attempts at persuasion won him no friends amongst the Arminians, but he continued to pray for them and hope for them. He wrote to a friend in 1773 that 'The envy, malice, and fury of Wesley's party are inconceivable. But, violently as they hate me, I dare not, I cannot, hate them in return. I have not so learned Christ.—They have my prayers and my best wishes for their present and eternal salvation. But their errors have my opposition also.'[52]

Toplady's reputation has been unfairly maligned in my opinion because the extravagant Arminian eccentricities of the great and famous John Wesley have been hushed up or too easily excused — by Wesley, his followers, by Ryle, and others. It certainly does seem out of place for a man ordained nearly fifty years to behave the way Wesley did towards a fellow-Evangelical less than half his age. As Packer rightly says, Wesley's misrepresentations of Calvinism 'argue a degree of prejudice and closed-mindedness which is almost pathological.'[53] His heart was hot with hatred for Calvinism.

Toplady wrote to a friend after all this, 'I believe Wesley to be the most rancorous hater of the gospel-system that ever appeared in this island. I except not Pelagius himself.'[54] But as a young man in his twenties he had held back from publishing his translation of Zanchi for nine long years, fearful of offending Wesley and those

---

[51] Toplady, *Complete Works*, 761, 756.

[52] ibid., 840. See also pages 46 and 839.

[53] J.I. Packer, 'Arminianisms,' in *Honouring the People of God: Collected Shorter Works of J.I. Packer Volume 4* (Carlisle: Paternoster, 1999), 300.

[54] Toplady, *Complete Works*, 847.

on his side.[55] If anything, Toplady seems for many years to have been guilty of an unwarranted deference to the older man's celebrity and intimidating influence.

Toplady once said that 'it is not necessary to be timid in order to be meek.'[56] And I guess that must be right, glancing at the inspired examples in Galatians 5:12 or Matthew 23:1-33. It should be seen in proper context though. Toplady thought it was the most fitting response to what had been said and done to him by Wesley. 'To have refuted the forgeries and perversions of such an assailant tenderly, and with meekness falsely so called,' he writes, 'would have been like shooting at a highwayman with a pop-gun, or repelling the sword of an assassin with a straw.'[57] If in later years this may have threatened to become an unhealthy fixation on demonstrating Wesley's perfidious errors, we can also see with crystal clarity that what also motivated Toplady was defending the gospel of God's mercy and grace. It was even his duty, he thought to pray for Wesley, writing, 'O, that He, in whose hand the hearts of all men are, may make even this opposer of grace a monument of almighty power to save! God is witness how earnestly I wish it may consist with the divine will to touch the heart and open the eyes of that unhappy man.'[58]

---

[55] He had fulfilled what Horace recommended (Horace, *De Arte Poetica*, 385-390): '*siquid tamen olim scripseris, in Meti descendat iudicis auris et patris et nostras nonumque prematur in annum membranis intus positis: delere licebit, quod non edideris, nescit vox missa reverti.*' Basically, if you write anything, let a few other trusted friends read it, and sit on it for nine years. You can always change or delete things which you haven't published yet, but you can't take it back once it's 'out there.' This is also recommended at the start of Quintillian, *Institutio Oratoria*, because it enables authors to let the excitement of writing cool down and gives time for dispassionate revision. Toplady says he delayed, however, not in order to come back to the work in a calmer mood, but because he was 'not sufficiently delivered from the fear of man'. There is much here for modern bloggers and writers to ponder!

[56] See Toplady, *Complete Works*, 46, 48.

[57] Toplady, *Complete Works*, 324.

[58] Quoted in A. Brown-Lawson, *John Wesley and the Anglican Evangelicals of the Eighteenth Century: A Study in Cooperation and Separation with Special Reference to the Calvinistic Controversies* (Durham: Pentland Press, 1994), 328.

Putting the Daggers Away: Simeon and Wesley

I originally thought of giving this chapter the somewhat more sensationalist title,'Celebrity Preachers in Calvinist Cover-Ups.' The extent of Wesley's Arminianism and bad behaviour has for too long been covered up. We have explored some reasons why already, but much of the blame for downplaying things here might fairly be laid at the door of another evangelical Anglican hero, Charles Simeon.

In November 1787, nearly a decade after Toplady died, a young Charles Simeon, destined to be the leader of the Evangelicals into the next century, met with the ageing John Wesley. The conversation (though it is not recounted in Wesley's journal) has often been cited as evidence that Calvinists and Arminians are in essence agreed on fundamentals:

> Simeon: Sir, I understand that you are called an Arminian; and I have been sometimes called a Calvinist; and therefore I suppose we are to draw daggers. But before I consent to begin the combat, with your permission I will ask you a few questions, not from impertinent curiosity, but for real instruction. Pray, Sir, do you feel yourself a depraved creature, so depraved, that you would never have thought of turning unto God, if God had not first put it into your heart?

> Wesley: Yes, I do indeed.

> Simeon: And do you utterly despair of recommending yourself to God by any thing you can do; and look for salvation solely through the blood and righteousness of Christ?

> Wesley: Yes, solely through Christ.

> Simeon: But, Sir, supposing you were first saved by Christ, are you not somehow or other to save yourself afterwards by your own works?

Wesley: No, I must be saved by Christ from first to last.

Simeon: Allowing then that you were first turned by the grace of God, are you not in some way or other to keep yourself by your own power?

Wesley: No.

Simeon: What then, are you to be upheld every hour and every moment by God, as much as an infant in its mother's arms?

Wesley: Yes; altogether.

Simeon: And is all your hope in the grace and mercy of God to preserve you unto his heavenly kingdom?

Wesley: Yes; I have no hope, but in him.

Simeon: Then, Sir, with your leave, I will put up my dagger again; for this is all my Calvinism; this is my election, my justification by faith, my final perseverance: it is, in substance, all that I hold, and as I hold it: and therefore, if you please, instead of searching out terms and phrases to be a ground of contention between us, we will cordially unite in those things wherein we agree.[59]

If this account is accurate and does actually relate to Simeon himself,[60] we ought to notice that Simeon begins not by claiming to *be* a Calvinist but by saying he has 'sometimes' been called one. Normally, he did not want to identify either with Calvinists or Arminians, claiming to be 'no friend to systematizers in Theology.'

---

[59] The conversation is recounted in C. Simeon, *Helps to Composition, or Six Hundred Skeletons of Sermons* 1st American ed. (Philadelphia, 1810), Volume 1, xviii note o.

[60] The dialogue is prefaced, 'A circumstance within the Author's knowledge reflects so much light upon this subject, that he trusts he shall be pardoned for relating it. A young minister, about three or four years after he was ordained, had an opportunity of conversing familiarly with the great and venerable leader of the Arminians in this kingdom; and, wishing to improve the occasion to the uttermost, he addressed him nearly in the following words…' It seems likely that it does refer to Simeon himself, but a small doubt remains due to the third person references.

He had 'no doubt that there is a system in the Holy Scriptures; (for truth cannot be inconsistent with itself),' but he was 'persuaded that neither Calvinists nor Arminians are in exclusive possession of that system.'[61]

Wesley, on the other hand, although he does not recount the conversation, identified Simeon, on both occasions when the two met, as very much like his own designated successor as leader of the Arminians, J. Fletcher of Madeley. Simeon and Fletcher are 'two kindred souls,' he says in 1784. Simeon 'breathes the very spirit of Mr Fletcher,' he repeated in his journal in 1787.[62] That is not to say that Simeon was an Arminian, of course. I don't believe he was. Yet here his Calvinism was either unseen or sufficiently confused as to not attract the attention of the very man who had been Calvinism's self-proclaimed nemesis for fifty years and had made such harsh pronouncements against it.

Perhaps Simeon was somewhat naïve in his youthful enthusiasm to sidestep decades of serious discussion and be considered (like a consummate ecclesiastical politician) sympathetic to both sides. Yet the debate was not, as many may wish it to be, one merely of timing and where to place the emphasis—as if Calvinists like Whitefield held to divine sovereignty but did not appeal for human decisions, or that they simply ignored parts of Scripture that did not at first blush seem to fit their preconceived system, or that they were abstract theologisers who needed Arminians to teach them how to speak to real people. That caricature certainly does not fit George Whitefield, the greatest evangelist of the eighteenth century.

To say Arminian doctrines of free will could be used alongside Calvinist teaching concerning divine providence and grace as if

---

[61] C. Simeon *Horae Homileticae or Discourses (in the Form of Skeletons) upon the Whole Scriptures* (London, 1819), Volume 1, 4-5.

[62] *The Works of John Wesley*, 4:294, 403. Since Simeon was ordained deacon in 1782 and priest in 1783 the conversation (if between Simeon and Wesley) took place between 1785-1787 (3-4 years after he was ordained, as he says), and hence the November 1787 meeting is the most likely occasion contra e.g. H. Moule, *Charles Simeon: Pastor of a Generation* (Fearn, Ross-shire: Christian Focus, 1997 [1892]), 83 who dates it to 1784.

they were not necessarily contradictory perhaps sounded irenic. Yet what are we to make of Simeon's comment that, 'It is supposed by many, that the doctrines of grace are incompatible with the doctrine of man's free-will; and that therefore the one or the other must be false. But why so?'—or his assertion that, 'it is possible, that the truth, may lie, not exclusively in either, nor yet in a confused mixture of both, but in the proper and seasonable application of them both.'[63] It seems likely that Simeon's misunderstanding that the two systems could be pastorally blended to obtain a supposedly better, more biblical, balance played straight into synergistic Arminian hands, and I suspect the more experienced Wesley was well aware of this. Toplady would have said something like, 'evangelical truth knows nothing of this harlequin assemblage.'[64] I refrain from speculating on what Luther's response might have been.

Second, it ought to be pointed out that Simeon, narrating events two decades previously, does most of the talking in this famous exchange, putting words into the older man's mouth. Hence we learn more here about Simeon than we do about Wesley (who had died by the time this account was published). Very skilfully, he skirts round some of the actual areas of contention to present *himself* in a very positive light. For example, he asks whether Wesley 'feels himself depraved' not whether he *is* or *was* totally depraved and unable to respond to God before his conversion which, because of his doctrine of prevenient grace or 'universal enablement,' he would not have been able to answer in the affirmative like a Calvinist.[65] As Charles Wesley's hymn appended to his brother's Free Grace sermon puts it:

> A power to choose, a will to obey,
> Freely His grace restores;
> We all may find the living way.

---

[63] Simeon, *Helps to Composition*, xvi, xxi.

[64] Toplady, *Complete Works*, 722.

[65] See e.g. *The Works of John Wesley*, 6:509, 512; 7:189; 10:229-230, 392.

And call the Saviour ours.[66]

As he re-sheaths his dagger Simeon declares, 'this is all my Calvinism; this is my election.' We should note, however, that he has at no point actually addressed the doctrine of election in the conversation! Presumably this is because he knew full well that Wesley believed in predestination on the basis of foreseen faith and perseverance, and not on the basis of God's gratuitous unmerited choice alone. As Charles Wesley would have us sing:

> Whom his eternal mind *foreknew*,
> That they the power would use,
> Ascribe to God the glory due,
> And not his grace refuse;
> Them, only them, his will decreed,
> Them did he *choose* alone,
> *Ordain'd* in Jesus' steps to tread,
> And be like his Son.

This is *conditional election based on foreseen faith* and the use of resistible grace by an unbound will. This was no small point, but goes to the very heart of the predestination debate. In his noble and heroic crusade for some kind of unity, however, Simeon evidently feels it is merely 'searching out terms and phrases to be a ground of contention.' Possibly by the late eighteenth century some may have gone too far into an unhealthy hyper-Calvinism or into arguing about words in an unwholesome way. Yet there was real gospel-minded concern at the heart of people's concerns about Wesley, which is not apparent from the way Simeon deals with him here.

Third, it is hardly right to acquit Wesley (and Arminianism) of synergistic views of salvation simply on the basis of his own protestations and denials. Which Christian theologian ever admitted openly to teaching salvation by works? Yet that is not to

---

66 Also found in volume 1 of Wesley's *Arminian Magazine* (1778). Later, it says: 'Lord, if indeed, without a bound, Infinite Love Thou art, The HORRIBLE DECREE confound, Enlarge Thy people's heart! Ah! who is as Thy servants blind, So to misjudge their God! Scatter the darkness of their mind, And shed Thy love abroad' (emphasis original).

say every Christian theologian avoids that trap or tendency as a clear implication of their system or in the minds of their less educated followers. Calvinists and Arminians alike need to guard themselves from inconsistency with their own profession and the dangers on either side of them.

Nevertheless, Simeon's view of Wesley and of Arminianism has become the dominant note in much of today's Evangelicalism. Differences between Calvinists and Arminians are too often evaded and fudged for the sake of unity and peace so that someone who dredges them up is considered factious and unnecessarily combative—'a cynic, a bear, a Toplady,' as Wesley put it in his usual sour way.[67] It is remarkable how often individuals have covered a drift towards different forms of liberalism 'with professions of indifference to theological aridities,' as one writer so strikingly puts it.[68] Yet questioning someone's teaching on predestination, justification, and sanctification is hardly equivalent to arguing about how many angels can dance on the head of a pin. These are the cornerstones of salvation.

Conclusion: Dealing with Celebrity Heroes

Wesley raised the temperature of debate amongst evangelicals in the eighteenth century. For one supposedly devoted to evangelical unity and peace, his heart and pen were strangely warmed against Calvinists and Calvinism. His behaviour and tone have too often been excused or covered up, and many have been blinded by his celebrity and reputation, or wanted to keep him and his followers onside. That has sometimes led to something of a whitewash. In response we must do better church history which, as Oliver Cromwell said about portrait painting, is best done 'warts and all.'

---

[67] *The Works of John Wesley*, 10:414. He thought becoming a Calvinist made one 'spiteful, morose, and touchy.' This may be true of some people, of course; and true also of fractious men and women of all parties.

[68] A. Cromartie, 'Hale, Sir Mathew (1609–1676),' *Oxford Dictionary of National Biography* (Oxford: Oxford University Press, 2004).

'Those who are for peace, will leave these things alone,' Wesley once said. Many feel the same way about the Arminian controversies which he stirred up—it is better not to get embroiled in such things. When he said those words, however, Wesley was not trying to calm a doctrinal debate (which he continued to fuel) but to deflect attention away from his scurrilous slandering of Toplady, which continued even after the younger man's untimely death. Wesley spread slanderous rumours that poor Toplady, on his deathbed aged only 37, had renounced his faith and wanted to repent of all he had said in opposition to Wesley. Toplady dragged himself out of bed to preach again, so as to refute this calumny. Once he was dead, Wesley spread further (false) rumours that he had died in black despair uttering blasphemies, and he even wrote to Toplady's friends commiserating with them that their friend had died 'a dud squib.' He was pursued for an apology for such gossipy aspersions and rather nasty partisan behaviour by Sir Richard Hill and others (who had actually been with Toplady when he died), but all he would say in response was 'Those that are for peace will let these things alone.'[69]

Party loyalty may sometimes be laudable, and there is a time and a place; but the idea that for the sake of 'evangelical unity' we must never question the behaviour of the big chiefs, however lamentable, is surely anathema to truth-loving Christians. Those that are for truth must sometimes touch the sore spot.

In my view, it is imperative that both Whitefield and Toplady are heard again in proper context by both Evangelicals and Anglicans. It is vital, as Paul Helm rightly notes, to see clearly that the Evangelical participants in the eighteenth century controversy, 'certainly did not think that what united them was greater than what divided them. The occurrence of the Calvinist-Arminian division was very serious, fairly permanent, and sad.'[70]

---

[69] For the whole sordid tale and Wesley's attempted cover-up, see Ella, *Augustus Montague Toplady*, 331-340.

[70] P. Helm, 'Calvin, A.M. Toplady and the Bebbington Thesis,' in M.A.G. Haykin and K.J. Stewart (eds.), *The Emergence of Evangelicalism: Exploring Historical Continuities* (Nottingham: Apollos, 2008), 215.

Many would not have considered themselves Evangelical first and Reformed second if that meant unity with the domineering Wesley was the touchstone issue. George Whitefield may acknowledge some common ground with Wesley, but he resisted the idea that the issues at stake between them on predestination, the atonement, perfectionism, original sin, and justification were of only secondary importance, to be placed on one side for the sake of a common witness. He told Wesley in 1741 that they were preaching two different gospels.[71]

Fred Sanders, a well-known and much respected Arminian Wesleyan, recently attacked Toplady in a blog post. Toplady wrote the hymn *Rock of Ages*, he said, 'out of spite', and was 'a bitter and narrow-minded young man who couldn't keep his personal hatred from over-flowing into his prayers and songs.' Well, Toplady did indulge in some florid rhetoric at times, for which he cannot be entirely praised. Sometimes, like Luther, he didn't wrestle enough with 2 Timothy 2:22-26. But I think on this occasion my friend Professor Sanders is perhaps guilty of selective historical judgment. Again, Toplady is excoriated (and not always fairly) while the great and famous John Wesley is almost automatically exonerated from his nefarious crimes! Dr Sanders does, however, have these very helpful words of application, for both sides in the debate:

> When publicly disagreeing with other believers, try to keep some sense of perspective. If a Wesleyan is the worst thing you can imagine, you have a weak imagination. Wesley's influence is not what's driving the godless spirit of the age. The same moral applies, of course, to Arminians, too: If you think the main problem with the world today is Calvinism, you should get out more.[72]

---

[71] *The Works of John Wesley*, 1:305.

[72] Fred Sanders, 'Hit 'em with the Rock of Ages' at http://scriptoriumdaily.com/hit-em-with-the-rock-of-ages/ (accessed on November 11th, 2010).

That being said, for Whitefield and his friends, the confessionally Anglican and evangelical testimony to God's saving grace in the gospel must remain unadulterated. Unconditional election and justification *sola fide* are too important to push conveniently to one side. A time may come when even friends or allies must be taken to task for 'softening' gospel truths or adding spurious practices to them.[73] We forget this at our peril, and must not let pragmatism ('but they are so used by God!') or the politicians' fallacy ('does it matter how they behave in their private lives?') blind us to the New Testament's teaching on the consistent Christian living required of leaders. They may have the 'will to power,' as Nietzsche termed it, but they are emphatically not beyond good and evil. We should not excuse or ignore reprehensible behaviour in the heroes of the past, because to do so only encourages it in the heroes of the present (and their imitators).

---

[73] Whitefield was equally candid with Count Zinzendorff, often associated with Wesley and the Methodist movement, being astonished at the Moravian's use of images of Christ, incense, and other superstitious and idolatrous practices. See *The Works of the Reverend. George Whitefield: Volume IV*, 253-261 (in a letter from April 1753).

Scripture Index